100 HIKES IN SOUTHERN CALIFORNIA

SAN BERNARDINO
MOUNTAIN TRAILS

100 HIKES IN SOUTHERN CALIFORNIA

SAN BERNARDINO
MOUNTAIN TRAILS

John W. Robinson
and
David Money Harris

7th Edition

 WILDERNESS PRESS... *on the trail since 1967*

SAN BERNARDINO MOUNTAIN TRAILS: 100 HIKES IN SOUTHERN CALIFORNIA
Seventh edition, first printing
Copyright © 2016 by John W. Robinson and David Money Harris

Copyright © 1972, 1975, 1979, 1986, 2003, 2006 by John W. Robinson
2004 update by Rick Whitaker
Sixth edition by David Money Harris

Editor: Lady Vowell Smith
Project editor: Ritchey Halphen
Cover design: Scott McGrew
Cartography: Scott McGrew and Chris Salcedo/Blue Gecko, using data from John Robinson
    and David Money Harris, Laurence Jones, and USGS topos
Text design: Annie Long
Cover and interior photos: Copyright © 2016 David Money Harris, except where noted
Proofreader: Rebecca Henderson
Indexer: Sylvia Coates

Cataloging-in-Publication Data is on file with the Library of Congress.

ISBN: 978-0-89997-807-9; eISBN: 978-0-89997-808-6

Manufactured in the United States of America

 WILDERNESS PRESS
An imprint of AdventureKEEN
2204 First Ave. S., Suite 102
Birmingham, AL 35233
800-443-7227; fax 205-326-1012

Visit wildernesspress.com for a complete listing of our books and for ordering information.
Contact us at info@wildernesspress.com, facebook.com/wildernesspress1967, or twitter.com
/wilderness1967 with questions or comments.

Distributed by Publishers Group West

Cover photo: Approaching San Bernardino Peak on the Great San Bernardino Divide
    (see Hike 48, page 121)
Frontispiece: Deep Creek (see Hike 10, page 54)

SAFETY NOTICE Although Wilderness Press and the author have made every attempt to ensure
that the information in this book is accurate at press time, they are not responsible for any
loss, damage, injury, or inconvenience that may occur to anyone while using this book. You are
responsible for your own safety and health while in the wilderness. The fact that a trail is described
in this book does not mean that it will be safe for you. Be aware that trail conditions can change
from day to day. Always check local conditions, and know your own limitations.

▪ Contents ▪

▪ PART ONE: THE SAN BERNARDINO MOUNTAINS 25

■ part two: THE SAN JACINTO MOUNTAINS 139

■ part three: THE SANTA ROSA MOUNTAINS   229

▪ Prefaces ▪

Preface to the Seventh Edition

IT IS AN HONOR to continue updating John Robinson's iconic guidebook. My goal is to be faithful to the original flavor of the book while keeping it accurate and current.

I moved to Southern California from the Bay Area 17 years ago and have been hiking the local mountains ever since. Every author needs a lucky break to get started, and in 2005, I received my break when Wilderness Press asked me to update this book for the sixth edition. Since then, I've had a remarkable opportunity to explore, research, and write about the magnificent mountains and deserts of Southern California, leading to five books with Wilderness Press.

As John Robinson points out, change is constant. In this edition, I eliminated eight trips, mostly because they became overgrown after the wildfires that have swept the San Bernardino Mountains or because summits can be reached by road. In their place, I have added worthy trails, especially in the popular Lake Arrowhead and Big Bear resort areas.

I would like to thank Jeannette Granger, Audrey Scranton, and Richard Wilkerson for their assistance in reviewing the manuscript and for sharing their knowledge of the mountains. Lady Smith provided a thoughtful copyedit. The remaining errors are my own.

—*David Money Harris*
Upland, California
January 2016

Preface to the Sixth Edition

THE SAN BERNARDINO and San Jacinto Mountains have always held a special fascination for me. It's been more than half a century since I first ventured, on foot, from Poopout Hill to what we then called Slushy Meadows, up to Dollar Lake, and on to the gravelly summit of San Gorgonio Mountain. Many times since, I have explored this wonderful high country, where stately lodgepole pine is the dominant conifer, snow patches linger into early summer, and the air is crisp with the chill of elevation. I have equally enjoyed the "sky island" of the high San Jacintos, its boulder-strewn ridges, and lush meadows. For more than five decades, I have walked the forest trails, forded the creeks, and scrambled up the peaks for far-reaching vistas.

In 1971, after completing *Trails of the Angeles,* a hiking guide to the San Gabriel Mountains, I suggested to Tom Winnett that Wilderness Press publish a trail guide to San Bernardino National Forest. Tom enthusiastically approved, and a year later *San Bernardino Mountain Trails* appeared.

Over the next 33 years, I rechecked the driving directions, rewalked the trails, reclimbed the peaks—all in an effort to keep the guidebook up to date. These were years of strenuous work. Unlike a novel, a trail guide is never finished; change is constant. Still, it was a labor of love, doing what I enjoy most, experiencing nature's beauty, meeting new friends.

Now, because of advancing age, the time has come to relinquish my work on *San Bernardino Mountain Trails.* My successor is a young, energetic hiker who has already proved his worth by checking out many of the trail trips and making necessary revisions. David Money Harris, a professor of engineering at Harvey Mudd College in Claremont, spends many of his nonteaching days rambling through the Southern California mountains.

I offer a heartfelt farewell to the many friends I have met, over all the years, on the trails. May you continue to enjoy walking the footpaths of the mountains we all love.

—*John W. Robinson*
Fullerton, California
September 2005

Overview of Hikes

OVERVIEW OF HIKES

NUMBER	HIKE	DISTANCE (miles)	ELEVATION GAIN (feet)	TRAIL TYPE	DOGS ALLOWED	GOOD FOR KIDS	MOUNTAIN BIKING	BACKPACKING
1	Pacific Crest Trail to San Andreas Rift Viewpoint	6.5 mi.	1,000'	✓	✓			
2	Cajon Mountain	3 mi.	500'	✓	✓	✓	✓	
3	Heart Rock	1 mi.	300'	✓	✓	✓		
4	Deep Creek Hot Springs from Bowen Ranch	4 mi.	900'	✓				
5	Deep Creek Hot Springs from Kinley Creek	5.5 mi.	1,900'	✓				
6	The Pinnacles	3.5 mi.	1,000'	✓	✓	✓		
7	Metate Trail	0.8 mi.	100'	✓	✓	✓	✓	
8	Tunnel Two Trail	1 mi.	100'	✓	✓	✓	✓	
9	Little Bear Creek	4 mi.	800'	✓	✓			
10	Deep Creek	6 mi.	600'	✓	✓			✓
11	Holcomb Creek	12 mi.	2,200'	✓	✓			✓
12	Heaps Peak Arboretum	0.7 mi.	100'	✓	✓	✓		
13	Upper Deep Creek	5 mi.	800'	✓	✓	✓		✓
14	Holcomb Crossing Trail Camp	6 mi.	900'	✓	✓			✓
15	Shay Mountain	7 mi.	1,100'	✓	✓			
16	Cox Creek	12 mi.	1,200'	✓	✓			✓
17	Exploration Trail	4.5 mi.	1,300'	✓	✓		✓	
18	Little Green Valley	3 mi.	700'	✓	✓	✓	✓	

OVERVIEW OF HIKES

NUMBER	HIKE	DISTANCE (miles)	ELEVATION GAIN (feet)	TRAIL TYPE	DOGS ALLOWED	GOOD FOR KIDS	MOUNTAIN BIKING	BACKPACKING
19	Siberia Creek Trail Camp from Snow Valley	6 mi.	2,200'	✓	✓			✓
20	Grays Peak	7 mi.	1,200'	✓	✓		✓	
21	Delamar Mountain	5.5 mi.	1,000'	✓	✓			
22	Bertha Peak	7 mi.	1,400'	✓	✓			
23	Gold Mountain	3 mi.	1,000'	✓	✓			
24	Silver Peak	4 mi.	1,000'	✓	✓			
25	Whitewater Canyon View Loop	3.5 mi.	600'	✓	✓	✓		
26	Castle Rock	2 mi.	700'	✓	✓	✓		
27	Champion Lodgepole Pine	0.6 mi.	100'	✓	✓	✓	✓	
28	Siberia Creek	14 mi.	2,900'	✓	✓			✓
29	Grand View Point	6.5 mi.	1,100'	✓	✓		✓	
30	Skyline Trail	14 mi.	1,800'	✓	✓		✓	
31	Sugarloaf Mountain from Green Canyon	10 mi.	2,700'	✓	✓		✓	✓
32	Sugarloaf Mountain from Wildhorse Meadows	7 mi.	1,300'	✓	✓		✓	✓
33	Wildhorse Creek	8 mi.	1,400'	✓	✓		✓	✓
34	Santa Ana River Headwaters	10 mi.	1,000'	✓	✓		✓	
35	Fish Creek Meadow	5 mi.	650'	✓	✓			
36	Fish Creek	12 mi.	1,900'	✓	✓			✓

OVERVIEW OF HIKES

NUMBER	HIKE	DISTANCE (miles)	ELEVATION GAIN (feet)	TRAIL TYPE	DOGS ALLOWED	GOOD FOR KIDS	MOUNTAIN BIKING	BACKPACKING
37	Ponderosa Nature Trail	0.7 mi.	150'	loop	dog	kids		
38	Siberia Creek Trail Camp from Seven Pines	8 mi.	1,300'	out-and-back	dog			backpacking
39	South Fork Meadows	8 mi.	1,400'	out-and-back	dog			
40	Dollar Lake	12 mi.	2,800'	out-and-back	dog			backpacking
41	Dry Lake	10 mi.	2,300'	out-and-back	dog			backpacking
42	San Gorgonio Mountain via Dollar Lake Saddle	20 mi.	4,700'	out-and-back	dog			backpacking
43	San Gorgonio Mountain via Mine Shaft Saddle	22 mi.	4,700'	out-and-back	dog			backpacking
44	North Fork Meadows	19 mi.	4,600'	out-and-back	dog			backpacking
45	Johns Meadow	6 mi.	800'	out-and-back	dog			backpacking
46	San Bernardino Peak Divide from Forsee Creek	15 mi.	4,000'	out-and-back	dog			backpacking
47	San Bernardino Peak	16 mi.	4,700'	out-and-back	dog			backpacking
48	The Great San Bernardino Divide	28 mi.	6,200'	out-and-back	dog			backpacking
49	Mountain Home Flats	3.5 mi.	1,100'	out-and-back	dog			backpacking
50	San Bernardino Peak Divide from Mill Creek	14 mi.	5,200'	out-and-back	dog			backpacking
51	Alger Creek Trail Camp	7 mi.	2,100'	out-and-back	dog			backpacking
52	Dollar Lake Saddle from Mill Creek	18 mi.	4,700'	out-and-back	dog			backpacking
53	Big Falls	0.6 mi.	200'	out-and-back	dog	kids		
54	San Gorgonio Mountain via Vivian Creek	17 mi.	5,500'	out-and-back	dog			backpacking

OVERVIEW OF HIKES

NUMBER	HIKE	DISTANCE (miles)	ELEVATION GAIN (feet)	TRAIL TYPE	DOGS ALLOWED	GOOD FOR KIDS	MOUNTAIN BIKING	BACKPACKING
55	Galena Peak	8 mi.	3,200'	↗	🐕			
56	Black Mountain	7.5 mi.	2,700'	↗	🐕			🥾
57	San Jacinto Peak via Fuller Ridge Trail	15 mi.	4,100'	↗				🥾
58	Indian Mountain	5.5 mi.	1,300'	↗	🐕		⚙	
59	North Fork San Jacinto River	1.4 mi.	400'	↗		👪		
60	Seven Pines Trail	7 mi.	2,400'	↗				🥾
61	San Jacinto Peak via Marion Mountain Trail	13 mi.	4,600'	↗				🥾
62	Webster Trail	5 mi.	1,900'	↗	🐕		⚙	
63	Suicide Rock	7 mi.	1,900'	↗	🐕			
64	Strawberry–Saddle Loop	10 mi.	3,400'	↗	🐕			🥾
65	San Jacinto Peak from Idyllwild	18 mi.	5,200'	↗				🥾
66	Skunk Cabbage Meadow	6.5 mi.	1,700'	↗	🐕			🥾
67	San Jacinto Peak from Humber Park	14 mi.	4,400'	↗				🥾
68	Jean Peak and Marion Mountain	16 mi.	4,600'	↗				🥾
69	Humber Park– Round Valley Loop	14 mi.	3,600'	↺				🥾
70	Tahquitz Valley	6 mi.	1,700'	↗	🐕			🥾
71	Caramba	14 mi.	3,300'	↗	🐕			🥾
72	Tahquitz Peak via Saddle Junction	8 mi.	2,400'	↗	🐕			🥾

OVERVIEW OF HIKES

NUMBER	HIKE	DISTANCE (miles)	ELEVATION GAIN (feet)	TRAIL TYPE	DOGS ALLOWED	GOOD FOR KIDS	MOUNTAIN BIKING	BACKPACKING
73	Lily Rock	2 mi.	1,600'	⤢				
74	Desert Divide	17 mi.	2,800'	⤢	🐕			🥾
75	Ernie Maxwell Scenic Trail	2.5 mi.	600'	⤢	🐕	👪		
76	Tahquitz Peak via South Ridge Trail	7 mi.	2,300'	⤢	🐕			🥾
77	Antsell Rock	15 mi.	4,000'	⤢				🥾
78	Apache Peak	11 mi.	2,600'	⤢	🐕			🥾
79	Palm View Peak	8 mi.	2,100'	⤢	🐕			🥾
80	Cedar Spring	6 mi.	1,700'	⤢	🐕			🥾
81	Thomas Mountain	12 mi.	2,400'	⤢	🐕		⊕	🥾
82	Cahuilla Mountain	6 mi.	1,400'	⤢	🐕			🥾
83	Long, Round, and Tamarack Valleys	5 mi.	800'	⤢		👪		🥾
84	San Jacinto Peak from the Tramway	10 mi.	2,600'	⤢				🥾
85	Lykken Loop	3.3 mi.	1,000'	↺				
86	San Jacinto via Skyline Trail	20 mi.	10,700'	⤢				🥾
87	Murray Canyon	4 mi.	500'	⤢		👪		
88	Lower Palm Canyon	4.5 mi.	600'	⤢		👪		
89	Fern Canyon Loop	6.5 mi.	1,000'	↺				
90	Jo Pond Trail	16 mi.	6,200'	⤢				🥾
91	Palm Canyon Traverse	15 mi.	–3,500'	⤢				🥾

OVERVIEW OF HIKES

NUMBER	HIKE	DISTANCE (miles)	ELEVATION GAIN (feet)	TRAIL TYPE	DOGS ALLOWED	GOOD FOR KIDS	MOUNTAIN BIKING	BACKPACKING
92	Pinyon Trail	8 mi.	1,400'	↗			⚙	
93	Desert Divide and Palm Canyon	19 mi.	2,900'	↗	🐕			🎒
94	Alta Seca Bench	2 mi.	800'	↗	🐕			🎒
95	Horsethief Creek	4.5 mi.	900'	↗	🐕			🎒
96	Cactus Spring Trail	18 mi.	3,000'	↗	🐕			🎒
97	Sawmill Trail	8 mi.	3,700'	↗	🐕		⚙	🎒
98	Rabbit Peak from Coachella Valley	16 mi.	6,700'	↗				🎒
99	Villager and Rabbit Peaks	21 mi.	7,900'	↗				🎒
100	Old Santa Rosa	20 mi.	2,800'	↗				🎒

■ TRIP-TYPE SYMBOLS KEY ■

Out-and-back   ◯ Loop   ↗ Point-to-point   🐕 Dogs allowed

🧍 Good for kids   ⚙ Mountain biking   🎒 Backpacking

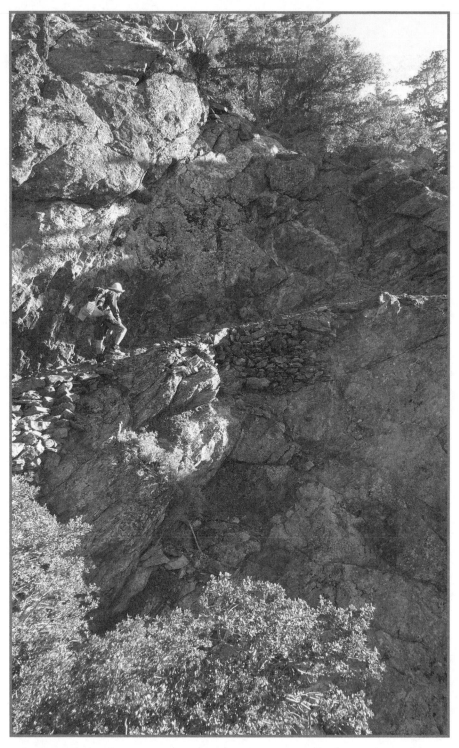

Pacific Crest Trail on the Desert Divide (see Hike 74, page 191)

▪ Introduction ▪

SAN BERNARDINO NATIONAL FOREST sprawls over a generous portion of Southern California's mountain landscape. It begins atop Old Baldy in the San Gabriel Mountains and ends on the desert-tempered slopes of Toro Peak and Martinez Mountain in the Santa Rosa Mountains—100 miles in a great northwest-southeast arc. Within its bounds are all or part of four distinct mountain ranges—the eastern San Gabriels, the San Bernardinos, the San Jacintos, and the northern Santa Rosas (five ranges, if you consider Cahuilla Mountain to be separate from the San Jacintos).

Within the San Bernardino National Forest is all manner of mountain country. There are gentle flatlands and rolling hills, and there are sheer escarpments and rock-ribbed peaks that soar above everything else in Southern California. There are hot slopes smothered in thorny chaparral, and there are cool alpine forests of pine and fir. There are places where snow almost never falls, and there are spots where snowbanks linger half the year. There are sparkling mountain lakes and boggy meadows, quiet brooks and rushing streams. Often there are barrel cactuses and Joshua trees in close proximity to Jeffrey pines and incense-cedars. Perhaps no other national forest in the United States contains such variety.

Humans have made an indelible mark on much of this landscape. We have built a maze of roads, and have erected a multitude of homes, resorts, and places of business high up in the forest country. Some areas—Crestline, Lake Arrowhead, Big Bear, Idyllwild—are so urbanized that they differ little from the cities below. About 46,000 people make their permanent home in the San Bernardino Mountains.

Yet there is wilderness here in these overused mountains, places where civilization—either by nature's design or human foresight—has left the mountains to themselves. Here, deep in the forest, alongside an alder-canopied stream or high on a rocky crag, you can relax and contemplate and enjoy nature's solitude. You can breathe the restoring scents of forest and chaparral, and listen to the quiet sounds of the earth. You can come to understand the true value of wilderness to a civilization that too often places artificial values before real ones.

The largest wilderness regions in San Bernardino National Forest are the wild areas around San Gorgonio Mountain and San Jacinto Peak, set aside to remain in their natural, pristine state. Here is the highest mountain country in

1

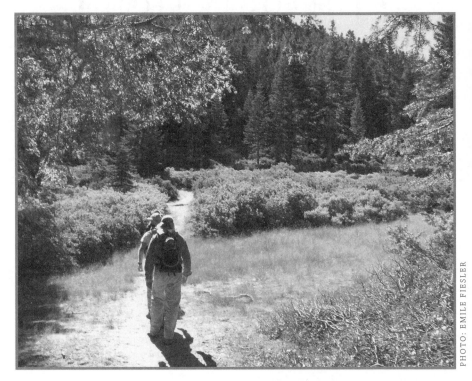

Entering the berry patch on the Fuller Ridge Trail (see Hike 57, page 159)

Southern California and, in the eyes of many, the most delightful. Besides these two official wild areas, there are many other parts of the mountains where, by reason of remoteness or difficulty of access, human touch has been minimal. These are scattered throughout the mountains, some of them quite close to overused areas—the Pinnacles country north of Lake Arrowhead, Holcomb and Deep Creeks, the bouldered slopes above Big Bear Lake, the Heart Bar country, Yucaipa Ridge, the palm-and-pinyon country on the desert slopes of the San Jacintos, the lonely Santa Rosas, to name the best.

This guidebook attempts to acquaint Southern Californians—and others—with the intimate parts of San Bernardino National Forest, the regions away from the highway where nature still reigns relatively undisturbed. The 100 hiking trips in this book take the reader and prospective hiker into almost every nook and cranny of the mountains. They vary from easy one-hour strolls to all-day and overnight rambles involving many miles of walking and much elevation change—excursions to satisfy the novice and challenge the veteran.

There is one overriding requirement: you must like to walk and be willing to forgo the comforts of civilization for periods ranging from a few short hours to several days.

Trails and fire roads crisscross much of San Bernardino National Forest, some well maintained and easy to follow, others almost-forgotten byways of the past, eroded and overgrown in spots. The great majority of trips in this guidebook are on maintained trails, and these should present no problems to the hiker. However, I have included a handful of cross-country scrambles and trailless peak climbs in areas well worth visiting but not served by standard routes. For these trips, directions have been presented in greater detail.

More so than any other national forest in California, and perhaps in the entire nation, San Bernardino National Forest is dotted with private holdings. This is particularly so in the urban belt of the San Bernardino Mountains that extends from Crestline eastward through Twin Peaks, Blue Jay, Lake Arrowhead, Running Springs, Green Valley, to Big Bear; and in the Idyllwild area of the San Jacinto Mountains. Besides these extensive developed areas, there are literally hundreds of private holdings ranging in size from 50 or more acres down to an acre or less. Only the San Gorgonio Wilderness, Mount San Jacinto State Park, the San Jacinto Wilderness, the Santa Rosa Wilderness, and the San Jacinto and Santa Rosa Mountains National Monument are relatively inviolate. Many trails have been removed from this guide over the years because of private property concerns.

As this book was going into production, President Obama designated the Sand to Snow National Monument spanning 154,000 acres from the San Gorgonio Wilderness to the edge of Joshua Tree National Park. The monument protects a critical wildlife corridor between the desert and mountains. Large portions of this land were privately acquired and then donated to the new monument to prevent development in sensitive areas; the Wildlands Conservancy plays a large role in this achievement.

I have walked, recorded, and researched all the trips in this guide. Every effort has been made to present the information as accurately and as explicitly as possible. Nevertheless, the prospective hiker should be aware that several factors—the rapid growth of chaparral, fire, flood, and the continual reworking of trails—may make some of this information out of date in a short time. Such changes will probably affect only a few of the trips described here, but if you are unfamiliar with the area in which you plan to hike, it is best to inquire at a ranger station before your trip.

The trail trips have been graded, based on my evaluation, as "easy," "moderate," "strenuous," or "very strenuous." An "easy" trip is usually 4 miles or less in horizontal distance, with less than 500 feet elevation gain—suitable for beginners and children. A "moderate" trip—including the majority here—is a 5-to-10-mile hike, usually with less than 2,500 feet elevation difference. You should be in fair physical condition for these, and children under 12 might find the going difficult. "Strenuous" trips are all-day rambles involving many miles of hiking and much elevation gain and loss; they are only for those in top physical condition and with hiking experience. "Very strenuous" trips involve at least a vertical mile of elevation gain and include some of the classic physical challenges of Southern California. The most important criteria for grading a trip are mileage covered, elevation gain and loss, and condition of the trail. Of less significance are accessibility of terrain, availability of water, exposure to sun, and ground cover.

Obviously, some of the latter criteria depend on the weather and time of year: a 3-mile hike over open chaparral slopes can be miserable under the hot August sun but delightful in January's cool breeze and cloudiness. A season recommendation is included for each trip.

This book is titled *San Bernardino Mountain Trails* because the mountain regions covered are predominantly in San Bernardino National Forest. There are two exceptions. The western end of San Bernardino National Forest extends into the San Gabriel Mountains, and this section is included in the companion volume, *Trails of the Angeles*. To make up for this absence, the entire Santa Rosa Range is covered in this guide, even though San Bernardino National Forest encompasses only the northern half. So the reader comes out even.

Hiking Hints

SOME HIKERS HAVE emerged from the mountains with the scent of laurel and pine on their clothing and with dust on their boots, tired but enriched—both physically and mentally—by their wilderness experience. Others have stumbled out of the mountains exhausted, footsore, sunburned, dehydrated, chilled, with clothing and skin torn by thorny chaparral, or soaked to the bone by an unexpected downpour, sadder but wiser for their ordeal. Some have had to be carried out. And a few have not come out.

Summit team, San Jacinto Peak

An outing in the mountains can be many things—fabulous, pleasant, unpleasant, harrowing, or disastrous. How it turns out depends to a large degree on you—your preparation, your clothing and equipment, your physical condition, and your good sense.

Following are some hints to make your mountain trip an enjoyable and rewarding experience.

PREPARATION

BECOME FAMILIAR WITH the terrain and landscape features of the area you plan to visit by studying a good map beforehand. It may be advisable to check with the Forest Service before your trip, particularly if you plan to walk a trail not regularly maintained (such trails are indicated in this guide).

PERMITS

IF YOU PLAN to visit the San Gorgonio Wilderness, San Jacinto Wilderness, or Mount San Jacinto State Wilderness, you must obtain a wilderness permit first. The permit is free to anyone who will agree to follow some simple rules intended to protect the visitor as well as the wilderness. Groups are limited to 12–15 people.

There are quotas on permits for some of the most popular trails and these quotas are often filled well in advance on summer weekends. For hikes in the San Jacinto Wilderness, a single wilderness permit from either the US Forest Service or California State Parks is sufficient for hikes spanning the two agencies.

If you plan to camp overnight in the San Bernardino National Forest, you are required to obtain a campfire permit, which is available from most ranger stations.

See Appendix 1 (page 251) for more information, including links to downloadable permit forms.

An **Adventure Pass** is required for all vehicles parking in developed areas of any of the four national forests of Southern California: Angeles, Cleveland, Los Padres, and San Bernardino. A one-day pass is $5; an annual pass is $30. The **Interagency Annual Pass** costs $80, but because it covers all national parks and many other federal lands, it may be a better deal than the Adventure Pass. These passes are available at Forest Service stations and some mountain stores; for more information, visit fs.fed.us/passespermits.

In the 2014 *Fragosa et al. vs. US Forest Service* decision, the California Central District Court ruled that visitors who do not use developed facilities and services (such as restrooms and picnic tables) cannot be required to buy a pass to park in or enter San Bernardino National Forest. At press time, the Forest Service had agreed to designate free parking within 0.5 mile of developed trailheads.

ACCESS TO TRAILHEADS

FINDING AND REACHING the trailhead may be half the challenge for many of these trips. The author has spent hours searching for dirt roads that are easy to miss from the highway. Fortunately, highways have mileage marker signs. For example, 038 SBD 53.50 is a marker at mile 53.50 on Highway 38 in San Bernardino County. Directions are often given relative to these markers.

The San Bernardino National Forest map, published by the Forest Service and available at most ranger stations, provides a reasonably up-to-date rendition of the dirt roads and trailheads in both the San Bernardino and San Jacinto

Mountains. AAA publishes a *San Bernardino Mountains Guide Map* that is also helpful, though less complete.

A smartphone or GPS receiver also can be helpful to locate trailheads. This edition provides GPS coordinates for all trailheads. Be aware, however, that automated guidance to obscure trailheads may be inaccurate or unsafe.

The condition of dirt roads changes rapidly. At the time of this writing, nearly all trailheads can be reached with an ordinary passenger car so long as it is driven carefully. On dirt roads listed as "fair" or "poor," a high-clearance four-wheel-drive vehicle is more likely to arrive unscathed. Exercise good judgment.

CLOTHING

MOUNTAIN WEATHER CAN vary considerably, even within a few hours. It is best to come prepared for both warm and cool temperatures with several layers of clothing—shirt, sweater, and windbreaker, for example—that can be put on or peeled off as needed. This is particularly advisable if you plan to climb any of the high peaks.

Short pants may be satisfactory when walking a fire road or rambling through an open forest at middle elevations, but they are miserable for thrashing through chaparral. If any part of your trip is through this elfin forest, wear sturdy long pants—and expect them to get torn.

Choice of headgear depends on the hiker. If you sunburn easily, you will probably want a hat with a generous brim. If the weather looks threatening, bring raingear.

Modern medical knowledge has linked skin damage and skin cancer with long periods of skin exposure to the sun. Long pants, a good hat, and generous sunscreen are recommended.

FOOTGEAR

TENNIS SHOES ARE adequate for most hikes on trails without snow. Indeed, most hikers taking the Pacific Crest Trail from Mexico to Canada wear running shoes the whole way. But if the trip is over rough or slippery terrain, a pair of sturdy boots, preferably with deep tread, should be worn.

Properly fitting shoes and close-fitting socks are essential to prevent blisters and sore feet. A mistake in footwear can ruin your trip. Break in new boots on short walks before you attempt a long hike. If you blister easily, carry moleskin, and use it at the first hint of oncoming trouble.

EQUIPMENT

A DAY HIKE in the mountains requires little in the way of equipment. It is surprising how many novices overburden themselves with large packs, excess clothing, too much or too heavy food, Rambo knives, and miscellaneous gadgets.

Still, there are essentials that all hikers should carry. These include a full water bottle, a first-aid kit, an area map, and some food. If you are doing any cross-country hiking, a compass is advisable and a topographic map is virtually a requirement. You will probably want to bring a camera. To carry all this, a lightweight daypack is advisable, preferably with a waistband to better distribute the weight.

An overnight outing, of course, requires more gear and preparation (see "Backpacking," page 12).

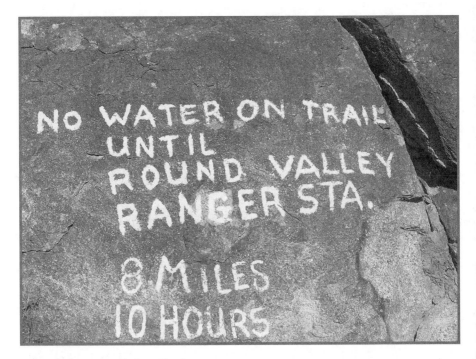

Scrawled sign on Skyline Trail

FOOD

TRAIL MENUS VARY considerably, and there is little agreement among experts about what foods are best. Sandwiches, cheese, fruit, nuts, cookies, and candy are probably the most popular trail foods. A planned, balanced diet is necessary only on an outing of several days.

What you eat is not nearly so important as how much you eat, and when. Small lunches plus snacks along the trail are best, because exertion after a feast causes competition for blood between stomach and hiking muscles, and leads to indigestion and weakness.

As important as food on a hike is liquid. Without enough water, exertion and heat dehydrate the body surprisingly soon and cause marked muscular weakness. Unless you are walking alongside a stream, bring a full water bottle—several if the weather is hot and your walk is long.

Giardia has made its appearance here. All water should be boiled, treated, or filtered first.

ON THE TRAIL

WALKING A MOUNTAIN trail is not as simple as one might think. An enjoyable hike requires proper pace and rest stops, knowledge of the terrain, correct reading of trail signs, and, above all, good judgment.

Unless you are training for the Olympics, a trail hike should not be a race to your destination and back. Start out slowly, easing your muscles into condition. Work up to the steady, rhythmic pace that suits you best. Your best trail speed is one at which you are working but not panting, and you feel you can continue almost indefinitely. When the trail steepens, shorten your steps but maintain your rhythm. Take short rests at moderate intervals, rather than stopping too frequently or for too long a time. If you are exceeding your ability, symptoms of exhaustion soon set in: sore or cramped leg muscles, profuse sweating, pounding pulse, headache, dizziness, redness of the face. Not only do these lessen your enjoyment, but a tired hiker is more accident-prone. The speedster who rushes up the trail, then collapses in a panting heap, is usually overtaken before long by the leisurely hiker. "Who goes into the mountains fast, comes out last," says an old proverb.

Stay on the trail. Shortcuts not only break down the trail (see "Mountain Courtesy," page 16) but can lead you astray. Probably the greatest temptation is to cut switchbacks—but sometimes the last zigzag doesn't zag, and you find yourself stumbling down a steep talus slope to nowhere, or thrashing through thorny brush in the wrong direction. When you finally realize your mistake, you are faced with the unpleasant necessity of churning back up the loose talus or beating through an ocean of chaparral—a painful, time-consuming object lesson in mountain sense.

When you come to a marked trail junction, read the sign carefully. If a junction is unmarked, consult your map and observe the surrounding landmarks to keep yourself oriented. If the trail seems to disappear in brush or boulders, look ahead for the way you think it should go; most trails take the obvious route. Look for "*ducks*" (several stones piled atop one another) that indicate the route. If you still can't find the trail and you are not experienced in cross-country travel, it is better to return the way you came rather than risk getting lost.

OFF THE TRAIL

ALTHOUGH TRAILS CRISSCROSS San Bernardino National Forest, there are some places they don't go—the upper section of Deep Creek in the San Bernardinos, and up Cornell Peak in the San Jacintos, for example. To reach these objectives, you must leave the established footpath and travel cross-country. Off-trail hiking, except for very short distances, is not for beginners.

Cross-country hiking in the San Bernardinos and San Jacintos is practical only in parts of the mountains—at higher elevations, along ridgetops, and along streambeds. In lower-elevation chaparral it is virtually impossible.

If you are planning a trip that is part cross-country, be sure you know the terrain, the landmarks, the ground cover, and the distance. Obtain a topographic map of the area and plan your route beforehand. Before you leave road or trail, make a visual survey of the region, noting the locations of landmarks. Continue this careful observation as you hike; look back at landmarks you'll want to use on the return trip—it's surprising how different the country sometimes looks when you're going the other way.

Without question, the most unpleasant type of cross-country travel is bushwhacking—an ordeal you should avoid whenever possible. One mile through unyielding chaparral is as difficult and tiring as 6 or 8 miles on trail, and much rougher on your clothing. If you must bushwhack, seek out terrain where the elfin forest is less dense—along ridges, in gullies, over recently burned areas. Chaparral also is thinner on shady, north-facing slopes than on sun-drenched, south-facing slopes. When entering a brushy area, secure loose items of clothing and equipment. It's mighty tough to retrace your exact route to find a lost camera or canteen.

On slopes of loose talus or scree, tread lightly; even the most careful walker cannot avoid dislodging a few rocks or triggering a slide. Solid-looking boulders may be precariously balanced; you must be ever-ready to leap nimbly aside when a foothold gives way.

Stream crossing is an art thoroughly mastered by few, and few hikers have never dampened their boots. If you can't find a dry crossing—a series of stepping-stones or a strategically located log—you must wade. It is better to wade the widest part of the stream, where the water is shallower and the current is slower. If the streambed rocks are smooth, wade across barefoot. If they are sharp-edged, remove your socks and wear your boots across. Then drain your boots, dry your feet, and replace socks and boots.

Hiking over snow can be a pleasure if the grade is gentle and the snow firm but not icy. It can be tedious if the sun has softened the snow so much that you break through at every step. And it can be extremely dangerous if the slope is steep and the snow icy, as it often is in higher elevations during late winter and spring. If you plan to snow-hike, you absolutely must wear a pair of boots with deep tread, preferably treated with a waterproof wax and worn with gaiters (waterproof leggings covering the upper part of the boot and part of the pant leg) to keep your feet dry. An ice axe, and knowledge of how to use it, is a requirement for steep snow slopes. Serious climbing on snow and ice, requiring ice axe, crampons, and rope, is only for skilled mountaineers. If you are interested, the Sierra Club offers a mountaineering course.

ROCK CLIMBING

ROCK CLIMBERS HAVE graded mountain routes into five categories, ranging from Class 1 (hiking) to Class 5 (climbing a vertical or overhanging cliff). You won't find much above Class 1 or 2 in these mountains, but there are some peaks whose ascent by certain routes involves some steep rock-scrambling—categorized as Class 3. The Pinnacles, Antsell Rock, and Cornell Peak are examples.

Class 3 climbing requires great caution. Move slowly, and test every handhold and foothold before shifting your weight. Take extra care on the descent, for this is when most accidents occur. Wear boots with good tread for traction on rock. Tahquitz Rock above Idyllwild is a favorite playground for advanced rock climbers.

BACKPACKING

SAN BERNARDINO NATIONAL Forest offers superb opportunities for overnight backpack trips—particularly in the San Gorgonio and San Jacinto Wilderness areas. The Forest Service maintains a number of overnight trail camps in these and other areas, many of them in delightful sylvan haunts away from the markings of civilization.

Most important is your choice of a pack itself. A wrong choice can cause an aching back and make backpacking a disagreeable experience. There are two main types of packs—internal frame and external frame packs—and each has its advantages. While both types of pack place most of the weight on your hips rather than on your shoulders, internal frame packs are superior for hiking over uneven terrain because they keep the load close to your body, allow for more upper-body motion, and have a lower center of gravity than external frame packs. They also can carry a heavier load. External frame packs hold the weight away from your back, making them cooler in warm weather. They provide more outside pockets and easier access to their contents, and are also less expensive than their internal frame counterparts.

For a good night's rest, you need a good sleeping bag. Down is the most efficient material for keeping you warm. Synthetic bags provide less warmth per unit of weight than down bags, making them heavier and bulkier. The advantages of synthetic bags are that they cost less, dry more quickly, and retain some insulating value when wet. For summertime trips in elevations below 8,000 feet, chances are that nights in these mountains will be mild, and a cheaper bag will be adequate. If you're a winter or spring backpacker, or if you plan to camp at any of the high trail camps in the two wild areas, better go with a down bag. "Mummy" and rectangular-shaped bags each have their adherents. Some people cannot tolerate the close fit of the mummy style, despite its superior thermal and weight characteristics.

Other backpacking essentials include warm clothing, raingear, plastic ground cloth, air mattress or foam pad, utensils, cooking gear, flashlight, first-aid

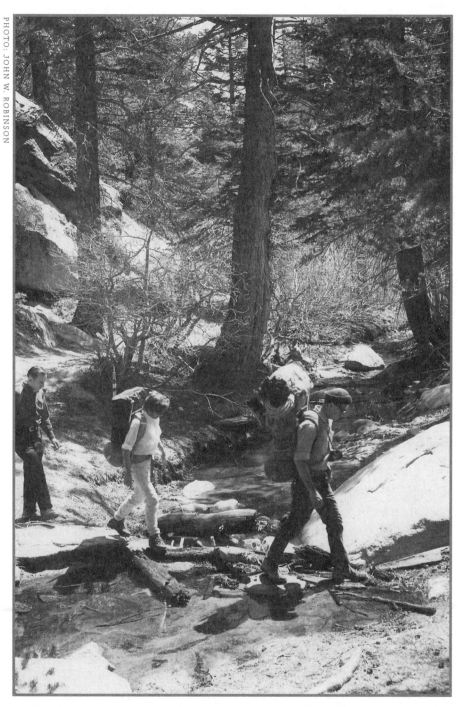

Backpackers cross Willow Creek in the San Jacinto Wilderness.

kit, snakebite kit, matches, and toilet paper. During the rainy seasons (winter and spring), tote a waterproof tent or—much less expensive—a plastic "tube tent" held up by nylon line.

CAMPING

YOU ARE REQUIRED to obtain a campfire permit, obtainable at most ranger stations, if you plan to use a camp stove or fire in San Bernardino National Forest. If your trip is in the San Gorgonio Wilderness (federal), the San Jacinto Wilderness (federal), or the Mount San Jacinto State Wilderness, you must obtain a wilderness permit (which includes permission for a campfire where applicable). Camp only in established trail camps, and build your fire only in campground stoves or fire rings; *open fires are not allowed.* Certain parts of the National Forest ban campfires entirely, especially during periods of high fire danger. In the San Jacinto Wilderness, the Forest Service has delineated camping zones; posts indicate camping areas within each zone. At present, you do not need to obtain a wilderness permit to enter the Santa Rosa Wilderness.

Portions of the National Forest have been ravaged by bark beetles, leaving stands of dead trees waiting to topple. It is prudent to camp and picnic away from these trees.

EMERGENCIES

THE SIERRA MADRE SEARCH AND RESCUE TEAM, without doubt the top mountain-rescue organization in Southern California, says that in the great majority of mountain emergencies in which a hiker is lost or injured, he or she (1) set off alone, (2) did not leave an itinerary or a planned return time, and/or (3) took a "shortcut" off the established trail. If you do all three and you're a relatively inexperienced mountaineer, you are inviting trouble. However, even the experienced and careful hiker may have a crisis. Knowing what to do in an emergency may save your life.

The first rule for survival in any outdoor emergency—be it losing your way, injury, snakebite, storm, or fire—is common sense: make a calm, reasoned judgment of the situation and act accordingly. The biggest threat to survival is panic. Panicky hikers have been known to throw away their supplies and wander aimlessly for miles. According to mountain-rescue experts, 8 out of 10 survival-situation fatalities could have been prevented if the hiker had known survival techniques and had used common sense.

Getting lost is by far the most common crisis faced by hikers. If you ever face this prospect, awareness of several basic rules should spare you unnecessary strain, fatigue, or injury, and maybe even your life. The minute you realize you are lost, stop and appraise the situation. If you are reasonably certain of your general location and have map and compass, try to retrace your steps, looking always for footprints and familiar landmarks. You may want to climb a nearby high point to survey the terrain for landmarks. Never take what you think is a "shortcut" over unfamiliar terrain; you stand a chance of becoming hopelessly tangled in thorny chaparral or slipping down a steep slope. If you are uncertain of your whereabouts, stay put. Never try to find your way at night.

If you've told people where you were going (and never enter the mountains on foot without telling someone your planned itinerary), a search will be made, probably the next day. Try to stay warm by huddling against a tree or by using branches, bark, or pine needles to build a primitive shelter. Don't search extensively for food; water is far more critical. To attract help from the air (search-and-rescue teams make much use of the helicopter nowadays) hang out bright-colored clothing or other objects, but do not start an uncontrolled fire— you could burn down the forest, endangering your life and the lives of many others. A common distress signal is three signs, visible or audible, repeated at intervals—for example, three bright objects placed in a row or three shouts. If you manage to find your way out on your own, immediately notify the Forest Service or sheriff's office so that the search can be ended.

The best way to avoid being trapped in a storm is to stay out of the mountains when the weather is threatening. If you are caught in a sudden blizzard at higher elevations, descend as rapidly as you can with safety, but don't start down unfamiliar slopes that might lead to drop-offs or to box canyons. Stay off ridges and open saddles, where wind velocity often becomes extreme. At lower elevations, your worry is water rather than snow or wind. Stay clear of canyon bottoms and gullies that are vulnerable to flash floods. If you're on the trail, stay on it. If you try a shortcut, your anxiety to get out, combined with the decreased visibility, could get you hopelessly lost. If you can't make it out, seek shelter in the hollow of a tree or under a rock overhang, away from the raging stream.

Fire in the Southern California mountains can be a fearful thing. Chaparral, especially when it's tinder-dry in late summer and fall, burns with unbelievable intensity, and wind can cause a brush fire to rampage at enormous speeds. If you see a fire in the mountains, even one that seems a safe distance away, get out fast and notify the Forest Service—the fire could be upon you before you realize it. If you are confronted by a close-at-hand brush fire, you must act fast. Determine the wind direction—fire moves much more rapidly downwind—and move laterally from that direction. Seek slopes and gullies where chaparral is sparse or absent—the fire may pass around these pockets. Or seek the refuge of a stream, preferably where brush does not crowd the banks. About 90% of Southern California forest and brush fires are caused by human carelessness, so make certain that no one in your party contributes to this tragic destruction.

Mountain Courtesy

TRAVELING A MOUNTAIN trail, away from centers of civilization, is a unique experience in Southern California living. It brings intimate association with nature—communion with the earth, the forest, the chaparral, the wildlife, the clear sky. A great responsibility accompanies this experience; you have an obligation to keep the mountains as you find them. Being considerate of the wilderness rights of others will make the mountain adventures of those who follow equally rewarding.

As a mountain visitor, you should become familiar with the rules of wilderness courtesy outlined below.

TRAILS

CUTTING SWITCHBACKS BREAKS down trails and hastens erosion. Take care not to dislodge rocks that might fall on hikers below you. Improve and preserve trails, as by clearing away loose rocks (carefully) and removing branches. Report any trail damage and broken or misplaced signs to a ranger.

OFF-TRAIL

RESTRAIN THE IMPULSE to blaze trees or to build ducks where it's not essential. Let other hikers find their own way as you did.

CAMPGROUNDS

SPREAD YOUR GEAR in an already-cleared area, and build your fire in a campground fire ring. Don't disarrange the camp by making hard-to-eradicate ramparts of rock for fireplaces or windbreaks. Rig tents and tarps with line tied to rocks or trees; never put nails in trees. For your campfire, use fallen wood or carry your own wood in rather than cutting standing trees or breaking off branches. Use the campground latrine. Place litter in the litter can or carry it out. Leave your campsite cleaner than you found it. Camp 200 feet or more from creeks and lakes.

FIRE

FIRE IS THE greatest danger in the Southern California mountains; act accordingly. Smoke only in cleared areas along the trail. Report a mountain fire immediately to the Forest Service. Campfires are not permitted in many portions of the San Bernardino National Forest, especially during times of high fire hazard in the summer and fall. Check regulations with the ranger station before planning to have a campfire.

LITTER

ALONG THE TRAIL, place candy wrappers, raisin boxes, orange peels, and other trash in your pocket or pack for later disposal; throw nothing on the trail. Pick up litter you find along the trail or in camp. More than almost anything else, litter detracts from the wilderness scene. Remember, you can take it with you.

NOISE

BOISTEROUS CONDUCT IS out of harmony in a wilderness experience. Be a considerate hiker and camper. Don't ruin another's enjoyment of the mountains.

GOOD SAMARITANSHIP

HUMAN LIFE AND WELL-BEING take precedence over everything else—in the mountains as elsewhere. If a hiker or camper is in trouble, help in any way you can. Indifference is a moral crime. Give comfort or first aid; then hurry to a ranger station for help.

Maps

WHEN YOU ARE hiking, it is important to know where you are in relation to roads, campgrounds, landmarks, and such and to know the lay of the land in general. For learning these things, there is no substitute for a good map. Unless your trip is very short, and over a well-marked route, you should carry a map.

Several types of readily available maps will give you the picture you need of San Bernardino National Forest and its adjacent mountain areas. Each type has its advantages and its disadvantages.

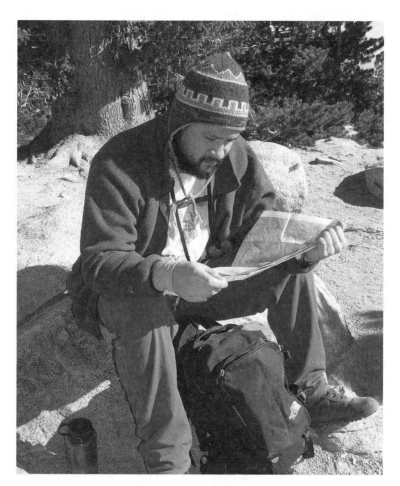

Studying a map at Wellman Junction (see Hike 69, page 181)

1. The large custom-designed **foldout map** packaged with this book shows all 100 of its hikes, including trailheads, access roads, and overlaps with forest roads and other trails, such as the Pacific Crest Trail. You'll also find points of interest mentioned in the text, watercourses, ranger stations, picnic and camping areas, and other information you might not find anywhere else. This map will help you locate trails and get the big picture. However, the topographic maps listed on the next page provide substantially more detail that is essential if you plan to hike off-trail.

2. **Tom Harrison Maps** produces topographic maps for the San Gorgonio Wilderness and San Jacinto Wilderness. These maps are laminated and show trail mileage. They can be purchased at most outdoor stores or from tomharrisonmaps.com. They are more convenient and withstand abuse better than the Forest Service wilderness maps.

3. *Santa Rosa and San Jacinto Mountains National Monument* is the best map of the monument. It has excellent coverage of trails and adequate coverage for basic cross-country travel. The map can be purchased at the monument visitor center at 51500 Highway 74, 4 miles south of Highway 111 in Palm Desert.

4. The **US Forest Service** sells topographic maps of the San Gorgonio, San Jacinto, and Santa Rosa Wildernesses. These maps can be obtained at most ranger stations, at outdoor stores, or at tinyurl.com/nationalforeststore.

5. **Earthwalk Press** publishes *Anza-Borrego Desert Region Recreation Map*, a laminated topographic map that covers the southern Santa Rosa region as well as the Anza-Borrego Desert. It is sold in local hiking stores or can be ordered online from Amazon.

6. The **US Geological Survey (USGS)** 7.5-minute series of topographic maps covers the entire region; each map covers an area of about 7 by 9 miles and has 40-foot contour intervals. They provide excellent detail but focus on such small areas that 29 separate maps are necessary to encompass all the hikes in this book. These maps are sold at some outdoor shops or at store.usgs.gov.

GPS AND ELECTRONIC MAPS

GPS RECEIVERS AND SMARTPHONES have revolutionized navigation. This edition brings you several options to take advantage of these tools, including the eTrails app and raw GPX-format tracks and waypoints.

If you are an iPhone or iPad user, download the free **eTrails** app. It contains high-resolution maps and tracks of the hikes in this book as well as an expanding list of other areas (including the Pacific Crest Trail and Orange County). The download size is large because all the maps are included, but you won't get caught out without a map. eTrails shows your position and the trail on a USGS base map and on an elevation profile, and links with Apple Maps to give you driving directions to the trailhead.

The GPX tracks and waypoints are also freely available at **eTrails.net.** With a bit of computer savvy, you can download them into your favorite navigation app or into your handheld GPS. Apps continue to evolve quickly, but at the time of this writing, my favorites are **BackCountry Navigator** for Android and **Gaia GPS** for iOS. You can also display the tracks and study the routes on **Google Earth** or other programs from the comfort of your home computer.

Finding the trailhead is often the hardest part of navigating. The GPS coordinates for each trailhead are listed for each trip. Even if you aren't using a mapping app, you can key the trailhead coordinates (or name) into a phone for guidance to the trailhead.

Handheld GPS receivers also continue to evolve. At the time of this writing, the Garmin eTrex units are light and cost-effective options. I have collected most of the data for this book on Garmin 60 and 62 series units, which are the gold standard for hiking GPS receivers. Compared with smartphones, dedicated receivers tend to have better battery life (about 15 hours), more resistance to the elements, and better reception in extreme conditions, which are seldom encountered in Southern California. However, smartphones have gotten good enough that they have largely replaced handheld GPS receivers for casual hiking.

Beware, though, of the many limitations of electronic navigation. A few of the trips in this book lack GPS data. GPS apps can drain batteries quickly and leave you without a map when your phone runs out of charge. Automated driving directions are handy but not always accurate, and might lead you down closed or impassable roads in remote areas. If you are using a commercial map program, remember to download the necessary tracks and base maps before you go because you may not have data coverage on the trail.

One Hundred Hikes

HOW THIS BOOK IS ORGANIZED

THE HIKING TRIPS in this guide are arranged by geographical area, generally northwest to southeast, from Cajon Pass at the west end of the San Bernardinos to Rabbit Peak at the southern end of the Santa Rosas. The first section covers the San Bernardino Mountains, with the largest concentration of hikes in the San Gorgonio Wilderness. The next section covers the San Jacinto Mountains, concentrated in Mount San Jacinto State Park and the San Jacinto Wilderness, along with a cluster in Palm Canyon. The final section covers the rugged Santa Rosa Mountains.

Information about each trip is divided into three parts:

The **Hike** section gives vital statistics: where the hike starts and ends; the walking mileage and elevation gain or loss; a rating of easy, moderate, strenuous, or very strenuous; the best time of year to make the trip; and the appropriate topographic map or maps.

The **Features** section tells something of what you will see on the trip, and gives information on the natural and human history of the area. It also contains suggestions for the particular trip, such as wear deep-tread boots or bring fishing rod.

The **Description** section details the driving and hiking route. The driving directions are kept to the necessary minimum, but the walking route is described in detail. Also, the hiking-route options that a trip offers are presented.

If you are a dedicated hiker who enjoys exploring the Southern California mountains on foot, the trips listed here are just a beginning. Many more than 100 hikes are possible, crisscrossed as these mountains are by roads, trails, and cross-country routes. Furthermore, various combinations of routes described here are possible, particularly if you can arrange car shuttles. You could spend a decade rambling through these mountains and still not fully know them.

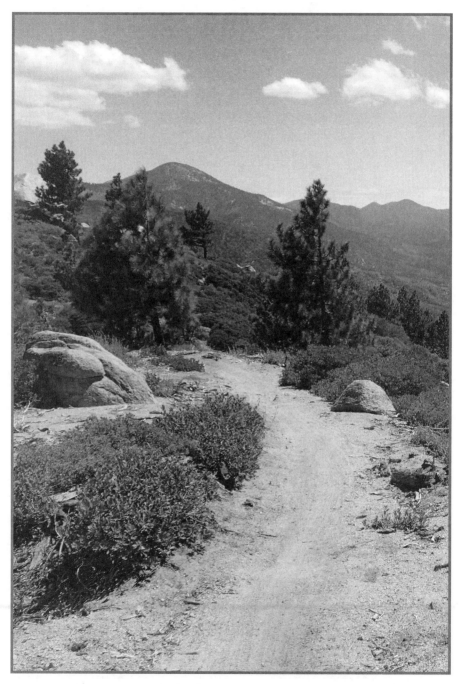

Santa Ana River Canyon, flanked by San Gorgonio and Sugarloaf Mountains, from the Skyline Trail (see Hike 30, page 87)

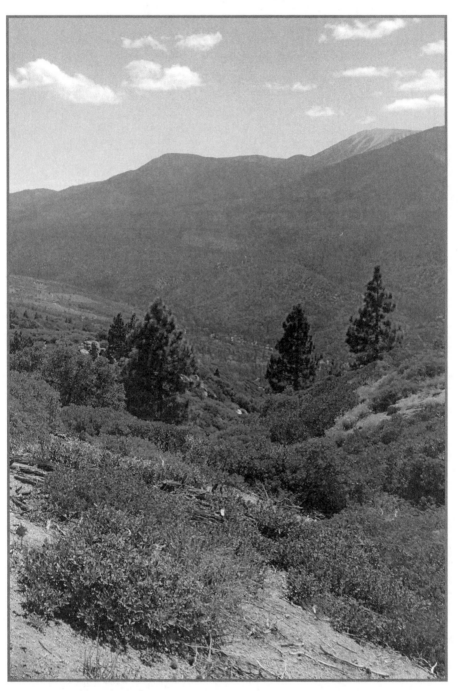

Another mountain vista from the Skyline Trail

PART 1

■ The San Bernardino ■ Mountains

Natural History of the San Bernardino Mountains

LAY OF THE LAND

From Cajon Pass and the slanted troughs of the great San Andreas Fault, the San Bernardinos rise, rather steeply at first, in chaparral-coated slopes, to the 5,000-foot summits of Cleghorn and Cajon Mountains. Eastward from here, for 30 miles, the crest of the San Bernardinos is remarkably uniform. Undulating ridges and tapered hillocks conceal within their folds forested glens and sparkling blue lakes. This is the Crestline–Lake Arrowhead–Running Springs–Big Bear country, the part of the mountains best known to thousands of Southern Californians. Here, among the lakes and streams that form the headwaters of the Mojave River, are summer homes, winter resorts, commercial centers, schools, paved roads by the mile—and only bits and pieces of wilderness.

From Big Bear Lake, the San Bernardinos veer southward and, beyond the deep valley of the upper Santa Ana River, reach their majestic heights in the San Gorgonio Wilderness. Here the hiker and the lover of pristine mountain country can rejoice. Under granite spines hammered up against the sky, lodgepole and limber pines grow sturdy and weather resistant, tumbling streams flow icy cold, and the thin air is crisp with the chill of elevation. Reigning over all is 11,502-foot San Gorgonio Mountain—or "Grayback," as it is known to thousands of hikers—the rooftop of Southern California. Early visitors possessed the foresight and initiative to forever preserve this high country in its primitive state.

South from Grayback, the mountains drop abruptly into the deep trench of Mill Creek, rise to rugged Yucaipa Ridge, and finally descend into the San Gorgonio Pass country.

Geologists place the San Bernardino Mountains, as well as the neighboring San Gabriels, in the Transverse Range province—a system of mountain chains that stretches west to east, athwart the general northwest-southeast structural grain of California. Like all the Transverse Ranges, the San Bernardinos were formed by intensive folding and faulting. The generally smooth summit region of the range—in marked contrast to the rough surface of the San Gabriels—reveals that the San Bernardinos were molded in comparatively recent geologic time. A complex network of faults separates the San Bernardinos from the surrounding landscape. Most pronounced is the great San Andreas Fault, which runs obliquely from northwest to southeast and forms the southern edge of the range. Adjoining the San Andreas is the Mill Creek Fault, which slices through the southern part of the mountains and forms the deep trough of Mill Creek. On the north side of the range, the fault lines, not so clearly evident, appear to be a series of short fracture zones. The largest on this flank is the Helendale Fault, which runs from the Mojave Desert up Cushenbury Canyon to the vicinity of Baldwin Lake. To the east is the Morongo Valley Fault. Other faults slice through the heart of the mountains. The surface rocks of the San Bernardinos are intermixed in great confusion, with granitic types and gneisses predominating, along with quartzite and crystallized limestone.

PLANT LIFE

The forest-and-brush cover of the San Bernardinos shows marked contrast. On the south slopes of the range, chaparral predominates. Covering most of the rolling crest of the mountains are lush stands of pine, cedar, and fir. Above 10,000 feet in the San Gorgonio Wilderness is boreal vegetation, sparse but hardy. Desert-facing slopes on the north and east are primarily pinyon–juniper woodland above and Lower Sonoran vegetation below.

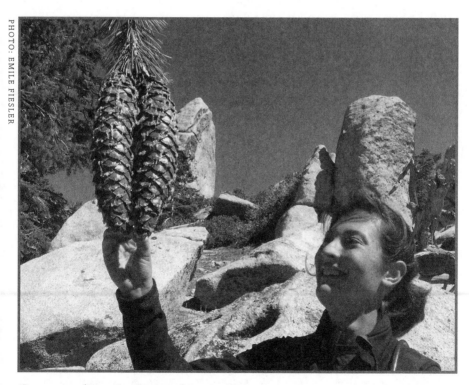

PHOTO: EMILE FIESLER

Sugar pine (Pinus lambertiana) *cones*

"Nothing seems more hauntingly Californian than the sight and aroma of chaparral drenched in sunlight," wrote a prominent western naturalist. What is chaparral? It is defined as "a dominant, deep-rooted, shrubby vegetation, chiefly evergreen, with leathery, often hard-surfaced leaves." The many-branched shrubs tend to look like miniature trees, and for this reason chaparral has been called "elfin forest." These shrubs can adapt themselves to a wide spectrum of soils, and can exist in terrain and climatic conditions that will support little else. The woodiness of trunks and stems and the thick, small leaves allow chaparral to conserve the moisture they absorb during the short rainy season through the long, hot, rainless summer, so they are ideally suited to Southern California hillsides. Shrubs collectively called chaparral include dozens of species, and many of them are present in the San Bernardinos. The most abundant types here are chamise, scrub oak, manzanita, California holly, and several forms of ceanothus. Hikers generally try to avoid chaparral; indeed, anyone so unfortunate as to become caught in its thorny maze will quickly come to curse it. But those who pay a friendly visit to the elfin forest instead of trying to thrash through it will come to see chaparral in a more favorable light. In bloom, many of the shrubs are sprinkled with colorful flowers. Yucca bursting with fragrant, creamy-white blossoms, ceanothus blooming misty blue or white, California laurel unfolding masses of yellow flowers, wild lilac giving forth its sweet aroma after a spring rain—these charms await the casual visitor. Chaparral is also valuable as a soil cover; where it has been burned off, rain rushes down the hillsides, causing severe erosion on the slopes and flooding in the canyons and lowlands.

Within the chaparral belt, in the watered canyons, is an association of plants that naturalists call streamside woodland. Lush, verdant growth is the chief characteristic of this habitat. Many varieties of ferns and rushes and a profusion of flowering herbs grow rich under a green canopy of sycamore, white alder, willow, big-leaf maple, and live oak. After one has slogged for several miles through the elfin forest, reaching this streamside woodland is a special treat—particularly on a warm summer day. The streamside woodlands of Bear and Siberia Creeks are particularly delectable.

Amid this ocean of chaparral, nestled on sun-sheltered slopes, are sometimes found islands of bigcone Douglas-fir, the lowest-growing conifer in the Southern California mountains. Easily identifiable by its long, horizontal branches and its sparse foliage, this adaptable tree is found from elevations as low as 2,000 feet up into the main mountain forest at 6,000 and 7,000 feet.

The crest of the San Bernardinos from Crestline to Big Bear Lake is blessed by a forest as magnificent as any in Southern California. Here grow dense and stately stands of Jeffrey pine, ponderosa pine, sugar pine, Coulter pine, knobcone pine, white fir, and incense-cedar. Adding a beautiful touch of color is the California black oak, its leaves sprouting pink in springtime, light green in summer, and turning a striking yellow in autumn. Beneath ponderosa pine and incense-cedar, we find Pacific dogwood, and no other forest flower equals the ethereal grace of the dogwood's white blossoms. Walking beneath the canopy of this mountain forest can be a refreshing and enriching experience.

High up in the San Gorgonio Wilderness—on the granite slopes of Grayback and Mount San Bernardino, in the Dry Lake basin—is what naturalists call boreal or subalpine forest. The predominant conifer here is lodgepole pine: tough, cold-resistant, erect where sheltered or twisted and bent where exposed to nature's high-altitude fury. Limber pines, gnarled and ground-hugging, live a marginal existence on the loftiest ridges. The high-altitude chaparral, composed in part of manzanita, snowbrush, bush chinquapin, is rich and green, and waist high. In season, alpine wildflowers burst forth in splashing colors. This is delightful hiking country, a touch of the High Sierra in Southern California. May it ever stay wild.

The back side of the San Bernardinos shows the strong influence of the desert. Here, just over the ridge from the main mountain forest, lying in the "rain shadow" of the range, are extensive stands of pinyon pine and western juniper. Lower down grows that shaggy monarch of the high desert, the Joshua tree. Hardwooded mountain mahogany thrives on the higher desert-facing slopes. Along Deep Creek and the West Fork of the Mojave grow Fremont cottonwood, desert willow, and velvet ash. Mesquite and several varieties of sage are the dominant shrubs below 5,000 feet. This desert slope of the San Bernardinos sees few hikers; this is a shame, for during the cooler months this is an enchanting landscape.

WILDLIFE

The wildlife of the San Bernardino Mountains is timid and, for the most part, scarce. Man has killed off or driven out many species that once roamed in abundance. Grizzly bears, which were thick in these mountains during pioneer times, have been gone for a century. Black bears—misnamed, for most of them are brown—were once near extinction, but seem to be on the increase. Naturalists estimate that there are around 200–250 in the range. On desert-facing slopes live a handful of statuesque bighorn sheep, extremely shy and seldom seen except on the cliffs above Whitewater Preserve. There are perhaps 15 mountain lions in the San Bernardinos. Rare is the hiker who spies one of these big cats romping through the forest, although its large and unmistakable track is sometimes seen

*Pinion jay (*Gymnorhinus cyanocephalus*)*

on the trail. The most abundant large mammal in the range is the California mule deer. Several thousand head roam the San Bernardinos from top to bottom, feeding on a great variety of plants and sometimes being fed upon by the mountain lion. Smaller mammals include the bobcat, ring-tailed cat, gray fox, coyote, opossum, raccoon, skunk, weasel, and a host of squirrels and chipmunks. Although bald eagles were wiped out from Southern California by the 1950s, a breeding pair reestablished a nest near Grays Peak in 2012. The only creature considered dangerous to man in these mountains is the western rattlesnake, abundant below 6,000 feet, sometimes seen up to 8,000 feet. However, most rattlers are not very aggressive and will crawl away if given half a chance.

These, then, are the San Bernardinos—overused yet possessing prime wilderness, smothered with elfin forest below and rich with conifers above, sea-influenced on one side and desert-facing on the other, the highest mountain country in Southern California and some of the most gentle. These are the aspects of the San Bernardinos that have lured visitors into the high country for decades. Come up and sample its delights.

WILDFIRES

In recent years, drought and fires have been a major part of the story of the San Bernardino National Forest. A century of well-intentioned fire suppression led to thick buildups of forest litter so that fires today spread rapidly and do great damage. This problem has been compounded by recent droughts that have weakened trees, allowing bark beetles to invade and kill mature trees. These trees in turn become more tinder for fire. Major fires of recent years include the following:

1999 WILLOW FIRE 63,000 acres north of Lake Arrowhead, caused by arson

2003 OLD FIRE 91,000 acres around Lake Arrowhead, caused by arson, leaving at least 5 people dead and 993 homes destroyed. Rickie Lee Fowler, a violent meth addict, was sentenced to death in 2012 for starting the fire.

2006 ESPERANZA FIRE 40,000 acres south of Banning, killing 5 firefighters. Serial arsonist Raymond Lee Oyler was sentenced to death in 2009 for starting the fire.

2006 SAWTOOTH COMPLEX FIRE 61,000 acres west of Yucca Valley, caused by multiple lightning strikes

2007 SLIDE AND BUTLER II FIRES 26,000 acres west of Big Bear Lake, caused by lightning

2013 MOUNTAIN FIRE 27,000 acres on the Desert Divide, caused by electrical equipment malfunction

2015 LAKE FIRE 32,000 acres on the north side of the San Gorgonio Wilderness east to the Onyx Peak area, caused by humans

The Forest Service fire suppression budget rose from 16% of its annual expenditures in 1995 to 50% in 2015 and continues to rise. Traditional functions of the Forest Service such as maintaining and patrolling trails and assisting visitors are now done largely by volunteers or not at all.

The Forest Service now tends to close severely impacted areas for five years or more after a major fire to allow vegetation a chance to recover and avoid humans and ATVs developing unauthorized trails. Many hikes in this book are closed at the time of this writing as they recover from the Lake and Mountain Fires.

Human History of the
San Bernardino Mountains

*I only went out for a walk and finally concluded to stay out till sun-
down, for going out, I found, was really going in.*

—John Muir, who visited the
San Bernardino Mountains in 1896

Mountains have always held a special significance to humans. They have inspired
in us awe and fear and wonder, and filled us with curiosity and longing. They have
affected our climate and helped to shape our way of life. They have afforded us
livelihood, refuge, pleasure, and peace. They have been objects of affection and
worship. In all, mountains have been a great source of human fulfillment.

The San Bernardino Mountains have been important to us since our ances-
tors first set foot in Southern California. To the Serrano and Cahuilla tribes, they
were a source of food, water, and materials. Spanish explorers and Californios,
the Mexican Californians, sought water and timber. American pioneers expanded
the use of water and timber, and added a feverish quest for gold. The mountains
continue to entice people to build homes here and find natural areas for recreation, solitude, and relaxation.

A complete history of the San Bernardino Mountains would be a monumental work, covering all of the varied and sometimes hectic human activities in the
range. Like the neighboring San Gabriels, the proximity of the San Bernardinos to
centers of civilization has resulted in their being swarmed over, dug into, and built
upon to a degree equaled by few other mountain ranges in the West. All we have
space for here are the highlights of this activity, a sketch to give you a general idea
of what humans have done to these mountains.

FIRST PEOPLES

For untold centuries before the arrival of Europeans, Native Americans lived in
and below the San Bernardino Mountains. The mountains provided them acorns,
pinyon nuts, berries, and other wild fruits, together with such game as they killed
with their bows and arrows or caught in their snares and traps. The mountains
were thick with wildlife. Native Americans avoided bears, but relished deer and
rabbits, both for their food and their skins. In the mountains they gathered fibers
for ropes and baskets, willow splints for arrow shafts, and greasewood for any
number of uses.

To make their way through the mountains, Native Americans forged a network of trails. Hunting trails, food-gathering trails, and trading trails crisscrossed much of the range. The most important of these trade routes was the ancient Mojave Trail, which led up the Mojave River into the mountains, up Sawpit Canyon to the crest of the range near today's Monument Peak, and down the south slope via the ridge just west of Devil Canyon. This famous pathway, along with another route through Cajon Pass, was used for centuries by desert Native Americans to trade with peoples living in the San Bernardino Valley and coastal plains.

The Spaniards gave the name *Serrano*—meaning "mountaineer"—to these native peoples of the San Bernardino Mountains. Most of the Serrano villages were located below the south slopes of the range, although some groups apparently lived most of the year well up in the mountains. In the Big Bear region dwelled the Pervetum people, and around Little Bear Valley (now Lake Arrowhead) lived the Kaiwiems. South of the Santa Ana River were villages of the Wanakik or (Pass) Cahuillas, one of the three branches of this widespread Native American group. North and east of the mountains—in the desert and along the Colorado—lived the Mojave people.

EARLY EXPLORERS

The Spanish soldier Pedro Fages entered the scene in 1772—the first European known to have reached the mountains. Fages was pursuing army deserters from San Diego; he followed them as far as the Colorado Desert. Evidently the desire to do some more exploring seized him, for he turned north and skirted the San Jacinto Mountains by a route Juan Bautista de Anza was to travel two years later. Fages entered the San Bernardino Valley, crossed the mountains in the vicinity of Cajon Pass, and made his way northwest along the south edge of the Mojave Desert to the Tehachapis, the southern San Joaquin Valley, San Luis Obispo, and eventually Monterey.

Fages was followed four years later by the intrepid missionary-explorer-martyr Fray Francisco Hermenegildo Garcés, who crossed the San Bernardino Mountains on his way from the lower Colorado River to Mission San Gabriel in 1776. From his diary, it appears that he used the ancient Mojave Trail over the mountains, rather than Cajon Pass. (In 1931, the San Bernardino County Historical Society erected a monument to mark the point where Garcés crossed the crest of the range.)

In a notable 1806 expedition, Fray Jose Zalvidea started from Mission Santa Barbara, explored the southern San Joaquin Valley, crossed the Tehachapis to the desert, and skirted the northern foothills of the San Gabriel and San Bernardino Mountains. Fray Zalvidea and his party entered the latter near the junction of

Deep Creek and the Mojave's West Fork, then traversed through Summit Valley and Coyote Canyon into lower Cajon Canyon before continuing on to San Gabriel.

Four years later—on May 20, 1810, the feast day of Saint Bernardino of Siena, a Franciscan preacher of the 15th century—a party from Mission San Gabriel set up a temporary chapel in the valley south of the mountains.[1] From this came the name "San Bernardino." This original chapel was evidently short-lived, but in 1819 Spaniards came into the San Bernardino Valley to stay. An *asistencia* of Mission San Gabriel was established southeast of the present city of San Bernardino.

The Spaniards, and a short time later the Californios,[2] soon were engaged in agriculture in the San Bernardino Valley. To bring water to the lands under cultivation, a *zanja* (irrigation ditch) was built from Mill Creek into the valley in 1820. This was the earliest known use of water from the San Bernardino Mountains for irrigation. Timber was taken out also by the Californios. In 1830, mountain hemlock was cut in Mill Creek for use in building the San Bernardino *asistencia*— the earliest known logging in the mountains. Other than taking out water and carrying on some small-scale lumbering, the Spaniards and Californios put the mountains to very little use.

Until the 1840s, only the foothills and low western regions of the San Bernardino Mountains were known to nonnatives; the higher country to the east was virtually unexplored. It remained for Benjamin D. Wilson to make known the area now occupied by Big Bear Lake. In the summer of 1845, Wilson, who owned part interest in the Jurupa Rancho (Riverside), led a troop of Mexican cavalry in search of cattle rustlers. Setting out toward the desert, where it was believed the rustlers had headed, Wilson divided his command. Most were sent through Cajon Pass, while Wilson took 22 troopers directly across the mountains. After two days of strenuous travel, Wilson's party reached a wooded valley and a small lake inhabited by scores of grizzly bears. The soldiers formed pairs, and they bagged and skinned 11 bears. Then they continued across the mountains, rejoined the main party, and surprised the rustlers along the Mojave River. Afterward, Wilson and his 22 troopers returned home via the mountain lake. Here they lassoed 11 more bears, enough for each man to have a bearskin trophy as a remembrance of the trip. Wilson gave the name "Bear Lake" to the little body of water high in the mountains, and later the grassy basin south of the lake became known as Bear Valley. Years later the name of the body of water Wilson discovered was changed

---

1   The establishing of this chapel in 1810 is disputed by historians. The original diary reporting its founding has long been lost.

2   This term refers to Mexican Californians. In 1820, Mexico won independence from Spain and by 1823 had established hegemony over California.

to Baldwin Lake, but the name he gave survives in Big Bear Lake, created when a dam was built at the lower end of Bear Valley in 1884.

The 1840s were watershed years in the history of the mountains. Already mentioned was Wilson's expedition, opening up a part of the range little known before. This was the decade that saw the last of the Native American raids across the mountains, when Wak (or Walkara), a crafty Ute chieftain, led marauding bands through Cajon Pass and over the Mojave Trail, making off with livestock and striking fear in the hearts of rancheros as far as Claremont and Azusa. These raids caused authorities to station soldiers near Cajon Pass. The attacks continued into the 1850s, but on a diminished scale. In 1848, California became part of the United States, and with the coming of the American settlers from the east, the mountains began to receive much more attention.

During these years, the mountains became known by the name they hold today—the San Bernardinos. Thomas Coulter, in his *Notes on Upper California: A Journey from Monterey to the Colorado River in 1832,* published by the Royal Geographical Society of London in 1835, refers to the "great snowy peak of San Bernardino." Coulter, an Irish botanist, is remembered in the name of the Coulter pine. Charles Wilkes's map of 1841 labeled San Bernardino Peak "Mt. Bernardino," and by 1849 most maps showing the mountains used this name or "San Bernardino."

LOGGING IN THE SAN BERNARDINOS

It was the Mormons, who lived in the San Bernardino Valley from 1851 until 1857, who really opened up the mountains. The Mormon settlers needed lumber for building their town of San Bernardino, and what better place to get this lumber than from the rich stands of pine and cedar in the nearby mountains? Their first efforts were directed toward Mill Creek; here Daniel Sexton built the sawmill in 1852 that gave Mill Creek its name. A second mill was built farther up the creek the following year, known as Mormon Mill. Stumps discovered years later revealed that lumbering was undertaken as far up-canyon as the site of present-day Fallsvale, well up under the shoulder of San Gorgonio Mountain.

Mill Creek met the Mormons' lumber needs for several months, but soon their eyes turned to the much richer stands of timber on the mountain crest to the north. But first a road would have to be built up the steep south slopes of the range. This was accomplished through back-breaking efforts in 1853, by "every man leaving his family in camp and freely laboring and camping upon the road incessantly until finished." This first road onto the crest of the San Bernardinos climbed directly up Hot Springs (later Waterman) Canyon and gave access to Seely and Huston Flats, then heavily timbered. Charles Crisman built the first sawmill here within 10 days of the road's completion, dragging up an engine and boiler for this small, portable operation. The first major sawmill on the mountain crest was erected by the brothers David and Wellington Seely in the summer of 1853; they used waterpower from the creek flowing through Seely Flat. Oxen hauled the cut wood down to San Bernardino. By the middle of 1854, the Mormons had six mills operating in the San Bernardino Mountains—four on the mountain crest and two on Mill Creek. Most of the lumber was used in San Bernardino, but some was hauled as far away as Los Angeles.

The Mormons returned to Utah in 1857, but the mountain sawmills remained, and more were built in ensuing years. Strawberry Valley, Grass Valley, Little Bear Valley (later Lake Arrowhead), Hooks Creek, Twin Peaks, Green Valley, Snow Valley, Big Bear, Holcomb Valley, and Barton Flats all were the scene of lumbering operations, some of them continuing into recent years. Most ambitious were the activities of the Brookings Lumber Company at Fredalba, near today's Running Springs,

PHOTO COURTESY OF TOM CORE

Logging train of the Brookings Lumber Company, 1904

in operation from 1898 until 1910. Robert Brookings built a narrow-gauge logging railroad network that gave access to most of the timber between Heaps Peak and Arrowbear Lake—quite an expanse of mountain country (see photo on previous page). Remnants of this turn-of-the-20th-century operation are still visible.

SOUTHERN CALIFORNIA'S GOLD RUSH

Timber was the first magnet that lured nonnatives into the San Bernardino Mountains; gold was the second. The precious metal was reportedly found in the mountains as early as 1857, and some prospecting activity took place in 1859, but not until William F. Holcomb made his famous discovery in Holcomb Valley in 1860 was there a real gold rush. The story goes that Holcomb and a companion named Ben Chouteau, members of a prospecting party in Bear Valley, crossed the ridge that separates the waters of the Santa Ana River from those of the Mojave River during a hunting trip and shot two bears. The next day they returned to secure the animals, and in addition to obtaining bear meat they discovered something much more thrilling—gold! Within a week the entire Holcomb party had moved into the gold-laden basin—later known as Holcomb Valley—and were feverishly digging for placer gold. The news of the discovery spread to San Bernardino, and by early July Holcomb Valley was swarming with prospectors, who were making $5–$10 a day. A boomtown sprung up in short order; the miners named it Belleville, in honor of little Belle Van Dusen, whose mother had furnished a flag for a patriotic occasion. More gold was discovered across the ridge in Bear Valley, and by the fall of 1860 the entire mountain region was overrun with gold seekers.

The original route to the mines was by wagon road from San Bernardino to the mouth of Santa Ana Canyon, then by steep pack trail up the Santa Ana River to Seven Oaks and over the ridge into Bear Valley. Bringing in provisions by this route was difficult and expensive, so the miners subscribed $1,500, which they gave to a Mr. Van Dusen to build a new wagon road. Van Dusen wisely decided that the south slope of the range below Bear Valley was too steep and rugged for such a road; instead he built his road northwesterly from Holcomb Valley down to the Mojave River, then southwest to near the head of Cajon Pass, where it met the toll road through the pass into the San Bernardino Valley just completed by John Brown. By this roundabout route, all types of supplies were transported to the mines.

Through most of the 1860s, mining activities involving hundreds of men continued in Holcomb and Bear Valleys. At one time the population in Holcomb Valley alone is said to have reached 2,000. These were years of stormy excitement and controversy. Ruffians and outlaws came in large numbers, and during the Civil

Rare photograph of Gold Mountain Mill in operation, circa 1910

War, Southern sympathizers were vocal and active. As many as 40 men and probably many more met violent deaths during this frenzied period. But gradually the placer gold gave out and the miners drifted away to new diggings elsewhere in the West. By 1870, Belleville was a ghost town and Holcomb Valley's hectic era was history.

Although the placer gold was gone, many quartz-gold prospects remained, hidden in canyons and hillsides throughout the Holcomb Valley–Bear Valley area. The last three decades of the 1800s saw the development of many of these hard-rock prospects—the Osborne Mine northeast of Holcomb Valley, the Ozier on John Bull Flat, the Rose Mine southeast of Baldwin Lake, the Santa Fe group in Blackhawk Canyon, and, most productive of all, Lucky Baldwin's Doble Mine on Gold Mountain. Gold was mined and milled at these and other prospects well into the 20th century.

BLUE GOLD

Water was the third lure that brought outsiders into the San Bernardino Mountains. The streams gushing down from the high country had been utilized for domestic purposes and irrigation since settlers had first made homes in the San Bernardino Valley. But most of the water was wasted, flowing out to sea during the wetter months, and not available during the hot months when many of the streams dried up. The possibility of using Bear Valley as a storage reservoir was brought to public attention in 1880, when a state engineer's survey said the basin was one of the best sites for such a reservoir in Southern California. In 1883, the founders of the new colony of Redlands incorporated the Bear Valley Land and Water Company, intent upon impounding water in a mountain reservoir for use on the newly developed valley land. A single-arch, stone-and-cement dam was completed at a cost of $75,000 the following year; thus was born Big Bear Lake. Although the mountain lake was now reality and the dam (to the surprise of many engineers) held, the water company was flooded with a mass of litigation over water rights that lasted for decades. In 1910–11, a second, stronger dam was constructed just below the original one; this is the dam the highway crosses today, holding back a lake 8 miles long, containing 72,000 acre-feet of water.

Lake Arrowhead was formed in much the same way. In 1891 a group of Ohio businessmen organized the Arrowhead Reservoir Company, and two years later began construction of a dam across Little Bear Creek. The dam was completed in 1908, and tunnels were dug to divert the waters from their natural flow (northward) to the San Bernardino Valley. But a mass of litigation was involved here, too. The state supreme court doomed the irrigation project by ruling that water could

PHOTO COURTESY OF BIG BEAR VALLEY HISTORICAL SOCIETY
MUSEUM, KENDALL STONE COLLECTION

The Talmadge Sawmill in Little Bear Valley (now under the waters of Lake Arrowhead), 1870s

not be diverted from one watershed to another. But Little Bear Lake remained, to be renamed Lake Arrowhead in 1922.

During this era a number of toll roads were built into the mountains. The first ones were the Daley Road up Twin Creek Canyon, built in 1859, and the Cajon Pass Toll Road constructed by John Brown two years later. During the 1890s four new ones appeared—the Bear Valley, City Creek Canyon, Devils Canyon, and Arrowhead Reservoir Company toll roads. On the desert side the Johnson and Cushenbury Grades were gouged out and another route opened into the high country. Then came the most famous road of all, the Rim of the World Highway (Highway 18), 101 miles long, completed in 1915.

TODAY'S GOLD: RECREATION

With the roads came people, and with people arose the fourth lure of the mountains: recreation. At first there were cabins, then hotels and stores and saloons. Gus Knight Jr. built the first mountain resort at Big Bear Lake in the 1890s. Pine Knot was the first lakeside community here. Down in the canyon of the Santa Ana River was Seven Oaks, a popular tent camp in the 1890s. In the 1920s Lake Arrowhead became a resort community, and subdivision for residential purposes began. Then came the development of Crestline, Lake Gregory, Running

Road to Forest Home

PHOTO: G. E. SCHMIDT

Entering Mill Creek Canyon with San Bernardino Peak in the distance, 1915

Springs, Green Valley, and many more centers of civilization in the high country. The mountains were being overrun by people.

Fortunately, humankind includes those who work to protect and preserve as well as those who might pillage and destroy. By 1890 it was evident to many far-sighted people that the San Bernardino Mountains needed federal protection. Even those with myopic vision could see that reckless cutting of timber was destroying the mountain watershed. As a result of strong pressure from conservation-minded citizens, President Benjamin Harrison signed an act creating the San Bernardino Forest Reserve on February 25, 1893. In 1898 the first rangers were assigned to the reserve and a patrol system was established. Unfortunately, large areas of the high country were already in private ownership and outside their jurisdiction. But the lands within the forest reserve were zealously guarded, and, starting about 1902, burned areas were reforested. In 1908 the San Bernardino Forest Reserve was joined with the Angeles and the designation was changed from forest reserve to national forest. This union lasted until 1925, when San Bernardino National Forest again became a separate entity. In 1931 the highest and most primitive part of the mountains was set aside as the San Gorgonio Primitive Area (since 1964, the San Gorgonio Wilderness), to be forever preserved in its natural state.

Today, the San Bernardinos receive annually about 15 million visitors, making them one of the most heavily used mountain regions in the nation. With this many people motoring, sightseeing, picnicking, camping, horseback riding, boating, skiing, and hiking in the mountains, nature is hard-pressed to hold its own.

Even areas considered inviolate face pressures generated by the people explosion. During the early 1960s, commercial skiing interests waged a determined and almost successful effort to "open up" the heart of the San Gorgonio Wilderness to roads, resorts, and ski lifts. Conservationists, led by the Defenders of the San Gorgonio Wilderness, barely won that battle. Now the problem is not skiers but hikers—too many of them swarming over wilderness trails and into campgrounds. To save the wilderness from the perils of overuse, the Forest Service in 1971 instituted the wilderness permit system. Permits are now rationed in most wilderness areas, allowing only a limited number of people to enter the area at one time.

Regardless of the history, the future of these mountains rests with the people who frequent them. They are the ultimate guardians of Nature's handiwork.

■ Hike 1 PACIFIC CREST TRAIL TO SAN ANDREAS RIFT VIEWPOINT ⤢ 🐐

HIKE LENGTH 6.5 miles out-and-back; 1,000' elevation gain
DIFFICULTY Moderate
SEASON October–May
TOPO MAP *Cajon* (7.5-minute)

■ FEATURES

The San Andreas Fault, perhaps the most famous fault in the world, has carved a badland beneath the Cajon Pass between the San Bernardino and San Gabriel Mountains. This hike climbs the Pacific Crest Trail (PCT) from Interstate 15 to the ridgeline. It offers terrific views, both of the natural features that the fault has carved and of the complex lifelines that man has built through this gap between the mountain ranges.

■ DESCRIPTION

From Interstate 15, turn east onto Highway 138. Immediately turn right onto the Wagon Train frontage road and follow it 0.3 mile south past gas and fast food to the Pacific Crest Trail Trailhead at the end (**GPS N34° 18.362' W117° 27.969'**).

Follow the trail northeast up a shallow canyon. In 0.7 mile, cross a gas pipeline road. Just beyond, cross seasonal Crowder Creek beneath some cottonwoods. The PCT now begins a long climb up the ridge to the east.

In another 0.2 mile, pass under the first of three sets of high-voltage transmission lines that run along this side of the freeway. The trail now loosely follows and occasionally crosses Forest Road 3N44, which services these power lines. Soon pass the second set of transmission lines.

Views expand as you continue up the ridge. Whipple yuccas dot the slopes and put up an impressive show of blossoms in late spring after a good winter's rain. At the top, reach a breathtaking view atop heavily eroded cliffs (**GPS N34° 19.029' W117° 26.198'**).

From here, you can take in the handiwork of nature and man. The San Gabriel Mountains, pushed up as the Pacific and North American Plates crash together and buckle, represent one of the fastest-growing (and fastest-eroding) mountain ranges in the world. Mount Baldy is the highest point, surrounded by a host of subsidiary summits. The jagged sandstone slabs in the San Andreas Rift Zone are called the Mormon Rocks to commemorate these early American settlers who crossed this pass in 1851 en route from Salt Lake City to San Bernardino.

Through this landscape run dozens of lifelines connecting people, goods, energy, and data between the Los Angeles Basin and the desert. Native Americans

Eroded cliffs near the rift vista

have used this trade route for untold centuries. Spanish officer Pedro Fages crossed the Cajon in 1772 on a lengthy exploration while looking for deserters. Jedediah Smith was the first American explorer to cross the pass in 1826. Route 66 through the pass began as a wagon toll road in 1861, and the Atchison, Topeka, and Santa Fe Railroad laid tracks through the pass in the 1880s. Today, Interstate 15 and the BNSF and Union Pacific tracks wind their way down the pass, and 500-kV transmission lines carry power from the Hoover Dam. Hidden beneath the surface, two 36-inch high-pressure natural-gas pipelines and two smaller petroleum pipelines carry fuel to Las Vegas and the desert military bases. Five fiber-optic conduits carry data to and from the basin.

It is possible to continue up another 0.4 mile to the third set of transmission lines beneath Forest Road 3N22 on the ridgeline. However, this road attracts a contingent of folks fooling around with guns, and is neither particularly scenic nor safe.

■ Hike 2 CAJON MOUNTAIN 🐾 🐕 👫 ☸

HIKE LENGTH 3 miles out-and-back; 500' elevation gain
DIFFICULTY Easy
SEASON October–May
TOPO MAP *Cajon* (7.5-minute)

■ FEATURES

Cajon Mountain (5,310 feet) towers over the lower end of the Cajon Pass area, and its summit offers a sweeping panorama of the great fault-carved passage through the mountains. From here you can see the San Andreas Fault, its strange slanting ridges and twisted rock formations all bearing in a northwest-southeast direction. Directly below is the Blue Cut, where Cajon Canyon narrows to a gorge and crosses the fault. The view beyond is equally grand, with Mount San Antonio (Old Baldy) and the cluster of high peaks at the east end of the San Gabriels looming massive and grayish.

This trip is all on fire road. In the winter and early spring, the eastern peaks of the San Gabriels are dazzling in their mantle of whiteness, and the foothills are velvet-green.

Cajon Mountain at sunset

■ DESCRIPTION

From Interstate 15, turn northeast onto Highway 138 and proceed 11 miles to the signed Cleghorn Road exit just beyond mile marker 138 SBD 26.18. Note that this Cleghorn Road is Forest Road 2N49, not to be confused with the other Cleghorn Road, 2N47, coming up from Interstate 15. Turn right (west) and drive past group camps. Cleghorn turns into a poor dirt fire road (2N49) 0.9 mile from the highway. Continue 5.6 miles, crossing Cleghorn Pass, to a junction with Cajon Mountain Road, on your right (west). Park outside the locked gate (**GPS N34° 16.240' W117° 24.241'**).

Proceed past the locked gate, following Cajon Mountain Road through a delightful forest of oak, bigcone Douglas-fir, and incense-cedar, as it descends to a saddle, then climbs across chaparral-clad slopes to the summit of Cajon Mountain, 1.5 miles (**GPS N34° 16.266' W117° 25.454'**). A fire lookout tower once stood here. This area burned in the 2003 Old Fire. Enjoy the superb panorama; then return the same way.

■ Hike 3 HEART ROCK 🥾 🐕 🧍

HIKE LENGTH 1 mile out-and-back; 300' elevation gain
DIFFICULTY Easy
SEASON All year
TOPO MAP *Silverwood Lake* (7.5-minute)

■ FEATURES

Seeley Creek descends the north slope of the San Bernardinos, from its source west of Crestline to Miller Canyon, and eventually into the Mojave River. This short, delightful forest walk follows a stretch of the bubbling creek under a canopy of very tall Jeffrey pines, incense-cedars, and black oaks. You end up alongside two limpid pools with a natural waterslide between. Nearby is Heart Rock, with a heart-shaped hole in the middle through which water sometimes splashes. For an introduction to the San Bernardinos, you can do no better than this magnificent forest stroll. The creek was misnamed in memory of David and Wellington Seely, brothers who established a saw mill in 1853.

Thoughtless people leave their litter beside the pools on the creek. If you bring a trash bag and carry some of it out, you'll help keep the creek beautiful for all of us.

■ DESCRIPTION

From Crestline, take Highway 138 northwest, down to the Camp Seely entrance road at mile marker 138 SBD 35.00. Turn left, then left again just outside the gate

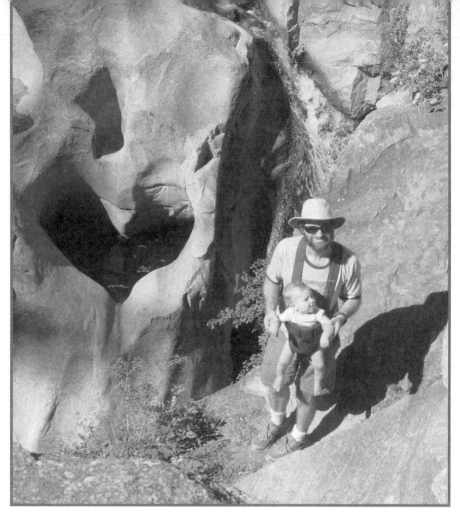

Heart Rock

to Camp Seely, and follow the narrow paved road to a parking area on your right, marked with a metal pole with 4W07 (the trail number) on it, 0.4 mile from the highway (**GPS N34° 15.426' W117° 18.350'**).

    Walk down the broad trail as it descends north, through a shady forest of Jeffrey pine and incense-cedar, just above the creek. After 0.5 mile, your pathway climbs a slight rise and forks as Seeley Creek abruptly drops. To your right, a short walk gets you to a rocky outcropping directly above Seeley Creek, where you look down on Heart Rock (**GPS N34° 15.732' W117° 18.293'**). Return to the main trail and follow it steeply down to the creek. Here, deep in the forest, are two pools with a natural waterslide between.

    Return the same way.

■ Hike 4 DEEP CREEK HOT SPRINGS FROM BOWEN RANCH ↗

HIKE LENGTH 4 miles out-and-back; 900' elevation gain

DIFFICULTY Moderate

SEASON All year

TOPO MAP *Lake Arrowhead* (7.5-minute)

PERMIT Fee for entering via private Bowen Ranch

■ FEATURES

Deep Creek, on the north slope of the mountains, boasts the only genuine hot springs in the San Bernardinos. As many as 20 hikers bathe in the three warm pools beside the cold creek on winter weekends. During the summer, Deep Creek offers swimming holes and sandy beaches near the springs. Overnight camping is prohibited at the hot springs, but you may camp at Bowen Ranch. Please protect the hot springs: do not bring glass and make a special effort to leave the place cleaner than you found it.

■ DESCRIPTION

From Interstate 15, 6 miles north of Cajon Summit, turn right (east) onto Main Street in Hesperia. Proceed 7.2 miles, and then bear left (east) on Rock Springs Road where Main Street curves south. Cross the dry bed of the Mojave River and follow Rock Springs Road east to a junction where its name changes to Roundup Way, 10.2 miles from the freeway. Continue east on Roundup for 4.4 miles, then turn right

Cold pool beside Deep Creek Hot Springs

(south) onto the good dirt Bowen Ranch Road. Proceed up the latter, staying right at a junction with Coxey Truck Trail at 2.1 miles, and right again in 1.9 miles at another junction with Oak Springs Road, to Bowen Ranch, on the left 5.4 miles from Roundup Way.

You must stop at the ranch house, register, and pay a modest fee. Camping is allowed 0.5 mile beyond the ranch house. The trail begins at road's end atop a hill (**GPS N34° 21.510' W117° 09.881'**). You descend south, pass through a gate onto Forest Service land, and veer left, then right down a wash. You traverse a ridge, then drop steeply down to Deep Creek. The hot springs are across the creek, which can be a cold and difficult ford in the winter (**GPS N34° 20.364' W117° 10.641'**).

The hottest pool is enclosed in rocks above the creek. Lukewarm pools are below, separated from the creek by a constructed rock barrier. Don't submerge your head in hot pools, which contain elevated levels of fecal coliform. A bather died in 1991 after becoming infected here with *Naegleria fowleri*, a rare brain-eating amoeba that lives in warm waters and enters through the nose.

Return the way you came. Remember, it's all uphill on the way back.

■ Hike 5 DEEP CREEK HOT SPRINGS FROM KINLEY CREEK ⬈

HIKE LENGTH 5.5 miles out-and-back; 1,900' elevation gain
DIFFICULTY Strenuous
SEASON October–May
TOPO MAP *Lake Arrowhead* (7.5-minute)

■ FEATURES

This alternate approach to Deep Creek Hot Springs is more strenuous but avoids the use fee at Bowen Ranch and the cold ford of Deep Creek. Thus, it is a preferable route during the winter. This is not an official Forest Service trail and is extremely steep in places; it is not recommended for those unsure of their footing. The steep, shadeless canyon is an oven in summer. Remember that Deep Creek Hot Springs is a special place; camping and glass bottles are prohibited.

■ DESCRIPTION

From Lake Arrowhead, follow Highway 173 north 5 miles to the Rock Camp Forest Service Station, then 2.5 miles farther to the bridge over Kinley Creek. If the highway turns to dirt, you have gone 0.2 mile too far. Park on the shoulder of the highway (**GPS N34° 19.081' W117° 11.753'**).

Look for the trail on the northeast side of the road. The trail immediately passes a gate with a sign reading Bradford Ridge Path to Deep Creek. Round a corner and look left for a waterfall on Kinley Creek. The 1999 Willow Fire ravaged more than 60,000 acres, including almost everything along this trail, but look for the "Unburned Acre" where you can still see mature oaks as they once stood. Scrub oak and other chaparral are resprouting. Mature pines along the creek bottom also survived the inferno.

In 0.7 mile, the trail begins climbing steeply out of Kinley Creek. In another 0.7 mile, cross a minor saddle and start descending into a drainage leading down toward Deep Creek. In 0.4 mile, reach a junction by a gap in an old fence. A very steep side trail to the right shortcuts down, but the main trail leads straight down the ridge to the north and intersects the Pacific Crest Trail (PCT) in 0.4 mile at the toe of the ridge. Turn right and follow the PCT 0.5 mile to Deep Creek Hot Springs (**GPS N34° 20.364' W117° 10.641'**).

If you wish to return via the shortcut, it leaves the PCT at the first canyon west of the hot springs. Follow the canyon bottom southwest; then leave it and climb the steep, sandy trail back to the fence.

■ Hike 6 THE PINNACLES 🖈 🐐 👫

HIKE LENGTH 3.5 miles out-and-back; 1,000' elevation gain
DIFFICULTY Moderate
SEASON November–May
TOPO MAP *Lake Arrowhead* (7.5-minute)

■ FEATURES

The Pinnacles are an imposing stack of jumbo, weathered granite boulders cutting high over the badlands on the desert-facing slope of the San Bernardinos.

■ DESCRIPTION

From Lake Arrowhead, follow Highway 173 north 5 miles to the Rock Camp Forest Service Station, then 0.5 mile farther to a turnout on the left side of the road (**GPS N34° 17.657' W117° 12.796'**). If you reach the old trailhead a few yards south of the Arrowhead Rifle Range, you have gone 0.2 mile too far.

Walk through an opening in the fence and follow the trail north, crossing a dry wash. If the path seems to fork at times, follow the most used branch. In 0.3 mile, reach an unsigned junction with the old trail coming in on the right from the Arrowhead Rifle Range. Veer left and meander up a wash through chaparral and boulders until you can climb the steep hill to the Pinnacles. Continue northwest through scrawny chaparral and around large boulders to the foot of the main ridge.

The trail ascends the ridge to a plateau scattered with granite towers, the Pinnacles. The most prominent tower on the north side of the trail is called the Bong and features 5.10 to 5.12 routes for hard-core rock climbers.

The summit is about 0.25 mile farther northwest. The trail steepens abruptly near the end. Scramble up the summit boulders to an airy perch with outstanding views of the desert and mountains (**GPS N34° 18.433' W117° 13.689'**)

Descend the same way.

■ Hike 7 METATE TRAIL ♡ 🐕 👫 ☸

HIKE LENGTH 0.8-mile loop; 100' elevation gain
DIFFICULTY Easy
SEASON March–November
TOPO MAP *Lake Arrowhead* (7.5-minute)

■ FEATURES

For untold centuries, the Serrano people gathered each spring to harvest acorns and grind them into flour. One of their favored spots was the oak woodland north of present-day Lake Arrowhead, where the crop was plentiful and the weather was mild. The Metate Trail loops through these woods and you'll see the bedrock mortars where the women ground the acorns. Lake Arrowhead visitors will find this trip a family-friendly walk in the woods.

■ DESCRIPTION

From Lake Arrowhead, follow Highway 173 north 5 miles to the Rock Camp Forest Service Station. The trailhead parking is on the west side of the road across from the station (**GPS N34° 17.248' W117° 12.856'**).

Cross Highway 173 and walk through the Rock Camp Forest Service Fire Station to an INTERPRETIVE AREA sign. Take the wide trail east; then veer left at an immediate fork. The trail leads through an open forest of pine and oak.

In 0.2 mile, stay right at an unsigned junction with an ATV track. Just beyond, watch for a stone monument placed by the Woman's Club of Lake Arrowhead. Behind the monument (**GPS N34° 17.377' W117° 12.590'**), look for slabs of granite bedrock with deep holes called *metates* that were worn by generations of mothers and daughters grinding their family's food.

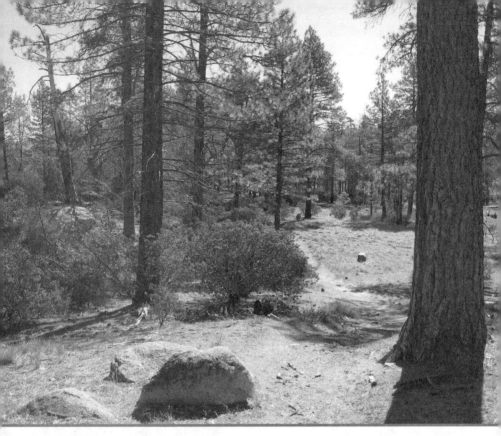

View through the pines on the Metate Trail

To complete the loop, continue east, keeping an eye out for more metates, and cross a seasonal tributary of Willow Creek. Stay on the main trail as it turns right, passes through a small meadow, recrosses the creek, and returns to the Forest Service Station at a green gate.

■ Hike 8 TUNNEL TWO TRAIL ⟳ 🐕 👫 ⚙

HIKE LENGTH 1-mile loop; 100' elevation gain
DIFFICULTY Easy
SEASON All year
TOPO MAP *Lake Arrowhead* (7.5-minute)

■ FEATURES

Lake Arrowhead was dammed in fits and starts between 1905 and 1923. Early plans called for diverting the water south through tunnels under the crest of the San

Bernardino Mountains to irrigate the valley, but ranchers in the high desert fought and won a legal battle to preserve their water rights. Before the litigation completed, 6 miles of a proposed 60-mile tunnel system were built. This short hike tours a scenic ridge named during the construction, though it does not actually visit a tunnel.

■ DESCRIPTION

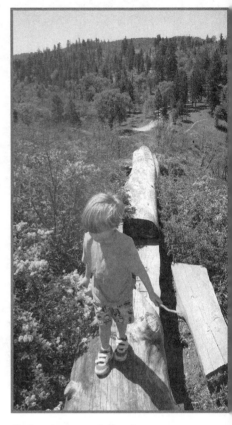

From the intersection with Highway 189 west of Lake Arrowhead, proceed north on Grass Valley Road for 0.5 mile. Turn left onto Club House Drive, and then take an immediate right onto Fairway Drive. In 0.4 mile, turn right on Brentwood Drive. In 0.8 mile, turn left onto Sonoma Drive, then immediately left again onto dirt Forest Road 2N34A. Follow it 0.4 mile to the signed trailhead at a T-junction with unsigned 2N34 (Tunnel Road) (**GPS N34° 15.771' W117° 13.816'**). High clearance may be necessary if the

Balancing on a fallen log

road is rutted, but you can also park at the end of the pavement and walk up 2N34A.

The Tunnel Two Trail (3W19) follows the ridge north paralleling Tunnel Road. The Grass Valley Fire swept through this area in 2007. Started when strong winds felled a power line, the fire burned nearly 200 houses as well as 12,000 acres of forest. Now you will see a mixture of mature oaks and pines that survived the fire, burned stumps logged after the fire, and buckthorn regrowing in the burned areas.

In 0.5 mile, come to a bench near the top of a low hill. From here, you can savor views over Miller Canyon and the headwaters of the Mojave River to Silverwood Lake. Mount Baldy, capped with snow in the winter, dominates the western skyline. In the spring, the black oaks and buckthorn bloom and chickadees and lizards are out looking for food. By October, the oaks put on a colorful show.

In another 0.1 mile, the trail ends at Tunnel Road. Turn right and walk back along the road to your vehicle.

■ Hike 9 LITTLE BEAR CREEK 🏃 🐕

HIKE LENGTH 4 miles out-and-back; 800' elevation gain
DIFFICULTY Moderate
SEASON All year
TOPO MAP *Lake Arrowhead* (7.5-minute)

■ FEATURES

The canyon of Little Bear Creek—just east of Lake Arrowhead—has always been a delight to visit. A small stream glides and dances over water-tempered boulders, shaded by magnificent Jeffrey and sugar pines and incense-cedars. Ferns and grasses once grew lush along the banks. Just over the ridge, civilization seems far away. The 2003 Old Fire incinerated almost everything on this trip. Consider this a unique opportunity to witness both the complete devastation of a major forest fire and the regeneration of the forest.

The trip descends from North Shore Campground, just east of Lake Arrowhead, to visit this verdant sanctuary and observe the regrowth.

Manzanita in bloom

▪ DESCRIPTION

From Highway 173, 2.8 miles northeast of the junction with Highway 189 at Lake Arrowhead Village, turn right (east) onto Hospital Road. Follow the latter 0.25 mile to the North Shore Campground entrance, opposite the hospital. The campground is open from May to October. If you park in the campground you must pay the day-use fee. You can park free outside the campground, but not in the hospital parking lot without permission.

Your trail (3W12) begins at the extreme eastern end of the campground by the Forest Service sign for the North Shore National Recreation Trail (**GPS N34° 16.021' W117° 09.771'**). Follow the trail downhill, crossing a dirt road, into the shady recess of Little Bear Creek. Now the trees are charred but the vegetation in the streambed is rapidly regrowing. The path follows the left (north) bank of the trickling creek, climbs 50 feet over a ridge to shortcut a horseshoe bend, and continues alongside the stream, before making an abrupt right turn and crossing the creek to Hooks Creek Road (Forest Road 2N26Y), 2 miles from the start.

You can return uphill the way you came, or have someone pick you up at your meeting with 2N26Y near the trailhead for Hike 10 (**GPS N34° 16.168' W117° 08.296'**).

▪ Hike 10 DEEP CREEK ↗ 🐕

HIKE LENGTH 6 miles out-and-back; 600' elevation gain
DIFFICULTY Moderate
SEASON All year
TOPO MAP *Lake Arrowhead, Butler Peak* (both 7.5-minute)

▪ FEATURES

Deep Creek cuts an impressive swath through the north-slope country of the San Bernardinos. The creek and its numerous tributaries drain most of the mountain region from Lake Arrowhead almost to Big Bear. Although not so named, Deep Creek is really the east fork of the Mojave River. Its abundant waters flow year-round, sometimes becoming a raging torrent in stormy times.

About midway between its headwaters and its junction with the West Fork of the Mojave, Deep Creek runs through rugged, rock-ribbed terrain. Its waters tumble and cascade among huge boulders, here and there pausing briefly in limpid pools. This is the Devils Hole country; the Devils Hole itself is in a narrow chasm just east of the creek.

Deep Creek

This is a trip for those who like to explore deep canyons and rushing creeks. It's easy walking on the slopes above Deep Creek on a section of the Pacific Crest Trail (PCT). Bring your fishing rod, for trout linger in some of the pools.

The 2003 Old Fire devastated the forest on the southern end of this trip and many homes in Cedar Glen. The PCT and the bridge across Deep Creek have been repaired.

■ DESCRIPTION

From Highway 173 1.6 miles northeast of the junction with Highway 189 at Lake Arrowhead Village, drive east on Hook Creek Road through the village of Cedar Glen for 2.3 miles to a gate at Forest Road 2N26Y. Continue 0.8 mile down the windy one-lane road (with speed bumps!) and cross Hooks Creek. Continue 0.1 mile on a good dirt road to a signed fork where 2N26Y meets a sharp bend in 3N34. Trail 3W12 from North Shore Campground (see previous hike) ends close to this point. Stay left at the junction on 3N34. Cross the creek again and make a right turn at 3N34C after 0.2 mile. Pass another gate and proceed 0.3 mile to the Splinters Cabin Trailhead where the hike begins (**GPS N34° 16.371' W117° 07.745'**).

If either gate is locked, park outside and walk from the gate, taking care not to block access to the gate or to private property on Hook Creek Road. Splinters Cabin has been the site of an unusual number of break-ins, so be especially vigilant to leave nothing of value in your vehicle.

Take the trail that leaves the north end of the parking area. You ford Little Bear Creek and reach the Pacific Crest Trail at the west end of the bridge spanning Deep Creek. Follow the PCT north as it climbs and then contours above Deep Creek, shaded by numerous live oaks. You then descend gently, matching the gradient of Deep Creek, and pass the confluence of Holcomb Creek, its waters churning in from the east beneath Deer Mountain. Continuing north on the PCT, you descend open slopes 150 feet above Deep Creek Narrows. Looking up a tributary creek to the east, you can see the tangled jumble known as Devils Hole (not for hikers). Your trail swings northwest, passing above some sandy flats ideal for sunbathing, and intersects the steep jeep trail (3N34D) coming down from Bacon Flats 3 miles from the start. Leave the PCT here and descend the jeep trail 100 yards to Deep Creek (**GPS N34° 18.087' W117° 07.716'**). There is a large pool here deep enough for swimming.

Return the way you came. Alternatively, hike west up the jeep road past Bacon Flats, then south on 3N34 back to the trailhead. This variation involves slightly more climbing and is not as scenic, but provides a loop trip. Another option requiring a car shuttle is to continue north and then northwest on the PCT to Deep Creek Hot Springs and then up to Kinley Creek, a 13-mile one-way trip (see Hike 5, page 48).

■ Hike 11 HOLCOMB CREEK ↗ 🐕 🚶

HIKE LENGTH 12 miles one-way; 2,200' elevation gain
DIFFICULTY Strenuous (1 day), Moderate (2 days)
SEASON April–October
TOPO MAPS *Lake Arrowhead* , *Butler Peak*, and *Fawnskin* (all 7.5-minute)

■ FEATURES

This is the longest hiking trip in the western half of the San Bernardinos. For 12 miles you follow the Pacific Crest Trail (PCT) through silent forests of pine, cedar, and oak, cross sparkling streams of cold water, and contour rocky slopes—quite an experience in this generally overused part of the range.

Most of the way you follow lower Holcomb Creek, either alongside the alder-shaded stream or a short distance above it. A third of the way, on a shady streamside bench, is Holcomb Crossing Trail Camp, the recommended overnight stop for those doing the trip in two days. A car shuttle between Hook Creek Road and Coxey Road is required.

Here the 2003 Old Fire burned the forest 1.6 miles to the east of Deep Creek. The 2007 Butler II Fire burned the upper portion of the Holcomb Creek drainage. This is an excellent opportunity for you to witness the devastation and regeneration of the fire cycle.

■ DESCRIPTION

Arrange your getaway vehicle at the junction of Holcomb Creek and Coxey Road (3N14). To reach this junction from Highway 38 in Fawnskin, turn northwest at the sign for Butler Peak onto Rim of the World Drive, which becomes 3N14. Follow it 4.4 miles from Fawnskin to the creek crossing and junction with 3N93 (**GPS N34° 18.010' W116° 58.915'**).

To reach the starting trailhead, return to Fawnskin and drive west to Lake Arrowhead. From Highway 173 1.6 miles northeast of the junction with Highway 189 at Lake Arrowhead Village, drive east on Hook Creek Road through the village

Holcomb Creek

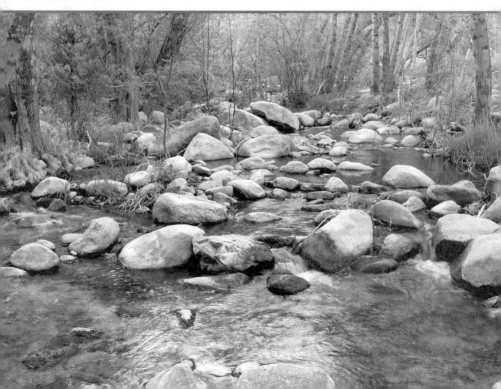

of Cedar Glen for 2.3 miles to a gate at 2N26Y. Continue 0.8 mile down the windy one-lane road and cross Little Bear Creek. Continue 0.1 mile on a good dirt road to a signed fork where 2N26Y meets a sharp bend in 3N34. Stay left at the junction on 3N34. Make a right turn onto 3N34C in 0.2 mile. Pass another gate and proceed 0.3 mile to the Splinters Cabin Trailhead where the hike begins (**GPS N34° 16.371' W117° 07.745'**). If either gate is locked, park outside and walk from the gate, taking care not to block access to the gate or to private property on Hook Creek Road. Splinters Cabin has been the site of an unusual number of break-ins, so be especially vigilant to leave nothing of value in your vehicle.

Take the trail north to a junction with the PCT, 0.25 mile, where the PCT crosses Deep Creek on a steel bridge. Cross the bridge and climb eastward through chaparral, scrub oak, and scattered burnt Jeffrey pines, with far-reaching views back over the Deep Creek drainage. In 2.5 miles you cross a ridge and begin a gentle descent into the Holcomb Creek watershed. You pass Trail 2W08, drop close to the creek, and then reach Bench Camp. Contour about 100 feet above the south bank to a junction with rutted ATV trail 1W17 to Crab Flats (see Hike 14, page 62). About 300 yards beyond is Holcomb Crossing Trail Camp, on a Jeffrey pine–shaded bench alongside the creek, with fire pits, 4.5 miles from the start.

Just east of the trail camp, the trail makes a bouldery crossing of Holcomb Creek. You climb the slope to pass some rocky narrows, then descend back to Holcomb Creek at a cedar-shaded bench, 0.7 mile from the trail camp. The old Cienega Redonda Trail used to depart here but was destroyed in the Willow Fire. You continue east up Holcomb Creek, climb 100 feet on a chaparral slope, and then return to the creek to a junction with Crab Flats Road (3N16) (**GPS N34° 16.529' W117° 03.048'**). This is an alternative endpoint if you prefer a shorter hike.

Make the easy ford of the creek on the roadbed. In 0.3 mile, cross back to the north side at the third and final ford, which can be difficult if Holcomb Creek is flowing high in the spring. Now you climb gradually eastward along the north slope, through chaparral and open groves of ponderosa pine and oak; then turn northeast and finally drop back alongside the alder-shaded creek. Your trail continues northeast close to the creek, paralleling 3N93 on the opposite bank. You pass several jeep tracks and reach a junction with Coxey Road (3N14). Here your transportation should be waiting. A longer option, recommended for three or four days, is to continue eastward on the PCT either to its crossing of Van Dusen Road (3N09) (11 additional miles) or to Doble on the Gold Mountain Road (3N08) (17.5 additional miles).

■ Hike 12 HEAPS PEAK ARBORETUM ⟳ 🐕 👥

HIKE LENGTH 0.7-mile loop; 100' elevation gain

DIFFICULTY Easy

SEASON April–November

TOPO MAP n/a

■ FEATURES

The Heaps Peak Arboretum offers a pleasant stroll through trees and wildflowers of the San Bernardino Mountains. It is situated just above where Fred Heaps established a pioneering ranch in the late 1800s. The area burned in 1922 and was replanted by the Lake Arrowhead Women's Club with the assistance of students from the Lake Arrowhead Elementary School. The site was abandoned in the middle of the century but was restored in 1982 by George Hesemann and the Rim of the World Interpretive Association, which now maintains the arboretum.

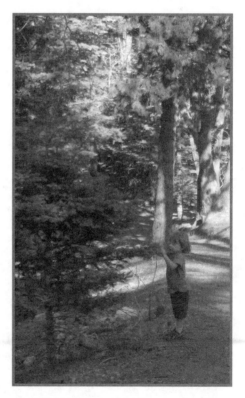

The kiosk at the arboretum contains a display of the western pine bark beetle that has been decimating the forests of the San Bernardino Mountains. The beetle preys on trees weakened by the lengthy drought. It leaves forests of dead trees in its wake, tinder for the Old and Butler II Fires and other fires yet to come.

■ DESCRIPTION

Park at a large turnout located on the north side of Highway 18 (**GPS N34° 14.025' W117° 09.642'**), 2 miles east of the Lake Arrowhead turnoff (Highway 173) and a quarter mile east of mile marker 27.00.

Getting to know white fir at Heaps Peak Arboretum

Pick up an interpretive trail guide at the Forest Information kiosk. The guide describes plants at 25 numbered posts along the loop. On weekends between 11 a.m. and 3 p.m., the Forest Information kiosk is staffed with volunteers when the weather permits.

The Sequoia Trail is a short loop featuring a sequoia grove, Arizona cypress, quaking aspen, California black oak, bracken fern, cinquefoil, rabbit brush, coffeeberry, potentilla, gooseberry, candytuft, and any number of wildflowers. The loop is also a good place for bird-watching.

■ Hike 13 UPPER DEEP CREEK

HIKE LENGTH 5 miles out-and-back; 800' elevation gain
DIFFICULTY Moderate
SEASON All year
TOPO MAPS *Butler Peak, Keller Peak* (both 7.5-minute)

■ FEATURES

This trip drops from the rolling high country north of Green Valley into the upper reaches of Deep Creek. The trail is well maintained, the views are far-reaching, and the creek is delightful. Along Deep Creek is Fisherman's Group Campground, a good place to seek trout.

Rockbound pool in Deep Creek

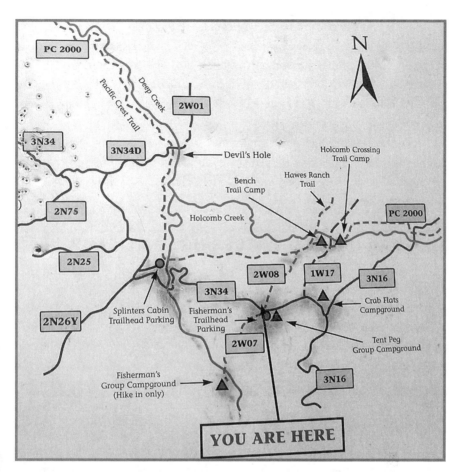

A helpful locator map of Deep Creek

■ DESCRIPTION

From the Rim of the World Highway (Highway 18), 2.9 miles northeast of the intersection with Highway 330 at Running Springs and just past mile marker 018 SBD 34.50, turn left (north) onto Green Valley Road. After 2.6 miles—just before you reach Green Valley Lake—turn left again onto Forest Road 3N16. Descend this good dirt road toward Crab Flats Campground, passing several side roads and crossing Crab Creek (impassable in high water). Reach the junction with Big Pine Flat Road after 3.8 miles. Stay left on 3N34, passing Crab Flats Campground after 0.2 mile. Another 1.1 miles farther down a bumpier road (high clearance recommended), park at a clearing and large VISITORS TO DEEP CREEK sign near Tent Peg Group Campground (**GPS N34° 15.679' W117° 06.108'**).

Follow Trail 2W07 from the south side of the road as it contours west around a ridge, with fine views over the Deep Creek drainage and the north-slope country. After 0.25 mile, the trail begins a descent into Deep Creek, crossing the small stream of Crab Creek after 1.2 miles, and reaching bottom 2.4 miles from the start (**GPS N34° 14.821' W117° 06.729'**). The Fisherman's Group Campground is across the creek and just upstream.

After trying your luck as an angler, return back up the same way. It is also possible to wade the obstacle-riddled creek 0.6 mile downstream to reach a two-tier waterfall. From here, a very steep use trail climbs 200 feet up to rejoin the main trail at a bend.

■ Hike 14 HOLCOMB CROSSING TRAIL CAMP

HIKE LENGTH 6 miles out-and-back; 900' elevation gain
DIFFICULTY Moderate
SEASON March–October
TOPO MAP *Butler Peak* (7.5-minute)

■ FEATURES

This is the easy way to reach the woodsy haunt of lower Holcomb Creek. You drop right down from Crab Flats to intersect the Pacific Crest Trail (PCT) west of Holcomb Crossing Trail Camp.

The trip is a living demonstration of how the forest changes with moisture and heat. Most of the way down from Crab Flats you are in what botanists call Transition zone—Jeffrey pines, California black and canyon live oak, a scattering of Coulter and sugar pine and incense-cedar—trees that require a moderate amount of moisture and coolness. Directly across the canyon is Upper Sonoran vegetation, including pinyon pine and juniper trees that grow in warm, semi-arid conditions found on such south-facing slopes. And along Holcomb Creek are the lush trees of streamside woodland—white alder, willow, and cottonwood—growing amid a verdant tangle of ferns, grasses, and flowering herbs. This area is popular with hunters in the fall, so wear something bright.

■ DESCRIPTION

From the Rim of the World Highway (Highway 18), 2.9 miles northeast of the intersection with Highway 330 at Running Springs and just past mile marker 018 SBD 34.50, turn left (north) onto Green Valley Road. After 2.6 miles—just before you reach Green Valley Lake—turn left again onto 3N16. Descend this good dirt

Holcomb Crossing Trail Camp

road toward Crab Flats Campground, passing several side roads and crossing Crab Creek (impassable in high water). Reach the junction with Big Pine Flat Road after 3.8 miles. Stay left on 3N34, passing Crab Flats Campground after 0.2 mile. Another 1.1 miles farther down a bumpier road (high clearance recommended), park at a clearing and large VISITORS TO DEEP CREEK sign near Tent Peg Group Campground (**GPS N34° 15.679' W117° 06.108'**).

The trail, 2W08, gently climbs over a broad forested ridge, then drops northeastward into the Holcomb Creek Canyon, passing areas charred by fire. In 1.5 miles, 2W08 ends at the PCT. Turn right (east). In 0.5 mile, pass a signed junction with 2W03 leading north to Hawes Ranch. In 0.3 mile, come to Bench Camp on a shady flat above the creek. In another 0.3 mile, pass an ATV track (1W17) climbing southward to Crab Flats. Shortly thereafter, arrive at Holcomb Crossing Trail Camp (**GPS N34° 16.618' W117° 04.563'**), located on a pine-canopied streamside bench.

You have several options on this trip: (1) return to Crab Flats the way you came; (2) climb the ATV track 1W17 steeply up 1.3 miles to Crab Flats, and then walk west on 3N34 0.8 mile to the trailhead; (3) follow the PCT west to Forest Road 3N34, and then hike this bouldery jeep trail southeast back to Crab Flats; (4) follow the PCT east to Coxey Road (see Hike 11, page 56); or (5) follow the Cox

Creek Trail north to Hawes Ranch (see Hike 16, next page). The last two require a car shuttle. Any way you do it, you are certain to enjoy this bit of canyon wilderness smack in the middle of the overdeveloped western half of the San Bernardinos.

■ Hike 15 SHAY MOUNTAIN 🥾 🐎

HIKE LENGTH 7 miles out-and-back; 1,100' elevation gain

DIFFICULTY Moderate

SEASON November–May

TOPO MAP *Butler Peak, Keller Peak* (both 7.5-minute)

▓ FEATURES

The long hogback of Shay Mountain (6,714 feet) looms high over the northside country of the San Bernardinos. From its broad summit one has panoramic views reaching from Lake Arrowhead almost to Big Bear and stretching far out over the Mojave Desert. This trip is part on trail, part cross-country scramble. But the scrambling is easy climbing over pinyon-dotted slopes. Do it in spring, when the northside country is damp and aromatic, and the high peaks to the southeast are glistening in their snowy mantle.

There have been lots of Shays in the history of the San Bernardinos. The particular Shay after whom the mountain is named is said to have been an early-day ranger at the old Coxey Ranger Station, Art Shay.

This area was badly burned in the 1999 Willow Fire. Nasty brush has grown back. Cross-country navigation skills are essential.

▓ DESCRIPTION

From the Rim of the World Highway (Highway 18), just past mile marker 018 SBD 34.50, turn left (north) onto Green Valley Road. After 2.6 miles—just before you reach Green Valley—turn left again onto Crab Flats Road (3N16). Descend 3N16 for 3.8 miles, passing several small side roads and crossing Crab Creek, to a signed junction with 3N34. Stay right on 3N16 and proceed for 8.3 more miles northeast to Big Pine Flat, watching the vegetation transition from forest to desert. Then turn left (west) on the Coxey Truck Trail (3N14) and follow it 3.4 miles to Little Pine Flat. Turn left on Hawes Ranch Road (3N41), and park in the clearing outside the locked gate (**GPS N34° 19.354' W117° 03.505'**).

Hike down the road 1.6 miles to Hawes Ranch and proceed westward up the unmaintained Muddy Spring Trail 0.9 mile to the ridgetop saddle. Then leave the trail and walk northwest up the slope to the summit, 1 more mile (**GPS N34° 18.503'**

W117° 05.175'). If you return to the trail saddle unfulfilled, scramble up the other direction (southeast) 0.75 mile to the top of Little Shay Mountain (6,635 feet).

■ Hike 16 COX CREEK 🥾 🐕 🚶

HIKE LENGTH 12 miles out-and-back; 1,200' elevation gain
DIFFICULTY Moderate
SEASON All year
TOPO MAP *Butler Peak, Keller Peak* (both 7.5-minute)

■ FEATURES

This is another route into the beautiful lower reaches of Holcomb Creek. You approach from the north, dropping down Cox Creek, then descending ridges and slopes into Holcomb Creek to Holcomb Crossing Trail Camp. Along Cox Creek are Jeffrey pines, but on the ridges and slopes you go through a semi-arid forest of pinyon pine and western juniper. In all but the hottest months, this is a pleasant trail trip, with options when you reach Holcomb Crossing.

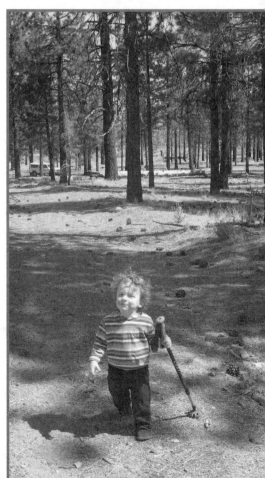

Little hiker at Little Pine Flat

■ DESCRIPTION

From the Rim of the World Highway (Highway 18), just past mile marker 018 SBD 34.50, turn left (north) onto Green Valley Road. After 2.6 miles— just before you reach Green Valley— turn left again onto Crab Flats Road (3N16). Descend 3N16 for 3.8 miles, passing several small side roads and crossing Crab Creek, to a signed junction with 3N34. Stay right on 3N16 and proceed for 8.3 more miles northeast to Big Pine Flat, watching the vegetation transition from forest to desert. Then turn left (west) on the

Coxey Truck Trail (3N14) and follow it 3.4 miles to Little Pine Flat. Turn left on Hawes Ranch Road (3N41) and park in the clearing outside the locked gate (**GPS N34° 19.354' W117° 03.505'**).

Hike down the road for 1.6 miles to Hawes Ranch. Continue south on the trail along the west side of Cox Creek, curving around Little Shay Mountain and Ingham Peak. Near the confluence with Holcomb Creek, the trail abruptly turns west and contours strangely for 0.7 mile before dropping down and crossing Holcomb Creek. Meet the Pacific Crest Trail (PCT) on the far side. Turn east and hike 1 mile to shady Holcomb Crossing Trail Camp (**GPS N34° 16.618' W117° 04.563'**), passing Bench Camp and ATV trail 1W17 along the way.

You can return the way you came. Or, with a car shuttle, you can take the PCT in either direction (see Hike 11, page 56) or, 300 yards west of the trail camp, find the eroded 1W17 trail that climbs southwest to Crab Flats (see Hike 14, page 62).

■ Hike 17 EXPLORATION TRAIL ↗ 🐕 ☸

HIKE LENGTH 4.5 miles one-way; 1,300' elevation gain
DIFFICULTY Moderate
SEASON April–November
TOPO MAP *Keller Peak* (7.5-minute)

■ FEATURES

The Exploration Trail was completed in August 2005 as part of the Forest Service Centennial Project to celebrate the 100th birthday of the Forest Service. It parallels the Keller Peak road through beautiful open oak and pine forest to the top of the road where it meets the National Children's Forest Interpretive Trail. For an easier trip, follow the trail in reverse, downhill all the way.

While you are in the area, consider visiting the historic Keller Peak Fire Lookout.

■ DESCRIPTION

From Highway 18 at a bend just east of Running Springs at mile marker 18 SBD 32.81, turn right (east) on the paved Keller Peak Road and drive 0.1 mile. Park at the signed Exploration Trailhead on the right (**GPS N34° 12.141' W117° 05.199'**). Leave another car or bicycle at the upper end of the trail, 4 miles up the paved Keller Peak Road (**GPS N34° 12.373' W117° 02.624'**). The trailhead is on the right side just beyond a fork in the road; the left fork leads to the National Children's Forest Interpretive Trail.

Pines and boulders along the Exploration Trail

Two trails depart from the lower trailhead; take the one on the right. The trail crosses Dry Creek, then climbs alongside it through an open forest of oak and pine past huge granite boulders for half a mile to a dirt road. Cross the road; then hike another quarter mile and cross a second road.

From here, the trail continues climbing, roughly parallel to the Keller Peak Road. It passes through fields of chaparral, then returns to open forest and contours across the northwest slopes of Keller Peak to its upper terminus at the paved road.

■ **Hike 18 LITTLE GREEN VALLEY** ↗ 🐕 👫 ⊚

HIKE LENGTH 3 miles one-way; 700' elevation gain
DIFFICULTY Moderate
SEASON April–November
TOPO MAP *Keller Peak* (7.5-minute)

■ FEATURES

Before the loggers and subdividers arrived on the scene, the top of the San Bernardinos from Crestline to Big Bear was heavily clothed in tall timber. Today, stands of magnificent pine, cedar, and oak, undisturbed by humans, are rare and widely scattered. One place where you can still find them, rich and tall and verdant, is on the ridges north of Snow Valley. This is a beautiful walk through the realm of these forest monarchs, on good trail or fire road all the way, and sometimes beside a trickling stream. Do it on a day when you have plenty of time, so that you can saunter, pause, and fully soak up nature's handiwork. The trip is especially pleasant in the spring when the creek is running and in the autumn when the oak leaves are turning yellow.

■ DESCRIPTION

You may wish to leave a getaway vehicle in Green Valley. From Highway 38 just east of mile marker 018 SBD 34.50, turn north on Green Valley Road and follow it 4.1 miles to Meadow Lane. Make a right and drive 0.3 mile to the unmarked dirt road 2N19 where Meadow Lane makes a sharp turn just beneath a water tank (**GPS N34° 14.587' W117° 04.139'**).

Little Green Valley

Return to Highway 18 and drive east to mile marker 038 SBD 37.24, 0.3 mile west of the Snow Valley parking area. A dirt road forks left (north) to some cabins; turn off the highway, and then turn left immediately again to park in the clearing on the left where you see the LITTLE GREEN VALLEY TRAILHEAD sign (**GPS N34° 13.491' W117° 02.477'**).

Follow the trail as it leads northwest, crosses a small brook, and gently climbs the slope. You cross two logging roads during the first 0.5 mile, the result of recent selective tree-cutting. After another 0.3 mile, stay left at an unmarked fork and climb the forested ridge to reach Little Green Valley. This is a good turnaround point if you want a short scenic walk without a car shuttle.

The trail briefly becomes indistinct as it traverses the south side of the marshy meadow and crosses a creek. Here you reach a dirt road 2N19 leading northwest to Green Valley Lake. Ignoring several forks, follow the dirt road across a ridge and down into the basin of Green Valley Lake. Pass just behind the Green Valley Public Campground, to Meadow Lane, 3 miles from the start.

If you have employed a car shuttle, your trip is over. Otherwise, return the way you came.

■ Hike 19 SIBERIA CREEK TRAIL CAMP FROM SNOW VALLEY 🐾 🐴 🚶

HIKE LENGTH 6 miles out-and-back; 2,200' elevation gain

DIFFICULTY Moderate

SEASON All year

TOPO MAP *Keller Peak* (7.5-minute)

■ FEATURES

A major fire raged through the Bear Creek drainage in 1971. Since then, the chaparral cover on the mountain slopes has grown back as vigorous as ever. On the lush canyon bottom, bigcone Douglas-fir, white alder, and canyon live oak protect the bubbling creek and its grassy banks from the sun's harshness.

Merging with Bear Creek just across from where the trail reaches canyon bottom is beautiful, woodsy Siberia Creek, probably the most delightful sylvan recess in the San Bernardinos outside of the San Gorgonio Wilderness. The little singing stream, shaded by an overarching canopy of green, is a favorite of hikers, campers, and fishermen alike. Here, smack in the middle of the overused San Bernardinos, nature reveals her quiet, pristine best.

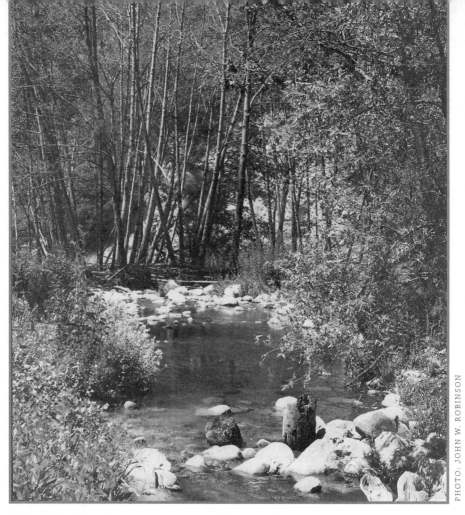

Siberia Creek

This trip leaves the Rim of the World Highway (Highway 18), drops down chaparral-clad slopes into Bear Creek, then continues into the deep, verdant oasis of Siberia Creek—miraculously untouched by the holocaust that ravaged the slopes just above. Here, just above the junction with Bear Creek, the Forest Service has placed Siberia Creek Trail Camp. Bring your fishing rod; rainbow trout swim in nearby Bear Creek.

This lightly maintained trail can be brushy. Long pants and sleeves are recommended.

■ DESCRIPTION

Drive 5.5 miles east of Running Springs (0.5 mile past Snow Valley) on Highway 18 to mile marker 18 SBD 38.00. Turn right onto the poor dirt Forest Road 2N97.

Low-clearance vehicles may wish to park near the highway. Otherwise, drive up the deeply rutted road, staying left at a fork, to a small parking area on the right on a ridgetop, 0.4 mile from the highway (**GPS N34° 13.473' W117° 01.460'**). The Camp Creek Trail (1W09) begins at an angler survey box.

Take the trail eastward, over the ridge, under scattered Jeffrey pines. In 0.5 mile you reach the 1971 burn, and the forest changes to chaparral. The trail now zigzags steeply down the brushy slopes to the welcome shade and cool water of Bear Creek. You cross Bear Creek, enter the mouth of Siberia Creek, and reach Siberia Creek Trail Camp, located on an alder- and oak-shaded bench just above the stream (**GPS N34° 12.574' W117° 00.699'**).

Return the same way. Or, with a car shuttle, take the trail northeast into Bluff Lake country (see Hike 28, page 84) or the trail south to Seven Pines (see Hike 38, page 99).

■ Hike 20 GRAYS PEAK 🥾 🐕 ☸

HIKE LENGTH 7 miles out-and-back; 1,200' elevation gain
DIFFICULTY Moderate
SEASON April–October
TOPO MAP *Fawnskin* (7.5-minute)

■ FEATURES

Forested 7,952-foot Grays Peak looms close over the western end of Big Bear Lake. The peak is named for Gray's Landing on the north shore of the lake, founded by Alex Gray in 1918 and still used by anglers.

This easy-graded, pleasant walk through stands of Jeffrey pine, black oak, and white fir, lies partly on trail, partly on fire road. Grays Peak is a bald eagle wintering habitat area and the trail is closed to public use from November 1 to April 1.

■ DESCRIPTION

Follow Highway 38 along the north shore of Big Bear Lake to the Grays Peak parking area (**GPS N34° 15.781' W116° 56.885'**) just west of mile marker 038 SBD 56.41, 2.7 miles northeast of Big Bear Dam, or half a mile southwest of Fawnskin. There are restrooms and picnic tables here, and many spaces for parking.

The signed trailhead is at the north edge of the picnic-parking area. Follow the pathway as it gently climbs through open forest to intersect a dirt fire road 2N04X, at 0.5 mile. Turn right onto the road, going straight ahead at a road junction with Forest Road 2N70, to a signed junction with the Grays Peak Trail, another 0.5 mile.

Grays Peak Trailhead

Turn left and follow the trail as it climbs, contours, and climbs again, circling around to the south flank of the peak. The trail ends 100 feet below the top (**GPS N34° 15.656' W116° 58.227'**); optionally work your way through buckthorn thickets and downed trees to the true summit. Views are limited by the forest cover, but you can make out shimmering Big Bear Lake to the south, and the rugged lower Holcomb Creek country to the north.

Return the way you came.

■ Hike 21 DELAMAR MOUNTAIN ↗ 🐕

> **HIKE LENGTH** 5.5 miles out-and-back; 1,000' elevation gain
> **DIFFICULTY** Moderate
> **SEASON** April–November
> **TOPO MAP** *Fawnskin* (7.5-minute)

■ FEATURES

Delamar Mountain stands 8,398 feet tall on the divide separating the Holcomb Creek drainage from Big Bear Lake. From its rocky, forested summit, you are rewarded with a superb panorama of the central San Bernardinos, with sparkling-blue Big Bear Lake immediately to the south and Holcomb Valley's historic gold country right below to the north.

This trip follows a stretch of the Pacific Crest Trail (PCT) for 2 miles, then climbs the east ridge of Delamar Mountain through an open forest of Jeffrey pine and white fir. Since part of it is trailless, wear boots with deep tread.

■ DESCRIPTION

From Highway 38, 2 miles east of Fawnskin at mile marker 038 SBD 54.04, turn north onto the good dirt Polique Canyon Road (2N09). At a fork in 1.5 miles with 2N71, stay right on 2N09 toward Holcomb Valley. Continue 0.8 mile to the top of the divide, where you will see the signed Holcomb View Trail, part of the PCT (**GPS N34° 17.021' W116° 55.034'**). Park here or on the side of the road where it becomes wider just beyond.

Walk west on the PCT, ascending gradually along the south side of the Big Bear–Holcomb Valley divide. You pass through an open forest of conifer and oak, with numerous views south to Big Bear Lake. In 1.5 miles you cross to the shadier north slope of the ridge and then contour northwest another 0.5 mile. At the point where the PCT begins a steady descent, leave the trail and climb westward on an easy cross-country ascent to Delamar Mountain's forested east ridge. Trudge up the trailless slope for 0.5 mile to reach the pile of granite boulders that is the summit (8,398 feet; **GPS N34° 17.452' W116° 56.726'**). For the best view southward over Big Bear Lake, scramble about 100 yards south to a slightly lower summit.

Return the same way, or continue westward on the PCT to Delamar Mountain Road, (3N12), 3.5 miles north of Fawnskin. A car shuttle is required for this option.

■ Hike 22 BERTHA PEAK 🡕 🐕

HIKE LENGTH 7 miles out-and-back; 1,400' elevation gain
DIFFICULTY Moderate
SEASON April–November
TOPO MAP *Fawnskin* (7.5-minute)

■ FEATURES

Like neighboring Delamar Mountain, Bertha Peak at 8,201 feet rises high on the forested ridge between Holcomb Valley and Big Bear Lake. From its rounded summit, you get a striking perspective over the gentle valley-and-ridge country of the central San Bernardinos.

This trip takes the Cougar Crest Trail from Highway 38, on the north shore of Big Bear Lake, to the Pacific Crest Trail (PCT), then ascends a steep dirt track to the electronic relay station on the summit. It is a pleasant and popular walk through an open forest of pinyon pine and juniper, climaxed by a panoramic view well worth the effort. Do it on a clear day, when almost the entire San Bernardinos sprawl below you, and the great Grayback–Mount San Bernardino ridge looms high and stark on the southeast skyline.

■ DESCRIPTION

From Fawnskin, drive east on Highway 38 for 2.5 miles to a large paved parking area on the north side of the highway near mile marker 038 SBD 53.50 with the sign COUGAR CREST TRAIL (**GPS N34° 15.844' W116° 54.653'**). (If you reach the Big Bear Discovery Center, you've driven 0.2 mile too far.) Park here.

Walk up the well-marked Cougar Crest Trail (1E22), through an open forest of pinyon pine, juniper, and scattered Jeffrey pines as you wind upward toward Bertha Peak's west ridge. Panoramic views open over the Big Bear Lake

View south from the PCT near Bertha Peak

Juniper at Cougar Crest

country as you gain elevation, and in 2.3 miles you intersect the PCT at a magnificent western juniper. This is a popular turnaround point for families and those looking for a casual hike. Turn right (east) and follow the PCT to a junction with a dirt road on the ridge crest, 0.5 mile. Walk up this dirt road, very steep in places, through pinyon pines and some rather large western junipers, to the summit relay station (**GPS N34° 16.981' W116° 53.962'**).

After taking in the 360-degree panorama, return the way you came.

■ Hike 23 GOLD MOUNTAIN 🥾 🐐

HIKE LENGTH 3 miles out-and-back; 1,000' elevation gain
DIFFICULTY Moderate
SEASON April–November
TOPO MAP *Big Bear City* (7.5-minute)

■ FEATURES

The eastern and northern flanks of the San Bernardino Mountains are honeycombed with abandoned gold prospects. No other mountain region in Southern California has seen so much mining excitement spread over so many years—from the 1850s well into this century.

Of all the lode-mining operations in the range, none was as storied nor as famous as Lucky Baldwin's Gold Mountain (or Doble) Mine high on the mountainside overlooking Baldwin Lake. The rich quartz ledges were discovered in 1873 by prospectors Barney and Charley Carter. Their discovery turned out to be a mountain of gold ore, and the rush was on. Elias J. "Lucky" Baldwin bought "Carter's Quartz Hill" for $6 million, and by 1875 he had constructed a 40-stamp mill to process the ore and had employed 180 men. Baldwin was not as "lucky" in this venture as he was in others, and it is doubtful that he ever saw a full return on his investment. During the early 1900s the mine was worked by several lessees, the most recent operation being in the late 1940s. The end finally came in 1951, when the equipment was removed and the property abandoned.

The site of the large mill and cyanide-processing plant can still be seen on the northeast slopes of Gold Mountain. This trip visits these storied ruins and climbs the pinyon-covered ridge of Gold Mountain for a panoramic view encompassing most of the old mining areas. For those with vivid imaginations, it is possible to look down over Doble Mine, Holcomb Valley, Arrastre Flat, and Van Dusen Canyon and visualize the feverish excitement and hectic activity that once occurred here. This trip is for those with such imaginations.

This route is a rough cross-country approach from Doble Mine. You can expect close encounters with mountain mahogany as you pick a path around brush and downed timber. If you prefer to avoid the brush, you can also climb the

Doble Mine

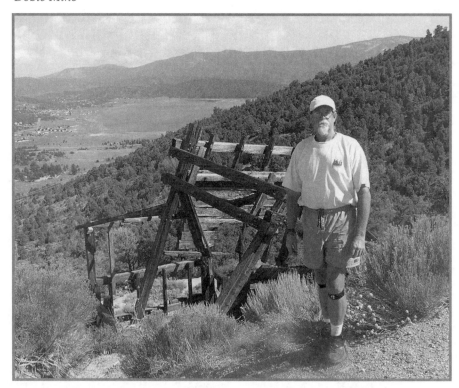

mountain from Holcomb Valley Road via the Pacific Crest Trail (PCT) and rough jeep road 3N69, an 8-mile out-and-back trip with 1,400 feet of climbing.

■ DESCRIPTION

From Highway 18 at mile marker 018 SBD 58.15 where it makes its loop around the north end of Baldwin Lake, turn left (north) onto Holcomb Valley Road. Drive up this paved road 0.9 mile. Just before the dump, turn left on the dirt Forest Road 3N16. After 0.8 mile, stay left on 3N16 at a junction. Climb 0.1 more mile and park in the clearing across from the old wooden "hopper" (**GPS N34° 18.179' W116° 49.764'**).

Before starting out on foot, look south along the mountainside, toward Baldwin Lake; the foundations and diggings you see are all that remain of this most famous lode mine in the San Bernardinos.

Walk up the dirt road about 300 yards; then start up the toe of the gentle, pinyon- and juniper-covered northeast ridge of Gold Mountain. The climb is trailless, and navigating through forest requires cross-country hiking experience and a good map. The pines are dense in places, so long pants and sleeves are recommended. Proceed around the right (north) side of a false summit to a junction with the PCT, 1 mile. Continue up the broad pinyon-clad ridge to the rocky 8,235-foot summit of Gold Mountain (**GPS N34° 17.309' W116° 50.367'**) for far-reaching views over this mine-poxed northeastern corner of the San Bernardinos.

Return the same way. An attractive option requiring a short car or bicycle shuttle (1.25 miles) is to descend via the PCT. You will get a good panorama of Baldwin Lake's usually dry playa, where Budd Doble, Lucky Baldwin's son-in-law, once trained racehorses. The PCT reaches Holcomb Valley Road 0.1 mile south of the dump (**GPS N34° 18.135' W116° 49.386'**).

■ Hike 24 SILVER PEAK 🥾 🐕

HIKE LENGTH 4 miles out-and-back from high-clearance trailhead; 1,000' elevation gain

DIFFICULTY Moderate

SEASON All year

TOPO MAP *Big Bear City* (7.5-minute)

■ FEATURES

The desert-tempered north slope of the San Bernardinos holds delightful surprises. When winter's snowy mantle grips the higher parts of the range, this land of pinyon, juniper, and Joshua trees is warm and inviting. This trip samples this

Mine on Silver Peak

semi-arid terrain. You climb the grayish hogback of Silver Peak—partly on old mining roads, partly by cross-country scrambling—for a far-reaching view over the Mojave Desert and its islands of treeless, steep-sided tawny mountain ranges.

Blackhawk Mountain (the summit of which is called Silver Peak) was once the scene of gold- and silver-mining activities. Abandoned diggings and shafts dot the slopes on all sides. The greatest activity was in Blackhawk Canyon, down the north side of the mountain. Gold deposits were discovered here in 1887 and developed soon afterward by the Blackhawk Mining Company, financed by English capital. Tunnels were dug and a 10-stamp mill erected, but high operating costs forced suspension of the venture within a few years. In 1921 the mines were reopened by the Arlington Mining Corporation, and they were worked continuously until 1940, yielding a reported $300,000. Since 1940 they have been idle.

Cactus Flat, where the hike begins, commemorates "Cactus Jim" Johnson, builder of the Johnson Grade road up Cushenbury Canyon to Baldwin Lake. Old

Cactus Jim selected his own burial site here, where his grave is now located and marked with a small sign.

■ DESCRIPTION

From the north shore of Big Bear Lake, proceed east on Highway 18. Low-clearance vehicles may park at mile marker 018 SBD 62.0 (**GPS N34° 19.319' W116° 49.094'**). Otherwise, turn east onto a poor dirt road. Follow this side road 0.3 mile to the first dirt road on the left; turn left and continue 0.2 mile to a small parking area before the road drops down a hill and deteriorates badly. Park here (**GPS N34° 19.669' W116° 48.954'**). Look north toward prominent white mine tailings at the toe of a ridge. Your route ascends the canyon behind these tailings, then follows the skyline to the summit.

Follow this dirt road 0.1 mile down into a gully; then turn left and hike up the gully 0.2 mile more to its end at another dirt road (a maze of old mining roads crisscrosses the mountain). Proceed right and follow this dirt road to the abandoned mine. Switchback northward through the white rock to the end of the path at an old mine shaft in the canyon. Turn up the canyon, roughly following a cable, to its top on the ridgeline. Climb up the spur ridge to the main ridge, where you will intersect another dirt road. Turn right (east) and follow the road up the main ridge to the 6,756-foot summit (**GPS N34° 20.259' W116° 48.627'**).

Return the same way, avoiding the private property area on the southwest flank of the mountain, where exploratory mining work is being done.

■ Hike 25 WHITEWATER CANYON VIEW LOOP
Q 🐕 🚶

HIKE LENGTH 3.5-mile loop; 600' elevation gain
DIFFICULTY Easy
SEASON October–April
TOPO MAP *Whitewater, Catclaw Flat, Morongo Valley* (all 7.5-minute)

■ FEATURES

The Whitewater River is the primary watercourse draining the south and east sides of the San Gorgonio Wilderness. Its frothing waters tumble down the mountain and rush across the desert before sinking into the sands near Palm Springs. The Wildlands Conservancy acquired the historic Whitewater Trout Farm in 2006 to prevent it from becoming a housing development. The canyon and many others are now within the Sand to Snow National Monument designated by President

Barack Obama in 2016, and Whitewater Preserve is one of the best places to experience the desert glory of the monument. This trip explores a short stretch of the canyon, briefly joins the Pacific Crest Trail (PCT), and follows a ridge with good views before returning to the canyon.

■ DESCRIPTION

This trip begins at Whitewater Preserve, which is open daily from 8 a.m. to 5 p.m. From Interstate 10, take Exit 114 north for Whitewater Canyon. Follow a frontage road east; then turn north onto Whitewater Canyon Road and proceed 4.9 miles to its end at Whitewater Preserve (**GPS N33° 59.358' W116° 39.371'**).

The trail begins at a kiosk on the north side of the parking lot and leads between a pair of palms. It turns west, turns right to briefly join an old jeep road, then turns left again at a signed junction and crosses the wide, ever-shifting wash. The trail becomes better defined on the far side and enters a grove of desert willows

Ranger Charlie leads an interpretive hike above Whitewater Canyon.

to join the PCT at the mouth of a canyon. You could turn south here and walk to Mexico, or go north and walk to Canada. This trip follows the PCT south up switchbacks for 0.7 mile to a junction with the Canyon View Trail. The spring wildflowers can be remarkable. Turn left and follow this trail south along a chamise-covered ridge, enjoying excellent views of Whitewater Canyon and the north face of San Jacinto. The chamise gives way to brittlebush as you switchback 0.6 mile down to the canyon floor. Turn left and follow Whitewater Canyon Road. Shortly after it crosses the river, look for a signed trail on the left that takes you directly back to the preserve headquarters.

Whitewater Canyon offers many options for those seeking a longer walk. Following the PCT 1.4 miles north brings you to Red Dome, a small volcanic lump beside the trail that makes a good picnic site. It is possible to continue along the PCT and then turn east to enter Mission Creek Preserve or west to visit Catclaw Flat and waterfalls along the Whitewater River and its Grape Canyon tributary.

■ Hike 26 CASTLE ROCK ↗ 🐐 🚶

HIKE LENGTH 2 miles out-and-back; 700' elevation gain
DIFFICULTY Moderate
SEASON April–October
TOPO MAP *Big Bear Lake* (7.5-minute)

■ FEATURES

South from Big Bear Lake, rising from the heavily forested ridge that divides the Big Bear basin from the canyon of the Santa Ana River, are a number of granite knobs and boulder outcroppings. Most impressive of these is a weather-eroded, knobby gendarme known as Castle Rock.

Castle Rock has long attracted attention because of its sentrylike position above the lower end of the lake and its unusual shape. Such qualities impress human imaginations, and from these imaginations legends arise that persist through the ages. The legend of Castle Rock is one of the most famous of those known to Native Americans who once made the San Bernardinos their home.

This trip climbs steeply up the forested mountainside. You follow a trail to the foot of the rock; then it is a Class 3 scramble to the summit. Wear boots with good tread. Do it when a breeze freshens the mountains; perhaps you will be able to hear the soft wail of the forlorn Serrano Indian princess who waited for her husband on Castle Rock.

◾ DESCRIPTION

From Highway 18 across from mile marker 018 SBD 45.50, 1.2 mile east of Big Bear Dam or 3 miles west of Big Bear Lake Village, the marked trail 1W03 starts up a forested gully. Park 100 yards east of the trailhead in a clearing on the north side of the highway (**GPS N34° 14.202' W116° 57.704'**).

The trail climbs steeply up the left (east) side of the gully through a magnificent forest of ponderosa pine, white fir, and incense-cedar, passing jumbo granite boulders. In about 0.7 mile the trail reaches a saddle and starts to descend. Castle Rock is the large outcropping immediately east of this saddle. Leave the trail here. The easiest way up the rock (Class 3) is to contour about 50 feet around the north and west sides of the outcropping, then climb up an indentation to the summit (**GPS N34° 13.872' W116° 57.694'**). There is one spot about halfway up where a belay may be warranted for the unsteady.

◼ Hike 27 CHAMPION LODGEPOLE PINE

🥾 🐕 🚶 ⚙

HIKE LENGTH 0.6 mile out-and-back; 100' elevation gain

DIFFICULTY Easy

SEASON May–October

TOPO MAP *Big Bear Lake* (7.5-minute)

◾ FEATURES

Lodgepole pines seldom grow taller than 70 feet, and in Southern California they are seldom seen below 8,000 feet. An exception to these rules occurs in the vicinity of Bluff Lake, a shallow body of water surrounded by lush forest and meadow country, 3 miles south of Big Bear Lake. Here, at 7,500 feet, grow the largest lodgepole pines in the world. The world champion, discovered in 1963, is a mammoth, double-topped tree standing 110 feet tall with a circumference of 20 feet. Its age is estimated at 400 years, meaning that the tree's life has spanned California's history since shortly after Juan Rodriguez Cabrillo's epic voyage into San Diego Bay in 1542.

Lodgepole—also known as tamarack—pines are readily identified by their thin, scaly bark and their paired needles (the only pine in these mountains with two needles per bundle). They are usually found only in high subalpine forests, just below timberline. This trip is a very short stroll through lush forest and grassland to the world champion. The trail is marked with several numbered posts. A pamphlet at the trailhead explains the sights at each post.

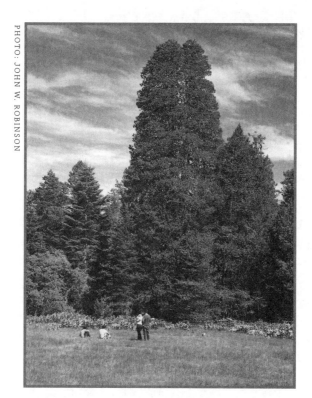

PHOTO: JOHN W. ROBINSON

World-champion lodgepole pine

■ DESCRIPTION

From the west end of Big Bear Lake Village at mile marker 018 SBD 47.45, at a sign pointing to Mill Creek Road and picnic grounds, turn south onto Tulip Lane. Proceed 0.4 mile; then turn right onto Mill Creek Road, which becomes good dirt Forest Road 2N10 in 0.7 mile. Proceed 3.8 miles, and turn right onto 2N11 at a sign pointing to Champion Lodgepole. Proceed 1.0 mile to a signed parking area on the right for the 1W11 Lodgepole Pine Trail (**GPS N34° 12.922' W116° 58.440'**).

Follow the trail west 0.3 mile alongside a trickling stream to a junction with 1W04 dropping to Siberia Creek. Then go right (north) 100 yards to Champion Lodgepole, near the east end of a meadow (**GPS N34° 13.132' W116° 58.376'**). Stay outside the wooden fence built by the Forest Service to protect the tree.

Return the same way. Or continue north and then east 0.3 mile to Bluff Lake Reserve, operated by the Wildlands Conservancy and free to the public for nature viewing during daylight hours.

■ Hike 28 SIBERIA CREEK ✎ 🐕 🚶

HIKE LENGTH 14 miles out-and-back; 2,900' elevation gain

DIFFICULTY Strenuous

SEASON April–October

TOPO MAPS *Big Bear Lake, Keller Peak* (both 7.5-minute)

■ FEATURES

Siberia Creek begins in the shallow pond known as Bluff Lake, on the high tableland between Big Bear Lake and the valley of the Santa Ana River. It flows southwest across this lushly forested tableland, through magnificent stands of white fir, ponderosa and lodgepole pine, and emerald-green meadows of tall grass, ferns, and flowering herbs. Then it abruptly drops down a boulder-filled gorge, finally to empty its spent waters into Bear Creek. Here, set amid alders, oaks, and spruces, is Siberia Creek Trail Camp.

A trail descends most of the length of Siberia Creek—from the west end of Forest Road 2N11 2 miles south of Bluff Lake all the way down to Siberia Creek Trail Camp, where it joins the trail up to the Rim of the World Highway (Highway 18) (see Hike 19, page 69). This trip follows this trail—first across the verdant tableland, then down around the steep slopes of Lookout Point to avoid the difficult gorge, and into lower Siberia Creek and its small trail camp. From here, options are available with a car shuttle (see next page).

Gunsight Notch

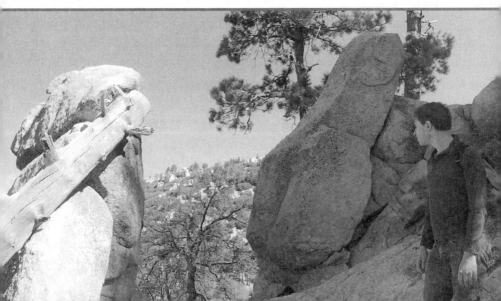

■ DESCRIPTION

From the west end of Big Bear Lake Village at mile marker 018 SBD 47.45 at a sign pointing to Mill Creek Road and picnic grounds, turn south onto Tulip Lane. Proceed 0.4 mile, and then turn right onto Mill Creek Road, which becomes good dirt Forest Road 2N10 in 0.7 mile. Proceed 3.8 miles; then turn right onto 2N11 at a sign pointing to Champion Lodgepole. Proceed 1 mile to a signed parking area on the right for the 1W11 Lodgepole Pine Trail (**GPS N34° 12.922' W116° 58.440'**).

From the parking area on 2N11, follow the Lodgepole Pine Trail 0.3 mile west, alongside a small creek, to a fork. Consider taking the 100-yard excursion to the right to see the Champion Lodgepole Pine (see previous hike). Otherwise, continue straight ahead on 1W04, alongside lush meadowland and through open forest. In 0.75 mile you cross Siberia Creek and follow its north bank downstream; 0.25 mile farther you recross the creek. Here the tableland ends and the stream abruptly drops into a boulder-stacked gorge by Gunsight Notch. Follow the trail as it contours out onto the open-forested slopes of Lookout Mountain, drops to a saddle, and zigzags down the steep ridge westward to a junction with the Seven Pines Trail (see Hike 38, page 99), 5 miles from the start. Turn right (north) and follow the latter 1 mile down to Siberia Creek Trail Camp, located alongside the stream to your left, just before Siberia Creek meets Bear Creek (**GPS N34° 12.574' W117° 00.699'**).

Return the same way, all uphill now. Or, with a car shuttle, ascend the Green Valley Trail to the Rim of the World Highway (Highway 18) (see Hike 19, page 69) or the Seven Pines Trail to Seven Pines (see Hike 38, page 99). Any way you do it, consider spending the night at Siberia Creek Trail Camp.

■ Hike 29 GRAND VIEW POINT 🐕 🐕 ⊛

HIKE LENGTH 6.5 miles out-and-back; 1,100' elevation gain

DIFFICULTY Moderate

SEASON May–October

TOPO MAP *Big Bear Lake* (7.5-minute)

■ FEATURES

This trip climbs from the Aspen Glen Picnic Area to the summit of the high ridge that separates Bear Valley from the basin of the Santa Ana River. En route you are rewarded with occasional views over Big Bear Lake and its crowded resort complex. From aptly named Grand View Point you look across the deep trench of the Santa

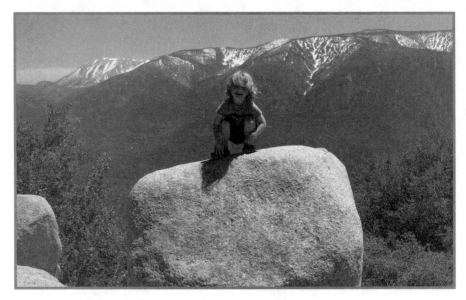

San Bernardino Peak Divide from Grand View Point

Ana to the lofty peaks and ridges of the San Gorgonio Wilderness. You're on trail or fire road all the way to Grand View Point. This trail is popular with cyclists and horseback riders. The USGS Big Bear Lake topographic map doesn't show the complete trail or all of the side trails.

■ DESCRIPTION

From the west end of Big Bear Lake Village at mile marker 018 SBD 47.45 at a sign pointing to Mill Creek Road and picnic grounds, turn south onto Tulip Lane. Proceed 0.4 mile; then stay left and continue 0.1 more mile to the Aspen Glen Picnic Area on your right (**GPS N34° 14.103' W116° 55.639'**).

The signed Pineknot Trail, 1E01, starts at the southern end of the picnic area. In 0.25 mile, stay left at a junction with the Cabin Trail. Cross a ridge, drop into Red Ant Canyon, and climb back out under a shady canopy of Jeffrey pine, black oak, and white fir. After crossing a spur road (2N08), the trail levels out, passes Deer Group Campground, and reaches Forest Road 2N10 at the top of the ridge. Cross the road and follow the marked trail 0.25 mile southeast to the summit of Grand View Point (**GPS N34° 12.696' W116° 55.419'**) for a panorama of the eastern San Bernardinos.

Return the same way, or cut the trip in half by having transportation awaiting you on 2N10.

■ Hike 30 SKYLINE TRAIL ↗ 🐕 ⊚

HIKE LENGTH 14 miles one-way; 1,800' elevation gain

DIFFICULTY Moderate

SEASON May–October

TOPO MAP *Big Bear Lake, Moonridge* (7.5-minute)

■ FEATURES

The Skyline Trail runs along the edge of the ridge south of Big Bear Lake, threading through scenic forest with wildflowers and boulder piles and offering great views of the San Gorgonio Wilderness across the Santa Ana River canyon. The trail, completed in 2015 through a partnership between the Big Bear Valley Trails Foundation and the Forest Service, has become an instant hit among mountain bikers, but is also an enjoyable trip for hiking and trail running.

The trail follows a preexisting firebreak bulldozed during the 2003 Old Fire to avoid creating new environmental impacts. As such, the trail passes over most

Cyclist on the Skyline Trail

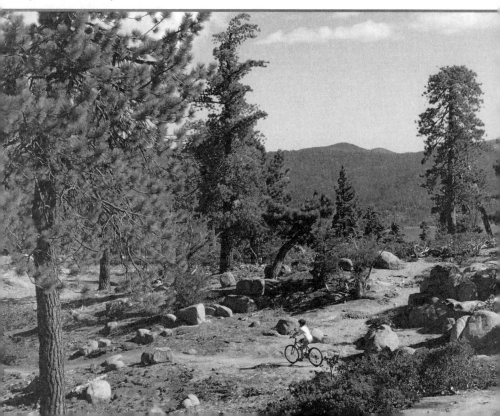

of the bumps on the ridge. Climbs are gently graded for intermediate mountain bikers and may feel a bit circuitous for hikers.

■ DESCRIPTION

Leave a getaway car or bicycle on Forest Road 2N10. From Highway 18 in Big Bear Lake at mile marker 18 SBD 48.0, turn south onto Mill Creek Road, which becomes good dirt 2N10. Park on the shoulder 2.6 miles from the highway at an inconspicuous sign for the Plantation Trail (1W12) (**GPS N34° 13.259' W116° 56.648'**). Return to the highway and drive east another 2.6 miles; then turn right onto Moonridge Road. In 1 mile, stay right on Club View Road. In 1.4 mile, reach the Skyline Trailhead where the road turns to dirt (**GPS N34° 13.627' W116° 52.030'**).

Multiple trails depart from the trailhead; be sure you take the signed Skyline Trail (1E12) uphill. Begin with an earnest climb, crossing Bear Mountain Road and reaching the ridge near the Radford Truck Trail (2N06) in 2 miles. From here, one could pick up the Pirate Trail and drop back to 2N10 to make a shorter loop.

The Skyline Trail continues west along the ridge, passing above Snow Summit. In 2.9 miles, pass a clearing with an excellent viewpoint over the Santa Ana River canyon. In 1.6 miles, come to a junction with the Grand View Point, Pine Knot, and Seven Oaks Trails. A short spur climbs to Grand View Point, but the views are no grander than what you have already been enjoying. In 2.5 miles, cross Clarks Grade Road (1N54). From here, one could veer north and shortcut down the Plantation Trail. However, the Skyline Trail continues west along the upper end of Bellyache Spring Road until the trail resumes in 0.1 mile.

In 0.8 mile, begin a long gradual descent through the open forest. In 0.7 mile, cross Forest Road 2N10; then in 1.6 mile, cross it again. In 1.4 mile, reach the Boulder Group Camp. Follow the 2N10B spur road 0.2 mile back to 2N10, where your getaway vehicle awaits at the intersection of the Skyline and Plantation Trails.

Purists may wish to follow the Skyline Trail another 1.1 miles as it winds through the woods to end at an easily overlooked post with limited parking near the intersection of 2N10 and 2N17. Perhaps this terminus will be developed further by the time you arrive.

■ Hike 31 SUGARLOAF MOUNTAIN FROM GREEN CANYON 🐾 🐕 ⊛ 🥾

HIKE LENGTH 10 miles out-and-back; 2,700' elevation gain
DIFFICULTY Moderate
SEASON May–October
TOPO MAP *Moonridge* (7.5-minute)

■ FEATURES

Sugarloaf Mountain—as the name implies—is a massive rounded lump on the main divide between the Big Bear country and the canyon of the Santa Ana River. From its 9,952-foot forested summit, you are treated to an all-encompassing vista over the whole eastern half of the San Bernardinos. It is the highest peak in the range outside of the San Gorgonio Wilderness.

For a mountain almost 10,000 feet high, Sugarloaf displays a surprising variety of flora. The usual Jeffrey pine, sugar pine, white fir, and incense-cedar

Sugarloaf Mountain from the southwest

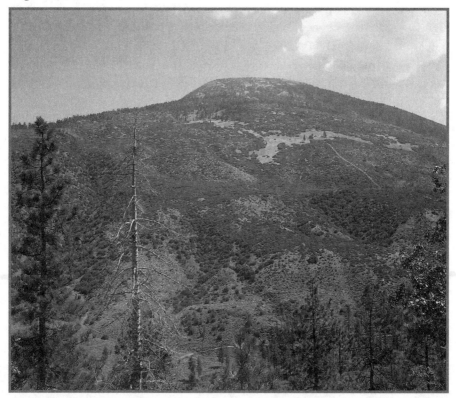

are found along the summit ridge and in sheltered recesses. Near the summit are some teepeelike western junipers. Pinyon pine, juniper, and mountain mahogany abound on the middle slopes, and purple sage and skeleton weed are prevalent in the sparsely forested sections. The rare black swallowtail butterfly, *Papilio bairdii*, can be seen on the summit in late August and early September.

This trail trip ascends beautifully forested Green Canyon to the top of the ridge, then follows the ridge westward to the summit. It is an ideal jaunt for a warm summer day, when the cool breezes along the ridgetop offer refreshing relief from the sweltering valley below.

■ DESCRIPTION

Drive east, then south on Highway 38 from Big Bear City. About 3 miles from town, turn right onto the good dirt Forest Road 2N93. The turnoff is across from Hatchery Road near the 038 SBD 45.75 mile marker. Follow 2N93, passing several small side roads, as it curves left and climbs along the mountainside to the Green Creek crossing. Park at the signed Sugarloaf Trail 2E18 (**GPS N34° 13.126' W116° 48.370'**), 1.3 miles from Highway 38.

Walk up the steep dirt road that turns to jeep tracks in a short distance, following alongside trickling Green Creek. In 2 miles, turn right off the dirt road at a signed trail leading up the hill. When you reach the saddle atop the ridge and a four-way trail junction, turn right (west) and follow the ridgetop trail 2E02 2.6 miles over and around bumps to the forested summit (**GPS N34° 11.934' W116° 48.854'**).

Return the same way. An option, requiring a shuttle, is to descend to the saddle junction, and then join Hikes 32 or 33.

■ Hike 32 SUGARLOAF MOUNTAIN FROM WILDHORSE MEADOWS 🥾 🐕 🚲 🚶

HIKE LENGTH 7 miles out-and-back; 1,300' elevation gain

DIFFICULTY Moderate

SEASON May–October

TOPO MAP *Moonridge* (7.5-minute)

■ FEATURES

This is the shortest and easiest way to climb Sugarloaf Mountain, but it involves a drive over a narrow and, in some places, rocky dirt road. You climb from Wildhorse Meadows up to the saddle east of Sugarloaf, then follow the ridgetop to the summit, on trail all the way. (For more on Sugarloaf Mountain, see Hike 31.)

Magnificent western junipers grow between Onyx Summit and Sugarloaf Mountain.

◼ DESCRIPTION

A high-clearance vehicle is usually required. From Redlands, drive east on Highway 38 through Barton Flats to the beginning of Forest Road 2N93 near mile marker 038 SBD 35.7. The fair dirt road is easy to pass by, so keep a sharp eye out for it on your left (north) immediately past a small wash. Drive up Forest Road 2N93 to Wildhorse Meadows, 5.5 miles. Continue up 2N93 for 0.6 mile beyond the meadow, to a fork on your left with an easily overlooked gated jeep road (**GPS N34° 12.333' W116° 45.908'**). This spot can also be reached from Highway 38 east of Big Bear Lake near mile marker 038 SBD 45.75 by driving up 2N93 for 5.5 miles.

Pass through a wooden break in the fence and walk west, following ducks up another faint jeep road, which becomes a trail. Continue west, atop the ridge, and then drop to a four-way trail junction in 1 mile. A sign indicates SUGARLOAF TRAIL leading west. Follow this good trail as it climbs, contours, drops, and climbs again to the forested 9,952-foot summit of Sugarloaf Peak (**GPS N34° 11.934' W116° 48.854'**), 3.5 miles from the start.

Return the same way. Or, with a car shuttle, descend Green Canyon to 2N93, 5 miles north of where you left it (see previous hike).

■ Hike 33 WILDHORSE CREEK 🪶 🐕 ⊚ 🚶

HIKE LENGTH 8 miles out-and-back; 1,400' elevation gain
DIFFICULTY Moderate
SEASON April–October
TOPO MAP *Moonridge* (7.5-minute)

■ FEATURES

The fault-carved canyon of Wildhorse Creek descends in an almost straight line from high on the Sugarloaf Ridge to the Santa Ana River. Near the head of the canyon is Wildhorse Spring, feeding the creek that runs full in spring but fades to a lazy trickle by late summer. The creek and the protective shade of the canyon walls nourish a lush forest of Jeffrey pine, white fir, incense-cedar, and several varieties of oak. For the most part, this forest is confined to the canyon bottom, and it stands in marked contrast to the sparse growth of scattered Jeffreys and semi-arid brush that dot the slopes above.

This trip follows a trail up over chaparral-coated ridges and down into upper Wildhorse Creek, superseding the old trail that followed the length of the creek. For an overnight stay there is Wildhorse Creek Trail Camp, nestled amid tall Jeffrey pines and white firs alongside the trickling creek. If you like solitude and nature's peace, this is the trip for you. In summer, when a multitude of hikers tramp through nearby San Gorgonio Wilderness, Wildhorse Canyon is usually left alone. I like it best in April or early May, when the air is crisp, Wildhorse Creek runs full, and Old Grayback sparkles under its snowy mantle.

■ DESCRIPTION

From Redlands, drive east on Highway 38 to the turnoff for the Wildhorse Trail, on your left just before mile marker 038 SBD 33.40 and 0.2 mile before the Heart Bar Campground road. Turn left (north) and drive about 20 yards up a dirt road to a signed parking area (**GPS N34° 09.772' W116° 47.317'**).

Follow the well-built trail, which for the first mile is an old jeep track, up through an open forest of Jeffrey and pinyon pine and western juniper. From the end of the jeep track, your trail winds steadily upward, over and around several ridges, leaving the forest behind. As you climb higher, snow-streaked Grayback Ridge begins to emerge from behind the forested slope of Grinnell Mountain, and views open up down the broad canyon of the upper Santa Ana River. After 3 miles you finally round the last ridge and then descend into the forested canyon of Wildhorse Creek. Another short mile brings you to Wildhorse Creek Trail Camp, located on a bench above the stream, shaded by tall Jeffrey pines (**GPS N34° 11.357' W116° 47.232'**). The creek usually runs all year, although fading to a trickle by late summer.

From the trail camp, you may retrace your steps. Or you can cross the creek and descend the unmaintained Wildhorse Creek Trail 2.25 miles to Highway 38 at a bridge at mile marker 038 SBD 31.77. This beautiful old trail stays within a few yards of the creek almost all the way down. It is clear for the first mile, then becomes fainter and occasionally brushy before eventually vanishing at the bottom. Arrange a car or bicycle shuttle or plan on a 1.6-mile trudge up the narrow highway shoulder back to the Wildhorse Creek Trailhead.

■ Hike 34 SANTA ANA RIVER HEADWATERS
🡕 🐐 ⚙

HIKE LENGTH 10 miles out-and-back; 1,000' elevation gain
DIFFICULTY Moderate
SEASON April–October
TOPO MAP *Moonridge* (7.5-minute), *San Gorgonio Wilderness* (Tom Harrison)

This area was impacted by the 2015 Lake Fire. As of 2016, the trail remains closed. Check with the Mill Creek Ranger Station at 909-382-2882 to determine if the trail has reopened.

■ FEATURES

The headwaters of the Santa Ana River, close under the forested and gravelly ridges of the San Gorgonio high country, are a delight to behold. The sparkling waters of the newborn river flow through verdant meadows and luxuriant streamside growth, amid a mixed forest of Jeffrey and ponderosa pine, white fir, and black oak. The trail weaves through a complicated maze of old dirt roads and side paths, so carrying a map is very helpful. Fortunately, the trail is mostly well marked with signs reading 2E03.

The Santa Ana River Trail also continues west from the trailhead, past Angelus Oaks and Morton Peak on the way to Mentone, but oddly never comes close to the river again before leaving the mountains. The trail eventually will continue all the way to the Pacific Ocean at Huntington Beach.

■ DESCRIPTION

From Redlands, drive east on Highway 38 to the paved Santa Ana River Trailhead parking area on your left (**GPS N34° 10.241' W116° 49.792'**) just past mile marker 038 SBD 30.74, 100 feet before the South Fork Campground turnoff to the right.

Your signed trail, 2E03, drops immediately to the river, passes under the highway bridge, and then turns sharply right at a junction and reaches a second trailhead just below the entrance to South Fork Campground. You switchback up the slope directly above your vehicle, then turn east. In 0.5 mile you reach a junction with the Lost Creek Trail (1E09), which branches right and climbs around the west slope of Grinnell Mountain to South Fork Meadows. You go left and continue eastward, through the forest, with the Santa Ana River down to your left. Continuing east, you enjoy views of 9,952-foot Sugarloaf Mountain on the northern skyline, and pass several side paths leading down to the river. After crossing Fish Creek, the trail follows the creek southward uphill 0.1 mile, then turns left at a junction and resumes its eastward progress overlooking the vast expanse of

Big Meadows

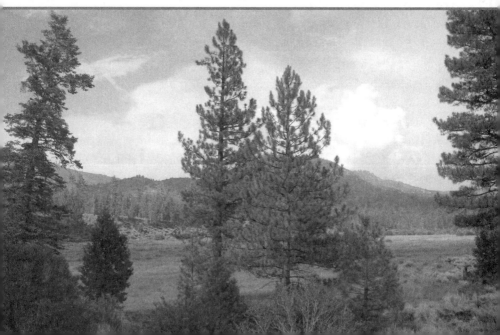

Big Meadows. You pass an unsigned side trail leading down to Big Meadows and on to Heart Bar Campground, but your trail continues east. Finally, cross Heart Bar Creek and reach the signed Santa Ana River Trailhead at Forest Road 1N05 (**GPS N34° 09.033' W116° 46.298'**). This trailhead is across from a dirt parking area 0.1 mile south of the junction with Forest Road 1N02.

Return the way you came, or arrange for a car or bicycle shuttle at Heart Bar Campground or Forest Road 1N05.

■ Hike 35 FISH CREEK MEADOW 🏃 🐕

HIKE LENGTH 5 miles out-and-back; 650' elevation gain

DIFFICULTY Easy

SEASON June–October

TOPO MAP *Moonridge* (7.5-minute), *San Gorgonio Wilderness* (Tom Harrison)

PERMIT San Gorgonio Wilderness Permit required

This area was impacted by the 2015 Lake Fire. As of 2016, the trail remains closed. Call the Mill Creek Ranger Station at 909-382-2882 for the latest information.

■ FEATURES

Fish Creek rises high on the massive slopes of Grinnell Mountain and Ten Thousand Foot Ridge, and cuts a deep swath before joining the Santa Ana River 2 miles east of Barton Flats. This all-year stream is shaded most of the way by a mixed forest of conifers and the largest grove of aspens in the San Bernardino Mountains. Verdant grasses carpet the creekside, particularly at Lower Fish Creek Meadow, an oval clearing where the canyon elbows from northeast to northwest.

This pleasant streamside trip follows the canyon through its middle reaches, where aspens quake in the cool mountain breeze and monkey flowers add a dash of color in early summer. In early autumn, the aspen leaves turn a brilliant golden yellow, in sharp contrast with the surrounding forest.

■ DESCRIPTION

From Redlands, drive east on Highway 38 to the entrance road to Heart Bar Campground and Fish Creek (1N02) just past the 038 SBD 33.48 mile marker. Turn right on 1N02, passing the campground entrance, and reach a junction in 1.3 miles. Go right, up 1N05, a fair dirt road, to the signed ASPEN GROVE TRAIL parking area, 2.7 miles from the highway (**GPS N34° 08.855' W116° 47.396'**).

Follow the old dirt road that leads southeast down to Fish Creek, 250 yards. You cross the creek and immediately reach the San Gorgonio Wilderness boundary. There are a few aspens here, but to see more of these lovely trees, take the side trail that goes right (northwest) 0.5 mile to Aspen Grove. The grove burned in the 2015 Lake Fire, but aspens resprout rapidly. The main trail passes the wilderness boundary sign and follows a sloping bench paralleling the creek on its west side. You climb gently through a beautiful forest of white fir, interspaced here and there with tall Jeffrey pines and incense-cedar. You pass the small clearing known as Monkey Flower Flat, then climb over a low ridge before dropping down to the creek. In 1.5 miles, your trail crosses Fish Creek to the east bank and, 0.75 mile beyond, reaches the grassy clearing of Lower Fish Creek Meadow and a junction with the upper Fish Creek Trail (see next hike; **GPS N34° 07.606' W116° 46.601'**).

Return the same way. Another option, requiring a car shuttle, is to go left at the junction to the upper Fish Creek roadhead, 0.3 mile (see next hike).

■ Hike 36 FISH CREEK 🏃 🐕 🥾

HIKE LENGTH 12 miles out-and-back; 1,900' elevation gain

DIFFICULTY Moderate

SEASON June–October

TOPO MAPS *Moonridge, San Gorgonio Mtn.* (both 7.5-minute), *San Gorgonio Wilderness* (Tom Harrison)

PERMIT San Gorgonio Wilderness Permit required

This area was impacted by the 2015 Lake Fire. As of 2016, the trail remains closed. Check with the Mill Creek Ranger Station at 909-382-2882 to determine if the trail has reopened.

■ FEATURES

This trip enters the back door of the San Gorgonio Wilderness, climbing up Fish Creek and over Fish Creek Divide into the northeastern corner of the wild area. Because driving access is difficult, few hikers use this route. But the forest of pine and fir is rich and green, the waters of Fish Creek are cold and sweet, and the high mountain air is thin and invigorating. For those who wish to linger awhile along Fish Creek, stay overnight at Fish Creek Trail Camp, with primitive facilities. With a car shuttle, many enjoyable options are available (see page 98).

■ DESCRIPTION

From Redlands, drive east on Highway 38 to the entrance road to Heart Bar Campground and Fish Creek (1N02) just past the 038 SBD 33.48 mile marker. Turn right onto 1N02, passing the campground entrance (on your right in 0.2 mile), to a junction in 1.3 miles. Go right, up the fair dirt road 1N05, bearing right at all road forks, to the signed Fish Creek Trail (1W07) parking area, 7.8 miles from the highway (**GPS N34° 07.471' W116° 46.028'**).

Walk west 0.6 mile on the well-defined trail (avoiding several other less-defined paths that lead in other directions), gradually descending, to a junction with the upper terminus of the Aspen Grove Trail, to your right (see previous hike). Continue straight ahead as your trail curves southwest into upper Fish Creek. Down to your right, as you near the creek, is a small, inviting trail camp shaded by Jeffrey pine and white fir. The trail then passes through an area of verdant growth, crosses two small side creeks, and climbs along the left (southeast) slope above the main creek, through a rich forest of Jeffrey pine and white fir. After several switchbacks to gain elevation, the pathway contours over into the main draw and reaches Fish Creek Trail Camp, 1.25 miles. The camp consists of several cleared flats amid rocky terrain, shaded by white fir. Water flows year-round in the stream just west of camp.

Beyond the camp, the trail starts climbing the broad slopes of Grinnell Mountain. As it rises above 9,000 feet, the view opens to the north and east, over the rugged east-end country of the San Bernardinos and out into the desert. Lodgepole pines begin to predominate. After four long switchbacks, you reach Fish Creek Saddle, on the high divide between Fish Creek and the South

Fish Creek to the left of Grinnell Mountain and San Gorgonio, with San Jacinto in the distance

Fork of the Santa Ana, 5.1 miles from the start. A 0.5-mile side trip north along the crest gets you to Grinnell Mountain for far-ranging views over the eastern part of the wilderness. (Grinnell Mountain is named for Joseph Grinnell, 1877–1924, a University of California zoologist who studied animals in the eastern San Bernardino Mountains during 1905–7.) From the saddle, the trail contours across the northwest slopes of Lake Peak, through a forest exclusively lodgepole, toward Mine Shaft Saddle, 0.8 mile to the Mine Shaft Saddle–North Fork Meadows trail branching left (southeast). Go right (west) 0.25 mile to Mine Shaft Saddle (**GPS N34° 06.631' W116° 49.188'**).

Here a number of options present themselves. You can return the way you came. You can take the Sky High Trail to the summit of San Gorgonio (see Hike 43, page 111). You can descend to Dry Lake and on out to Jenks Lake Road, requiring a car shuttle (see Hike 41, page 105). Or you can go down the North Fork of the Whitewater to North Fork Trail Camp (see Hike 44, page 113). With several days available for your outing, you can use this Fish Creek access to visit just about any part of the San Gorgonio Wilderness you desire.

■ Hike 37 PONDEROSA NATURE TRAIL
↻ 🐕 🚶

HIKE LENGTH 0.7-mile loop; 150' elevation gain

DIFFICULTY Easy

SEASON May–October

TOPO MAP *Big Bear Lake* (7.5-minute)

■ FEATURES

The Forest Service maintains a number of "nature trails" in San Bernardino National Forest that are designed to inform the visitor of the natural history of the San Bernardinos, pointing out the flora, the fauna, and landscape features. Walking these nature trails, seeing firsthand the various species and features, is the best way to learn nature's story in the mountains.

This short loop trail offers a fitting introduction to the nearby San Gorgonio Wilderness. In a 1-mile walk around a hillside and through the forest, you pass examples of most of the flora found in the lower half of the wilderness. Signs are posted every few hundred feet or so, describing what you see. This is a hike you should stroll rather than stride; go slowly, ponder nature's secrets, and you will more fully enjoy your next trip into the San Gorgonio Wilderness.

Santa Ana River Canyon and Slide Peak from the Ponderosa Nature Trail

◼ DESCRIPTION

From Redlands, drive east on Highway 38 to the beginning of the Ponderosa Nature Trail (1E19), marked by a large wooden sign on the left (north) side of the road (0.1 mile before the Jenks Lake turnoff at mile marker 038 SBD 25.51). Park in the adjacent clearing (**GPS N34° 09.839' W116° 54.703'**).

The well-graded trail climbs north along the slope, passing and describing various forms of vegetation, turns west and zigzags down into a forested shallow, then ascends southeasterly back to the parking area.

If you return to your car unfulfilled, cross the highway and sample the short (0.6-mile) Whispering Pines Nature Trail (1E33). An interpretive guide to the sights along the trail may be available at the start for a nominal fee.

◼ Hike 38 SIBERIA CREEK TRAIL CAMP FROM SEVEN PINES 🥾 🐕 🚶

HIKE LENGTH 8 miles out-and-back; 1,300' elevation gain

DIFFICULTY Moderate

SEASON All year

TOPO MAP *Big Bear Lake, Keller Peak* (both 7.5-minute)

■ FEATURES

This is the back-door approach to Siberia Creek, coming in from the valley of the Santa Ana River. A 1971 fire destroyed much of the forest cover, mainly live oaks and bigcone Douglas-fir. Now the first part of this hike is through open chaparral, exposed to the sun. For this reason, it is best done on a cool winter or spring day when the other approaches—via the Rim of the World Highway (Highway 18) (Hike 19, page 69) and Bluff Lake (Hike 28, page 84)—are snowed in. Fortunately, Siberia Creek was spared from the holocaust and is as delightful as ever.

Rock slides in 2005 damaged the trail. Numerous sections are washed out and some are brushy, but the route is still passable. In such condition, the trail is recommended only for the adventurous and surefooted; good boots and long pants are essential and a pair of garden pruners is helpful. Beware of deer ticks, especially in the spring. Ticks can carry Lyme disease, so if you develop a rash around the bite, see a physician promptly.

Siberia Creek

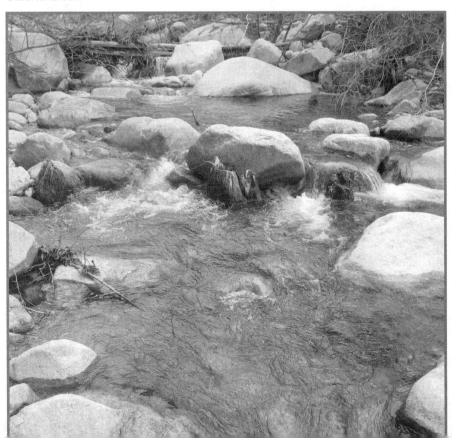

DESCRIPTION

From Redlands, drive 19 miles east on Highway 38 to Angelus Oaks. At a dirt turnout just beyond, turn left (north) and descend Middle Control Road (1N06), a good dirt road. In 0.5 mile, pass a waterfall at a bend in the road. Continue down to reach the Santa Ana River Road (1N09), 3.8 miles from the highway. Turn left (west) and drive 0.2 mile to a junction with the fair dirt Clark Grade Road (1N54). Turn right and ascend Clark Grade 1.8 miles to a junction with Forest Road 1N64. Turn left (west) and descend. Pass Clark's Ranch and two stream crossings that may be impassable in high water. After 1.7 miles, you will arrive at the Seven Pines Trailhead (1W10), marked by a broken signpost on the right. Park in a turnout just beyond (**GPS N34° 10.971' W116° 59.195'**). If you reach a side road to the top of a hill with a good view, you have gone too far.

The trail leads west along the hillside through dense scrub oak, manzanita, sage, buckthorn, and yucca. In a mile, it turns north and contours above Bear Creek. In 2 more miles, you intersect the trail coming down from Bluff Lake (see Hike 28). After the junction, the trail drops abruptly into the shady forest near the headwaters of Bear Creek. The trail can be difficult to follow in the fall when covered with a thick blanket of leaves. It crosses Siberia Creek and terminates at just above the confluence of the two creeks at Siberia Creek Trail Camp, recognizable by a small clearing and metal grill (**GPS N34° 12.574' W117° 00.699'**). Return the same way. Or you have the options mentioned above (see Hikes 19 and 28), both requiring a car shuttle.

◼ Hike 39 SOUTH FORK MEADOWS 🏃 🐕

HIKE LENGTH 8 miles out-and-back; 1,400' elevation gain

DIFFICULTY Moderate

SEASON May–October

TOPO MAP *Moonridge* (7.5-minute), *San Gorgonio Wilderness* (Tom Harrison)

PERMIT San Gorgonio Wilderness Permit required

This area was impacted by the 2015 Lake Fire. As of 2016, the trail remains closed. Check with the Mill Creek Ranger Station at 909-382-2882 to determine if the trail has reopened.

FEATURES

There is only one designated wilderness area in the San Bernardino Mountains. But for multitudes of hikers, it is the grandest in all of Southern California. This is

The Santa Ana River emerges from ferns at South Fork Meadow.

the 35,000-acre San Gorgonio Wilderness, a high mountain wonderland of granite peaks, forests of pine and fir, lush subalpine meadows, sparkling streams and placid lakes, and abundant wildlife. This region is set aside to be preserved forever in its pristine state. Here, under an evergreen canopy, alongside a singing stream or limpid pool, or high on a wind-washed ridge, you can find solitude and freedom, apart from the civilization so near yet seemingly a world away. The nourishment afforded by true wilderness should redeem and revitalize you. South Fork (also called Slushy) Meadows, on the north side of the wilderness, is fed by a multitude of springs. It was overused in the past, but is regaining its former glory. Casual hikers going only to the wilderness boundary do not need a permit. If you're proceeding beyond, to South Fork Meadows, you will need a wilderness permit, available at the Mill Creek Ranger Station, on Highway 38 a mile below the mouth of Mill Creek Canyon.

■ DESCRIPTION

From Redlands, drive east on Highway 38 to the Jenks Lake Road turnoff, 50 yards before mile marker 038 SBD 25.51. Turn right (southeast) and follow Jenks Lake Road 2.5 miles to the well-marked South Fork Trailhead (**GPS N34° 09.694' W116° 52.356'**). There is a large paved parking area with restrooms on your left.

Follow the well-built, easy-graded trail (1E04) as it winds up through stands of Jeffrey pine and white fir, passing the broad expanse of Horse Meadow, to the wilderness boundary at Poopout Hill, 2.2 miles and 1,000 feet of elevation gain. A sign points out a short side trail to the left leading to an outstanding view of San Gorgonio (**GPS N34° 08.887' W116° 51.290'**).

You contour eastward along the richly forested hillside, and after another mile begin to hear the rushing waters of the Santa Ana's South Fork down to your left. The trail climbs 200 feet in the last 0.25 mile and reaches South Fork Meadows, a sloping glen shaded by pine and fir, with lush ferns and grasses sprouting along the several converging streams and in the marshy cienegas (**GPS N34° 07.855' W116° 50.639'**).

Due to overuse, overnight camping in the South Fork Meadows area has been suspended indefinitely. Picnicking and day use are still allowed. Please take out everything you bring in.

Trails lead southwest to Dollar Lake (see next hike) and southeast to Dry Lake (Hike 41, page 105) and on to the summit of San Gorgonio Mountain (Hikes 42 and 43, pages 107 and 111). But this particular trail walk ends here at South Fork Meadows; so, after enjoying your stay, return the way you came.

■ Hike 40 DOLLAR LAKE ↗ 🐐 🚶

HIKE LENGTH 12 miles out-and-back; 2,800' elevation gain

DIFFICULTY Moderate (2 days), Strenuous (1 day)

SEASON June–October

TOPO MAP *Moonridge, San Gorgonio Mtn.* (both 7.5-minute), *San Gorgonio Wilderness* (Tom Harrison)

PERMIT San Gorgonio Wilderness Permit required

This area was impacted by the 2015 Lake Fire. As of 2016, the trail remains closed. Check with the Mill Creek Ranger Station at 909-382-2882 to determine if the trail has reopened.

■ FEATURES

High under the north face of the Grayback–San Bernardino Peak ridge, tucked snugly against rockbound slopes, is the tiny jewel called Dollar Lake. The little circular lake was so named because, when viewed from above on a sunny day, it shines like a silver dollar. Surrounding the lake is a healthy forest of lodgepole pine and white fir.

This trip follows the well-traveled pathway from Jenks Lake Road to Dollar Lake, where you may picnic but not camp. Overnight camping is allowed at Dollar Lake Forks, just northwest of the lake.

■ DESCRIPTION

From Redlands, drive east on Highway 38 to the Jenks Lake Road turnoff, 50 yards before mile marker 038 SBD 25.51. Turn right (southeast) and follow Jenks Lake Road 2.5 miles to the well-marked South Fork Trailhead (**GPS N34° 09.694' W116° 52.356'**). There is a large paved parking area with restrooms on your left.

Follow the excellent trail from Jenks Lake Road to South Fork Meadows, 4 miles (see Hike 39, page 101). The trail then skirts the west edge of the meadow for 100 yards and begins switchbacking up the ridge. You start out in a forest of ponderosa pine and white fir, but as you climb above 8,800 feet, lodgepoles begin to predominate. The trail then rounds the ridge and climbs along the west slope of the big draw leading to Dollar Lake Saddle, passing a grassy cienega and entering an area of waist-high manzanita. About 1.75 miles above South Fork Meadows, you reach a junction; go left on 1E03, dropping into the bowl above Dollar Lake. In 200 yards you reach another junction; again go left, and follow the trail down to the lake, 0.25 mile. The new trail camp is located 0.25 mile above (northwest of) the lake, adjacent to the junction of the Dollar Lake Saddle and Dollar Lake Trails.

Dollar Lake

Return the way you came. Another option is to climb San Gorgonio Mountain from here, making it a moderate two-day trip rather than a strenuous one-day scramble (see Hike 42, page 107).

■ Hike 41 DRY LAKE ✔ 🐕 🏃

HIKE LENGTH 10 miles out-and-back; 2,300' elevation gain

DIFFICULTY Moderate (2 days), Strenuous (1 day)

SEASON June–October

TOPO MAP *Moonridge, San Gorgonio Mtn.* (both 7.5-minute), *San Gorgonio Wilderness* (Tom Harrison)

PERMIT San Gorgonio Wilderness Permit required

This area was impacted by the 2015 Lake Fire. As of 2016, the trail remains closed. Check with the Mill Creek Ranger Station at 909-382-2882 to determine if the trail has reopened.

■ FEATURES

Dry Lake sits in a great amphitheater, surrounded on three sides by the lofty horseshoe crest of Grinnell, Lake, San Gorgonio, and Jepson Peaks. The lake is shallow, and in seasons of light precipitation, it dries up by midsummer—hence the name. But in early summer, after abundant rainfall, Dry Lake is full to the brim, and it beautifully mirrors the high granite ridges that soar above it. The forest cover on the surrounding slopes is almost exclusively lodgepole pine, with low clumps of chinquapin here and there. Dominated by the steep, gray-granite face of San Gorgonio, which is often snow-lined into midsummer, this delectable mountain basin approaches true alpine conditions and bears a striking resemblance to the High Sierra.

An excellent, easy-graded trail climbs from South Fork Meadows into Dry Lake basin, where two trail camps have been placed by the Forest Service—one just above the north shore of the lake, the other 0.25 mile beyond at Lodgepole Spring. For those who desire a small taste of the Sierra Nevada close to home, this is an ideal trip. Bring warm clothing and a good sleeping bag if you are going to stay overnight: nights can be nippy at 9,000 feet.

■ DESCRIPTION

From Redlands, drive east on Highway 38 to the Jenks Lake Road turnoff, 50 yards before mile marker 038 SBD 25.51. Turn right (southeast) and follow Jenks Lake Road 2.5 miles to the well-marked South Fork Trailhead (**GPS N34° 09.694' W116° 52.356'**). There is a large paved parking area with restrooms on your left.

Follow the trail from Jenks Lake Road to South Fork Meadows, 4 miles (see Hike 39, page 101). Leave the main trail here, which continues up to Dollar Lake

PHOTO: HARRY JAMES

Hikers wind around Dry Lake with San Gorgonio Mountain in the background (circa 1923).

and Dollar Lake Saddle (see previous hike), and cross to the southeast side of the meadows on any one of several beaten paths (a sign points to Dry Lake). Pick up the Dry Lake Trail (1E05) just past South Fork Meadows and follow it southeast into a draw. After about 100 yards, the trail turns left (northeast) and crosses the small stream coming down from Dry Lake basin. It then switchbacks up the mountainside through open stands of ponderosa and Jeffrey pine and white fir. After gaining 400 feet, the switchbacks end and your trail contours along the slope until it rejoins the floor of the draw. A short distance up the draw it reaches Dry Lake—1.2 miles from South Fork Meadows (**GPS N34° 07.302′ W116° 49.742′**). Here is a trail junction: right to Mine Shaft Saddle and San Gorgonio Mountain (see Hike 43, page 111), left to the two trail camps. You go left. In 0.1 mile the trail reaches Dry Lake Trail Camp, located in a grassy area surrounded by lodgepoles just above the northeast shore of the lake. A quarter mile farther, just inside the draw southeast of Dry Lake, is Lodgepole Spring Trail Camp, with water trickling from the small spring.

Return the way you came. Options include going on up San Gorgonio Mountain (Hike 43, page 111) and returning via Dollar Lake Saddle (see next hike), making a grand loop trip around the eastern part of the wilderness, or taking the new trail across the ridge to Fish Creek (Hike 36, page 96). Any way you do it, you will enjoy this alpine section of the highest wilderness in Southern California.

■ Hike 42 SAN GORGONIO MOUNTAIN VIA DOLLAR LAKE SADDLE 🥾 🐕 🚶

HIKE LENGTH 20 miles out-and-back; 4,700' elevation gain

DIFFICULTY Strenuous (1 day), Moderate (2 days)

SEASON June–October

TOPO MAPS *Moonridge, San Gorgonio Mtn.* (both 7.5-minute), *San Gorgonio Wilderness* (Tom Harrison)

PERMIT San Gorgonio Wilderness Permit required

This area was impacted by the 2015 Lake Fire. As of 2016, the trail remains closed. Check with the Mill Creek Ranger Station at 909-382-2882 to determine if the trail has reopened.

■ FEATURES

San Gorgonio Mountain crowns all of Southern California. No other peak south of the Sierra Nevada rises high enough to challenge its 11,502-foot elevation. Gleaming white in winter snows and somber gray during summer months, its massive granite bulk can be seen for 100 miles in many directions.

The great hogback mountain is the culminating hump of the 10,000-plus-foot, 7-mile-long, sky-piercing ridge that dominates the San Gorgonio Wilderness. Gravelly, boulder-strewn slopes and broad, shallow draws slant downward from the summit crest, dropping far into shadowy canyons. Snow patches linger well into the summer months. The air is crisp with the chill of elevation. The sky is deep blue, free of the urban-generated murkiness that clogs lower elevations.

Hikers on the summit of San Gorgonio

Wilderness boundary at Poopout Hill

Although a familiar sight to millions living below, only the hiker or horseback rider can really know the charm of this alpine island in the sky. Slopes that look barren and lifeless from the distance are actually spotted with hardy, weather-resistant life forms. Wind-buffeted dwarf lodgepole pines and limber pines hug the ground between boulders. Small clumps of high-altitude chinquapin sprout in protected hollows. Diminutive alpine wildflowers bloom colorfully in midsummer—most common are pink-flowered locoweed, alpine buttercup, and silver mat. Golden-mantle ground squirrels and grayish lodgepole chipmunks dart among the elfin trees. Red-tailed hawks and Clark's nutcrackers are occasionally seen flying above. Just east of the summit, on desert-facing slopes, dwell a handful of Nelson bighorn sheep.

The mountain received its name from Rancho San Gorgonio, the easternmost cattle ranch of Mission San Gabriel, established sometime before 1824 (located in today's San Gorgonio Pass). The rancho, in turn, was named for Saint Gorgonius, an obscure Christian martyr of the third century AD whose feast day is September 9. But for many years, the mountain was known by other titles. The Cahuilla people called it "Kwiria-Kaich," meaning "bald" or "smooth." Lieutenant Robert S. Williamson's Pacific Railroad Survey party of 1853 were the first to describe the mountain and called the whole ridge "Mount San Bernardino." In 1878 the US Army's Wheeler Survey saw in the great gray hogback a resemblance to a grizzly bear at rest and labeled it "Grizzly Peak" on their map. From the 1870s on, many San Bernardino Valley residents knew the mountain as "Grayback," a name that persists today. Not until E. T. Perkins, topographer for the US Geological Survey, surveyed the mountain in 1899 and placed the name "San Gorgonio Mountain" on the government topographical sheet did the latter become commonly accepted as the correct title for the peak.

The earliest known ascent of San Gorgonio Mountain was made by W. O. Goodyear of the California Mining Bureau and Mark Thomas of San Bernardino on June 2, 1872. Their route was up the south slope of the mountain from Mill Creek Canyon. Goodyear toted a mercury barometer to the summit and calculated its elevation at 11,600 feet—not a bad estimate considering his primitive instrument.

Since then, thousands have made the ascent in all kinds of weather conditions. Charles Francis Saunders, in his classic *Southern Sierras of California,* described a terrifying climb amid lightning, thunder, and dashing rain in 1904, in which one person was killed and another dazed by a lightning bolt. Because of the elevation and unstable winds, this type of weather occasionally occurs in the summertime. But most often the weather is clear and cool during the summer months, a welcome relief from the sweltering valley far below.

In 1875, Theodore Van Dyke proclaimed "He who has not ascended Grayback is like a savage who listens to the tuning up of an orchestra and goes off pleased— thinking he has heard the concert." This is a trip every Southern California hiker should make at least once. The trail is in excellent condition, the high-altitude atmosphere is invigorating, the alpine life forms offer a striking change from the usual Southern California pattern, and the view from the top encompasses a 360-degree panorama from the Mexican border to the southern Sierra Nevada, from the Pacific to the farthest reaches of the Mojave Desert.

You have a number of options. You can go up and back in one strenuous day. You can make it an overnight backpack by staying at one of several inviting trail camps. Or, with a car shuttle, you can go up this way and descend by another route. All of these options are outlined below.

DESCRIPTION

From Redlands, drive east on Highway 38 to the Jenks Lake Road turnoff, 50 yards before mile marker 038 SBD 25.51. Turn right (southeast) and follow Jenks Lake Road 2.5 miles to the well-marked South Fork Trailhead (**GPS N34° 09.694' W116° 52.356'**). There is a large paved parking area with restrooms on your left.

Follow the trail from Jenks Lake Road to South Fork Meadows, 4 miles (see Hike 39, page 101). The trail then climbs above the west edge of the meadow and begins switchbacking up the ridge. You start out in a forest of ponderosa pine and white fir, but as you rise above 8,800 feet, lodgepoles begin to predominate. The trail then rounds the ridge and climbs along the west slope of the big draw leading to Dollar Lake Saddle, passing a grassy cienega and an area of waist-high manzanita. Just beyond, you pass the junction of the trail going down to Dollar Lake.

Continue up the trail to Dollar Lake Saddle (10,000 feet; **GPS N34° 07.096' W116° 51.624'**), 2 miles from South Fork Meadows. Two small trail camps are just west of the saddle: Red Rock Flat (no water) and, 0.5 mile farther west, just south of the main divide trail, High Meadow Springs (always water), both shaded by lodgepole pines. If you are doing the trip in two days, stay overnight at one of these trail camps. Trails lead northwest along San Bernardino Peak Divide (see Hike 48, page 121), southwest down Falls Creek to Mill Creek Canyon (see Hike 52, page 130), and southeast to San Gorgonio Mountain. You turn left and take the latter trail. The pathway leads through a silent, stony forest of lodgepoles around the west and south slopes of Charlton Peak. In 0.5 mile you reach the steep side trail up to Charlton's summit (Charlton Peak is named for Rushton Charlton, supervisor of Angeles National Forest from 1907 to 1925, when the San Bernardinos were part of the Angeles). At 0.7 mile beyond the junction, the trail reaches the saddle between Charlton and Jepson Peaks, where you can look down into Dry Lake basin. Here is Dry Lake View Trail Camp, a small overnight stop amid stunted lodgepoles and granite boulders (waterless). The trail now climbs the treeless west slope of Jepson Peak (named for Willis Linn Jepson, 1867–1946, University of California botanist who made a botanical survey of the San Bernardino Mountains in the early 1900s and wrote *The Trees of California* and *A Manual of the Flowering Plants of California*), contours high on the south side through dwarfed and wind-bent lodgepoles, and reaches a junction with the Vivian Creek Trail, 3 miles from the saddle (see Hike 54, page 134). Continue upward and eastward. About 0.25 mile farther is a second junction, this one with the Sky High Trail leading down around the east slope of the mountain to Mine Shaft Saddle (see next hike). The trail now crosses nearly bare slopes, passes the top of Big Draw, crosses a slight rise, and climbs to the boulder-stacked summit of San Gorgonio Mountain, 10 miles from the start (**GPS N34° 05.954' W116° 49.495'**). Adjacent is Summit Trail Camp—no trees, no water, exposed to the elements, but a favorite of hardy backpackers who relish the mountaintop sunrise and don't mind below-freezing temperatures (a Southern California counterpart of sleeping on Mount Whitney's summit).

After taking in the all-encompassing view, return the way you came. Or you have several options. You can descend by the Sky High Trail to Mine Shaft Saddle and Dry Lake, and back to Jenks Lake Road, a 23-mile round-trip (see next hike). With car shuttles, you can descend the Vivian Creek Trail or the Falls Creek Trail into Mill Creek Canyon (see Hikes 52 and 54, pages 130 and 134). Or—very strenuous—you can follow the ridgeline trail westward over San Bernardino Peak and down to Angelus Oaks (see Hike 48, page 121). Any way you decide to do the trip, you will thoroughly appreciate this sky-reaching part of Southern California.

■ Hike 43 SAN GORGONIO MOUNTAIN VIA MINE SHAFT SADDLE 🥾 🐕 🚶

HIKE LENGTH 22 miles out-and-back; 4,700' elevation gain

DIFFICULTY Strenuous (1 day), Moderate (2 days)

SEASON June–October

TOPO MAPS *Moonridge, San Gorgonio Mtn.* (both 7.5-minute), *San Gorgonio Wilderness* (Tom Harrison)

PERMIT San Gorgonio Wilderness Permit required

This area was impacted by the 2015 Lake Fire. As of 2016, the trail remains closed. Check with the Mill Creek Ranger Station at 909-382-2882 to determine if the trail has reopened.

■ FEATURES

The Sky High Trail zigzags up the northeast and east slopes of San Gorgonio Mountain from Mine Shaft Saddle. When combined with the standard trail route from Dollar Lake Saddle, it makes for an ideal loop trip. You can go up one way and down the other, covering a good part of the unspoiled alpine country in the eastern half of the San Gorgonio Wilderness. The main attraction of the Sky High Trail is the superb view down over the Coachella Valley; on a clear day you can see to the Salton Sea and beyond. Be in top shape for this one, particularly if you plan to hike it in one day. It is more enjoyable as an overnight backpack, camping at Dry Lake or at one of the timberline trail camps.

■ DESCRIPTION

From Redlands, drive east on Highway 38 to the Jenks Lake Road turnoff, 50 yards before mile marker 038 SBD 25.51. Turn right (southeast) and follow Jenks Lake Road 2.5 miles to the well-marked South Fork Trailhead (**GPS N34° 09.694' W116° 52.356'**). There is a large paved parking area with restrooms on your left.

Follow the trail from Jenks Lake Road to South Fork Meadows, 4 miles (see Hike 39, page 101), then the trail to Dry Lake, 1.2 more miles (see Hike 41). If you plan to make this a two-day trip, you may want to camp overnight at Dry Lake, the last available seasonal water. Where the trail from South Fork Meadows reaches Dry Lake's outlet is a junction. Go right (south) along the west shore of the little

North face of San Gorgonio Mountain after a winter storm

lake, then right again in a quarter mile where the path veers off along the south shore to Lodgepole Camp. The trail enters a draw and climbs the ridge south of the lake, through a forest of almost exclusively lodgepole pines with clumps of chinquapin for ground cover. In 2 miles it reaches Mine Shaft Saddle, on the divide between Dry Lake basin and the desert-draining North Fork of the Whitewater River. Just beyond is a trail junction: left goes down to North Fork Meadows (see Hike 44, page 113) and Fish Creek Meadows (Hike 36, page 96); right is the Sky High Trail to San Gorgonio Mountain. Go right (southeast); a sign indicates SAN GORGONIO 3.5 MILES. The trail climbs eastward through granite boulder fields and a lodgepole forest, then makes eight switchbacks up the northeast slope of the mountain. You pass the wreckage of a C-47 that splattered against the mountainside on a stormy night in 1952. A Marine helicopter crashed shortly afterward while trying to reach the wreckage. Looking north, you see the undulating Ten Thousand Foot Ridge, where Frank Sinatra's mother died in a 1977 Learjet crash.

Finally, after gaining 1,000 feet, the trail rounds the east ridge of San Gorgonio and climbs westward up the south slope. Good views are obtained down into the rugged Whitewater country and beyond to the desert. When the trail intersects the main pathway from Dollar Lake Saddle, turn right (east) and climb 0.3 mile to the summit (**GPS N34° 05.954' W116° 49.495'**).

If you're doing the loop trip, descend via the Dollar Lake Saddle–South Fork Meadows route (see Hike 42, page 107). Or return the way you came. Other options include descending into Mill Creek Canyon via either Vivian Creek (see Hike 54, page 134) or the Falls Creek Trail (see Hike 52, page 130). Or, for a very long trip, follow the crest trail west to San Bernardino Peak and down to Angelus Oaks (see Hike 48, page 121).

■ Hike 44 NORTH FORK MEADOWS 🡕 🐕 🚶

HIKE LENGTH 19 miles out-and-back; 4,600' elevation gain

DIFFICULTY Strenuous (1 day), Moderate (2 days)

SEASON June–October

TOPO MAPS *Moonridge, San Gorgonio Mtn.* (both 7.5-minute), *San Gorgonio Wilderness* (Tom Harrison)

PERMIT San Gorgonio Wilderness Permit required

This area was impacted by the 2015 Lake Fire. As of 2016, the trail remains closed. Check with the Mill Creek Ranger Station at 909-382-2882 to determine if the trail has reopened.

■ FEATURES

The eastern end of the San Gorgonio Wilderness drops steeply toward the desert. Draining the 10,000- and 11,000-foot peaks of this eastern high country are the three forks of the Whitewater River, tumbling streams that through the ages have carved deep, V-shaped gorges from the high mountains down into arid Coachella Valley, where the spent waters sink into the desert sands and the river becomes a broad, gravelly wash. This lower part of the river is the Whitewater known to most people, drab and unimpressive. But the high Whitewater reveals a different character; it is a rugged, isolated wilderness, even today seldom trod by man. Here dwell Nelson bighorn sheep, the largest herds of these noble animals in the San Bernardino Mountains.

Very few trails enter the Whitewater country. One that samples a small bit of it is the overgrown pathway from Mine Shaft Saddle down into the headwaters of the North Fork to North Fork Meadows. Here, alongside the verdant meadow,

North Fork from Mine Shaft Saddle

with Jeffrey pines as a backdrop, the Forest Service has constructed Big Tree Trail Camp. This small campsite, easternmost in the San Gorgonio Wilderness, is well off the beaten track of most hikers. If you relish solitude and quiet beauty on your wilderness outings, this place should be one of your favorites.

Experienced mountaineers have descended the Whitewater all the way to the desert road end. It is a difficult, trailless venture. Don't do it unless you have done ample cross-country mountaineering, and then never attempt it alone.

■ DESCRIPTION

From Redlands, drive east on Highway 38 to the Jenks Lake Road turnoff, 50 yards before mile marker 038 SBD 25.51. Turn right (southeast) and follow Jenks Lake Road 2.5 miles to the well-marked South Fork Trailhead (**GPS N34° 09.694' W116° 52.356'**). There is a large paved parking area with restrooms on your left.

Follow the trail from Jenks Lake Road to South Fork Meadows (see Hike 39, page 101), then the trail to Dry Lake, 1.2 more miles (see Hike 41, page 105). At the outlet of Dry Lake is a junction; go right (south) and follow the trail up to Mine Shaft Saddle, 2 miles (see Hike 43, page 111). Here is another junction:

right up San Gorgonio Mountain (Hike 43), left down into the North Fork of the Whitewater River. Go left (east). The trail gradually descends through a lodgepole forest. In 0.25 mile you pass a trail leading left (northeast) to Fish Creek (see Hike 36, page 96); continue straight. Down to your right is Mine Shaft Flats, the scene of an unsuccessful turn-of-the-20th-century mining operation. Just beyond, the trail drops more steeply and leaves the lodgepole forest. You must now fight your way through buckthorn thickets down to the upper edge of North Fork Meadow, 2.6 miles from Mine Shaft Saddle. Here the trail deteriorates and you may encounter thick brush across the meadow to Big Tree Trail Camp, located under several large pines on the north edge of the meadow (**GPS N34° 06.107' W116° 48.121'**). Water runs year-round in the creek, but no wood fires are allowed.

Return the way you came. Alternatives include returning over San Gorgonio Mountain (see Hike 43) or via the Fish Creek Trail (see Hike 36). The latter requires a car shuttle.

■ Hike 45 JOHNS MEADOW 🥾 🐕 🚶

HIKE LENGTH 6 miles out-and-back; 800' elevation gain

DIFFICULTY Easy

SEASON May–November

TOPO MAP *Big Bear Lake* (7.5-minute), *San Gorgonio Wilderness* (Tom Harrison)

PERMIT San Gorgonio Wilderness Permit required

■ FEATURES

Johns Meadow is a good family destination for a picnic lunch or easy backpack. It offers a taste of the San Gorgonio Wilderness without the steep climbs required to reach the high mountains. The hike visits lush forest with several small creeks. Quiet hikers will come across squirrels, lizards, and birds. In midsummer, it features wonderful wildflowers and berries, especially where it crosses the creeks. The berries include blue currants (resembling small blueberries with crunchy seeds and a tart taste), small red currants, spiky red gooseberries (tasty after boiling to remove the thorns), and thimbleberries (red and delicious when ripe, related to raspberries and blackberries). Keep your eyes out for lupine, Indian paintbrush, ferns, and penstemon.

■ DESCRIPTION

From Redlands, drive east on Highway 38 to the Jenks Lake Road turnoff, just before mile marker 038 SBD 25.51. Turn right (southeast). After 0.3 mile turn right

Sugar-pine cones

again onto a fair dirt road where a sign reads FORSEE CREEK TRAIL. Drive 0.5 mile to the large parking area at the trailhead (**GPS N34° 09.618' W116° 53.976'**).

The trail starts steeply up the hillside. Pass the San Gorgonio Wilderness boundary marker in 0.3 mile. After another 0.1 mile, reach a signed junction. Turn right, toward Johns Meadow. The other path leads to Jackstraw Springs and up to the crest of the mountains (see Hike 47, page 119).

The trail now contours westward around the mountainside. It crosses Stetson Creek and another small creek, then climbs gently to a small saddle, 1.8 miles from the junction. Switchback steeply down to Forsee Creek for 0.5 mile. The slope beyond Forsee Creek was scoured by a snow avalanche in 2005, leaving a jumble of twisted tree trunks and debris. In 0.1 mile, arrive at Johns Meadow on a small bench (**GPS N34° 08.707' W116° 55.525'**).

Numerous tent sites are scattered across the bench. The trail becomes ill-defined as it wanders through the sites, but becomes clear again on the south-west side where it crosses another creek. Retrace your steps from Johns Meadow. Or continue up the unmaintained trail beyond the creek 1.5 miles to Manzanita Springs and on down the San Bernardino Peak Trail to Angelus Oaks (see Hike 47). This requires a car or bicycle shuttle.

■ Hike 46 SAN BERNARDINO PEAK DIVIDE FROM FORSEE CREEK ↗ 🐕 🚶

HIKE LENGTH 15 miles one-way; 4,000' elevation gain

DIFFICULTY Moderate (2 days), Strenuous (1 day)

SEASON June–October

TOPO MAP *Big Bear Lake, Moonridge* (both 7.5-minute)

PERMIT San Gorgonio Wilderness Permit required

This area was impacted by the 2015 Lake Fire. As of 2016, the trail remains closed. Check with the Mill Creek Ranger Station at 909-382-2882 to determine if the trail has reopened.

■ FEATURES

There are numerous opportunities for loop trips in the San Gorgonio Wilderness, laced as the region is with trails. This trip climbs the steep, heavily wooded north slope of San Bernardino Peak Divide via the Forsee Creek Trail, follows the divide trail east to Dollar Lake Saddle, and descends via South Fork Meadows to Jenks Lake Road. En route are several inviting trail camps for overnight stay, and three springs with icy-cold water. You pass through some lush forest country and are rewarded with far-ranging views from high on the 10,000-foot divide. This is one of the best circle trips in the wilderness. A 3-mile shuttle (or road walk) is necessary.

■ DESCRIPTION

Leave a getaway car or bicycle at the South Fork Trailhead. From Redlands, drive east on Highway 38 to the Jenks Lake Road turnoff, just before mile marker 038 SBD 25.51. Turn right (southeast) and proceed 2.5 miles to the signed South Fork Trailhead (**GPS N34° 09.694' W116° 52.356'**).

To reach the Forsee Creek Trailhead, drive back west 2.2 miles on Jenks Lake Road to a signed fair dirt road on the left. Follow this 0.5 mile to the large parking area at the trailhead (**GPS N34° 09.618' W116° 53.976'**).

The Forsee Creek Trail leads uphill through a forest of Jeffrey pine, incense-cedar, black oak, and white fir. In 0.4 mile you reach a trail junction; the fork to the right leads west to Johns Meadow Trail Camp (see previous hike). Continue straight ahead. In 1.7 miles you cross little Stetson Creek, trickling water until late summer. A mile farther up, the trail crosses a sloping bench, resplendent with grasses and ferns, spotted with Indian paintbrush and lupine. Beyond, the lodgepole pines begin to appear. Vistas open as the trail rounds the east side of the ridge. As you rise above 8,600 feet, lodgepole becomes the predominant forest tree. In 2.1 miles, a sign points right 100 yards to Jackstraw Springs Trail Camp (with wood, water, and little flats for sleeping). The trail now climbs the slope east of Forsee Creek and in 1.6 more miles reaches a junction with the lower branch of the San Bernardino Peak Divide Trail, traversing the mountain crest east and west. Just to the right (west) is Trail Fork Springs. Trail Fork Springs Camp (with primitive facilities) is on the lodgepole-shaded bench to your left.

Turn left (east); in 0.4 mile you reach a junction with the upper branch of the divide trail, which traverses close under Anderson Peak (named for Lew Anderson, district ranger at Barton Flats during the 1920s). Continue east through a parklike lodgepole forest, around the rocky north slope of Shields Peak (named for Leila Shields, manager of Camp Radford in the 1920s), and down to Shields Flat. There is a waterless campsite here, 80 yards south of the trail. Your trail climbs over a slight rise and drops to a junction with the side trail to High Meadow Springs. The spring and its cozy trail camp are 0.25 mile down the slope to your right (south). Water is always available here.

The trail turns southeast and descends 400 feet to Dollar Lake Saddle, 0.75 mile ahead (**GPS N34° 07.096' W116° 51.624'**). Here is a four-way trail junction and, just to the west, Red Rock Flat Trail Camp (no water). Trails lead southeast to San Gorgonio Mountain (see Hike 42, page 107), southwest down Falls Creek

Lodgepole pines on the Forsee Creek Trail

to Mill Creek (see Hike 52, page 130), and northeast to South Fork Meadows and Jenks Lake Road. Take the latter (see Hike 42 for description).

There are numerous ways to vary this loop trip. From Trail Fork Springs, you can turn west along the divide, cross San Bernardino Peak, and descend to Angelus Oaks (see Hike 48, page 121). From Dollar Lake Saddle, you can almost double the length of the loop by continuing on to San Gorgonio Mountain (Hike 42) and then descending the Sky High Trail to Mine Shaft Saddle, and on down past Dry Lake and South Fork Meadows to Jenks Lake Road (see Hike 43, page 111). With a car shuttle, you can descend the Falls Creek Trail into Mill Creek Canyon (see Hike 52).

■ Hike 47 SAN BERNARDINO PEAK 🡵 🐕 🚶

HIKE LENGTH 16 miles out-and-back; 4,700' elevation gain
DIFFICULTY Moderate (2 days), Strenuous (1 day)
SEASON June–October
TOPO MAP *Big Bear Lake, Forest Falls* (both 7.5-minute)
PERMIT San Gorgonio Wilderness Permit required

■ FEATURES

The men were exhausted. All day they had struggled up the rugged, trailless, brush-infested north slope of San Bernardino Peak, all the way from the canyon of the Santa Ana River. The important work they had been assigned to do would have to wait until the next day.

The men were Col. Henry Washington of the US Army, under contract with the US Surveyor General's Office; Mr. Gray, deputy surveyor; and 11 workmen. The date was November 7, 1852. Colonel Washington had been assigned the difficult task of establishing an initial point and erecting a monument from which an east–west baseline and a north–south meridian could be surveyed. Then land surveys for all of Southern California would be undertaken, based on Washington's pioneering calculations.

After thoroughly checking the rugged terrain around the peak, Colonel Washington selected a point overlooking the San Bernardino Valley about 0.5 mile west of the summit. Here he and his men erected an elaborate wooden monument 23 feet, 9 inches in height. Eleven bearings were taken to define the location of the monument, and here the surveyors ran into trouble. They found it impossible to obtain true fixes on distant triangulation marks because of shimmering heat waves from the valley. To overcome this problem, huge fires were lit atop San Bernardino Peak and at the other triangulation points, and the surveys were made at night.

Colonel Washington's monument

Upon the completion of this initial triangulation, Washington and his party commenced surveying Southern California. All land surveys in this part of the state have subsequently been based on Colonel Washington's baseline. Today, more than 150 years later, the wooden base and supporting rock cairn of Colonel Washington's monument remain intact, a few yards above the San Bernardino Peak Trail.

This trail trip visits this historic spot en route from Angelus Oaks to the summit of San Bernardino Peak. You pass through beautiful subalpine country in this western end of the San Gorgonio Wilderness. If the day is clear, views are breathtaking, extending over the foothills and across the vast San Bernardino Valley to the distant San Gabriel Mountains. Two delightful trail camps—Columbine Springs and Limber Pine Springs—offer opportunities for overnight stays. Both have water nearby. It's a long uphill climb, but one you shouldn't miss. Best do it on a cool early-summer or late-fall weekend; long stretches of the trail traverse open manzanita slopes and make for unpleasant walking on a hot day.

■ DESCRIPTION

From Redlands, drive east on Highway 38 to Angelus Oaks. Follow signs for the San Bernardino Peak Trail (1W07). First turn right from Highway 38 toward the fire station at mile marker 038 SBD 20.00. Then make an immediate left and drive 0.1 mile, passing the station. Make a right past the station at a sign indicating

1W07 on a fair dirt road. Stay right at two forks, and go 0.3 mile to a large dirt parking area with the signed SAN BERNARDINO PEAK TRAILHEAD (**GPS N34° 08.775' W116° 58.696'**).

The trail starts up through a forest of Jeffrey and sugar pine, white fir, and several species of oak. Soon you are switchbacking up a steep slope. In 2 miles you reach the boundary of the San Gorgonio Wilderness, marked by a wooden sign. A short distance beyond, the switchbacks taper off and you climb more gently through open stands of Jeffrey pine. As you near the top of a long 8,000-foot ridge, the Jeffreys become less numerous and the trail slices through oceans of manzanita. At 4.3 miles from the start is the Manzanita Springs junction just off the trail to the right (south). A side trail leads south down to Manzanita Springs and continues 0.25 mile to Columbine Springs Trail Camp (water unreliable). The main trail climbs up a slope covered with manzanita, snowbrush, and chinquapin, and in 1.4 miles reaches Limber Pine Springs Trail Camp. This campsite, located on a bench shaded by lodgepole pines, is the largest trail camp in the western half of the wilderness and is a favorite of Boy Scout groups. Water is usually available through the summer from Limber Pine Springs, 0.25 mile up the trail. From the springs, the trail turns south and climbs steadily to the top of the high ridge leading west from San Bernardino Peak. In 1.5 miles you reach the west ridge of San Bernardino Peak and climb eastward. Just 100 yards beyond, 50 feet to the right and above the trail, is Colonel Washington's initial baseline monument (**GPS N34° 07.219' W116° 55.859'**). The trail climbs eastward along the ridge and in 0.5 mile passes just north of the summit of San Bernardino Peak. A side trail ascends 150 yards to the 10,649-foot high point (**GPS N34° 07.341' W116° 55.345'**).

After fully enjoying the tremendous view and signing the summit register, return the way you came. An option is to continue eastward along the San Bernardino Peak Divide Trail (see next hike) and then descend to Jenks Lake Road or Mill Creek Canyon.

■ Hike 48 THE GREAT SAN BERNARDINO DIVIDE

HIKE LENGTH 28 miles one-way; 6,200' elevation gain

DIFFICULTY Moderate (3 days), Strenuous (2 days), Very Strenuous (1 day)

SEASON June–October

TOPO MAPS *Big Bear Lake, Forest Falls, Moonridge, San Gorgonio Mtn.* (all 7.5-minute), *San Gorgonio Wilderness* (Tom Harrison)

PERMIT San Gorgonio Wilderness Permit required

This area was impacted by the 2015 Lake Fire. As of 2016, the trail remains closed. Check with the Mill Creek Ranger Station at 909-382-2882 to determine if the trail has reopened.

▣ FEATURES

This long trail trip traverses the entire San Bernardino Peak–San Gorgonio Mountain ridge from west to east, covering a generous part of the San Gorgonio Wilderness. It is for experienced backpackers who relish long stretches of high-altitude walking. This is the rooftop of Southern California, the largest piece of subalpine wilderness south of the Sierra Nevada, and it is delightful summer hiking country, cool and refreshing. But the climb to this sky island is tough, involving over a mile of elevation gain. Be in good condition before you try it.

▣ DESCRIPTION

The trip ends at the South Fork Trailhead on Jenks Lake Road, so set up a car (or bicycle) shuttle there. From Highway 38 near mile marker 038 SBD 25.51, turn southeast onto Jenks Lake Road and then drive 2.5 miles to the trailhead parking (**GPS N34° 09.694' W116° 52.356'**).

Return to Highway 38 and drive west to Angelus Oaks. At the fire station at mile marker 038 SBD 20.00, turn left off the highway, and then immediately left again onto Manzanita Avenue. In 0.1 mile, make a right at a sign indicating 1W07 onto a fair dirt road. Stay right at two forks, and go 0.3 mile to a large dirt parking area with the signed SAN BERNARDINO PEAK TRAILHEAD (**GPS N34° 08.775' W116° 58.696'**).

Follow the San Bernardino Peak Trail 4.3 miles to the Manzanita Springs junction, then another 1.4 miles to Limber Pine Springs Trail Camp. (If you are doing the trip in the recommended three days, a first-night stop here is suggested.) Proceed 2.4 miles farther to San Bernardino Peak (see previous hike).

From San Bernardino Peak, the San Bernardino Peak Divide Trail leads east along or just north of the ridgetop, through an open forest of lodgepole pine. You drop 200 feet to a saddle, then climb up the slopes of San Bernardino East Peak, passing just north of the summit (10,691 feet). A side trail leads 100 feet to the top. About 0.25 mile beyond, you pass the unmarked junction of the Momyer Creek Trail coming up from Mill Creek Canyon (see Hike 50, page 126; **GPS N34° 07.599' W116° 54.403'**). In another 0.5 mile is a trail fork: left to Trail Fork Springs and a junction with the Forsee Creek Trail (see Hike 46, page 117), right for a traverse close under the slopes of Anderson Peak. The two forks rejoin after a mile. Almost pure stands of lodgepole pine cover the ridge from San Bernardino Peak eastward to the upper slopes of San Gorgonio. These hardy veterans of

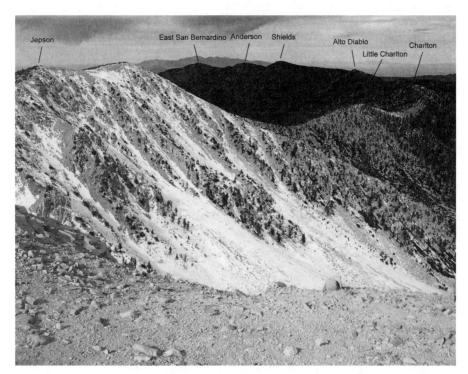

The peaks of San Bernardino Ridge

high elevations lack the sylvan greenery and underbrush of lower levels, forming a strange, open, stone-floored forest. Among them a profound silence reigns, occasionally broken by the rat-tat-tat of white-headed woodpeckers and the shrill chatter of chickadees, while toward evening the vesperlike antiphony of hermit thrushes is often heard.

The trail rounds the rocky slope of Shields Peak, drops to Shields Flat, crosses a rise, and reaches the High Meadow Springs Trail junction. The springs and trail camp are 0.25 mile to your right (south). The water here is the last before the climb of San Gorgonio, so fill canteens. (If you're doing the three-day trip, a second night's stay here is suggested.) The trail then descends to the four-way junction at Dollar Lake Saddle, 0.75 mile ahead (**GPS N34° 07.096' W116° 51.624'**). Continue southeastward along the divide trail, rounding the south slopes of Charlton Peak to Dry Lake View Trail Camp (no water) and then up around the bare slopes of Jepson Peak and on to the rocky summit of San Gorgonio (**GPS N34° 05.954' W116° 49.495'**), 3.6 miles and 17 miles from the start (see Hike 42, page 107, for detailed description).

You've now traversed the great San Bernardino Peak–San Gorgonio Mountain ridge. After taking in the summit view that encompasses half of Southern California, retrace your steps 0.25 mile to the Sky High Trail junction. Turn left (southeast) and follow the Sky High Trail down to Mine Shaft Saddle, then on down past Dry Lake and South Fork Meadows to the trip's end at Jenks Lake Road. This sky-high ramble is the longest in the wilderness, but the spectacular subalpine country you traverse makes the trip well worth the effort.

Alternatively, from Mine Shaft Saddle, descend east on the Fish Creek Trail to the Fish Creek Trail parking area (see Hike 36, page 96). This variation shaves off 3 miles and 1,100 feet of knee-pounding descent, while taking you across the entire San Gorgonio Wilderness from west to east. It requires a longer car shuttle.

The Nine Peaks Challenge is another variation on this trip, climbing all nine summits along the ridge. The San Gorgonio Wilderness Association sells an "I Climbed the Nine Peaks" arm patch. For many Boy Scouts, this three-day backpacking trip is a rite of passage. Serious peak-baggers and ultra-marathoners attempt it in one exhausting day. The nine peaks are, from west to east:

- **SAN BERNARDINO PEAK: 10,649' (GPS N34° 07.341' W116° 55.345')**
- **SAN BERNARDINO PEAK EAST: 10,691' (GPS N34° 07.482' W116° 54.588')**
- **ANDERSON PEAK: 10,864' (GPS N34° 07.479' W116° 53.659')**
- **SHIELDS PEAK: 10,701' (GPS N34° 07.631' W116° 52.931')**
- **ALTO DIABLO: 10,563' (GPS N34° 07.614' W116° 52.394')**
- **CHARLTON PEAK: 10,806' (GPS N34° 06.888' W116° 51.220')**
- **LITTLE CHARLTON PEAK: 10,696' (GPS N34° 06.622' W116° 51.027')**
- **JEPSON PEAK: 11,205' (GPS N34° 06.177' W116° 50.687')**
- **SAN GORGONIO MOUNTAIN: 11,502' (GPS N34° 05.954' W116° 49.495')**

■ Hike 49 MOUNTAIN HOME FLATS 🥾 🐕 🚶

HIKE LENGTH 3.5 miles out-and-back; 1,100' elevation gain

DIFFICULTY Moderate

SEASON April–November

TOPO MAPS *Big Bear Lake* (both 7.5-minute), *San Gorgonio Wilderness* (Tom Harrison)

▓ FEATURES

If you are seeking a short but wild backpacking trip or picnic destination where you can get away from the crowds, Mountain Home Flats is a great trip. The small trail camp is nestled beneath the pines, firs, and incense-cedars on a bench up a rugged canyon on a challenging trail.

Secluded campsite at Mountain Home Flats

■ DESCRIPTION

From Redlands, drive east on Highway 38. Take the huge hairpin turn at the mouth of Mill Creek Canyon, and then continue 3.4 miles to a bridge over Glen Martin Creek at mile marker 038 SBD 18.44 (**GPS N34° 07.632' W116° 59.017'**). There is very limited parking just south of the bridge, and more at a turnout 0.25 mile north. Do not mix up this trailhead with Mountain Home Creek, which is 1.5 miles farther south.

From the south end of the highway bridge, find the narrow trail leading east into Glen Martin Canyon. Follow it down to the floor of the creek; then briefly cross to the north side. When the creek divides, follow the south fork through a forest of Coulter pines.

The trail veers right and switchbacks steeply up to the canyon's south ridge. Take care to stay on the main trail, which is the easiest route. In 1 mile, cross the ridge and enter the upper reaches of Mountain Home Canyon. Be careful as you skirt the edge of a decomposing cliff before descending to a series of pools connected by a small waterfall.

The final stretch of trail switchbacks up again to reach the wooded campsite at Mountain Home Flats (**GPS N34° 07.726' W116° 57.674'**). The easiest access to water is a short but steep scramble north into Mountain Home Creek.

■ Hike 50 SAN BERNARDINO PEAK DIVIDE FROM MILL CREEK 🥾 🐎 🚶

HIKE LENGTH 14 miles out-and-back; 5,200' elevation gain

DIFFICULTY Very Strenuous

SEASON June–October

TOPO MAPS *Forest Falls, Big Bear Lake* (both 7.5-minute), *San Gorgonio Wilderness* (Tom Harrison)

PERMIT San Gorgonio Wilderness Permit required

■ FEATURES

From the fault-line gorge of Mill Creek Canyon, San Bernardino Peak Divide rises precipitously more than a mile above. This is one of the highest and steepest mountain walls in the San Bernardinos. Climbing directly up this towering slope in seemingly endless switchbacks is the Momyer Creek Trail, gaining 5000 feet in 7 miles. The trip presents a living demonstration of how the forest changes with altitude: first through brush and oak, then through belts of Jeffrey and ponderosa pine and white fir, then across manzanita slopes, and finally into the realm of lodgepole pine. There is no dependable water en route, unless you make the 2-mile round-trip to Alger Creek. This is a very steep trip for the well-conditioned hiker. Do it on a cool day, and get an early start, for much of the trail is open to the sun. The upper portion is not maintained, but is generally possible to follow. Wear long pants to fend off the brush. You will probably have the trail to yourself; few hikers use this tough route to the high country.

■ DESCRIPTION

From Redlands, drive east on Highway 38 to its junction with Valley of the Falls Road at the huge switchback 20 yards before mile marker 038 SBD 15.00. Turn right and continue east up Mill Creek Canyon to the large parking area for the Momyer Creek and Falls Creek Trails, on your left 100 yards before the fire station, 2.9 miles (**GPS N34° 05.250' W116° 54.863'**). Mill Creek Canyon is prone to dangerous floods, mudslides, and avalanches in times of heavy precipitation, and hiking is not recommended on those days.

Follow the trail down into the broad-shouldered wash of Mill Creek. The trail across the creek washes out every winter so some route finding is necessary. Go left at a hard-to-spot junction and traverse directly across the boulder maze to the north bank. Here the trail turns left (west) and climbs the open slope to a junction with the old beginning of the Momyer Creek Trail coming up from Torrey Pines Road. Turn right and follow the footpath as it switchbacks steeply up the divide

The San Bernardino Peak Divide towers above Mill Creek Canyon.

between Momyer Creek and Alger Creek, through chaparral and scrub oak. Soon you are climbing through a patchy forest of oak and Jeffrey pine. In 2.6 miles you reach a junction: a trail right goes 1 mile to Alger Creek Trail Camp (see next hike), but you should go left. Long switchbacks continue and the forest becomes richer—mostly Jeffrey and ponderosa pine and white fir. As the trail steepens, you cross slopes blanketed with manzanita, and some patches of snowbrush and chinquapin. You cross over the sharp south ridge of San Bernardino East Peak, pass more manzanita, and finally enter an open lodgepole forest. One final switchback gets you to the top of the divide 0.5 mile east of San Bernardino East Peak, where you meet the San Bernardino Peak Divide Trail (see Hike 48, page 121), 7 miles from the start (**GPS N34° 07.599' W116° 54.403'**).

You now have a number of options. You can return the same way. You can follow the divide trail west over San Bernardino Peak and down to Angelus Oaks (see Hike 47, page 119). You can take the divide trail east to Dollar Lake Saddle (see Hike 48), then down the Falls Creek Trail (see Hike 52, page 130) to Mill Creek Canyon, reaching the latter 0.5 mile east of the Momyer Creek Trail roadhead, making a 20-mile loop trip without a car shuttle. These are the most direct options; others will reveal themselves if you study the map.

■ Hike 51 ALGER CREEK TRAIL CAMP 🚶 🐕 🚶

HIKE LENGTH 7 miles out-and-back; 2,100' elevation gain

DIFFICULTY Moderate

SEASON June–October

TOPO MAP *Forest Falls* (7.5-minute), *San Gorgonio Wilderness* (Tom Harrison)

PERMIT San Gorgonio Wilderness Permit required

■ FEATURES

Alger Creek rises high on San Bernardino Peak Divide and flows steeply down the south slope into Mill Creek Canyon. Deeply recessed into the mountainside, shaded by rich stands of pine, fir, cedar, and alder, the little creek seldom suffers the full glare of sunlight. It is a delightful place to relax and keep cool and enjoy nature's sylvan charms on a hot summer day. The Forest Service has built a beautiful trail camp on a bench shaded by tall incense-cedars, just above the churning waters of Alger Creek.

This formerly was a loop trip, until a property owner's complaint cowed the Forest Service into closing the lower portion of the Falls Creek Trail—in spite of the fact that the trail, built by John W. Dobbs in 1898, has been a public thoroughfare for more than 100 years. Now you must go and return via the Momyer Creek Trail.

■ DESCRIPTION

From Redlands, drive east on Highway 38 to its junction with Valley of the Falls Road at the huge switchback 20 yards before mile marker 038 SBD 15.00. Turn right and continue east up Mill Creek Canyon to the large parking area for the Momyer Creek and Falls Creek Trails, on your left 100 yards before the fire station, 2.9 miles (**GPS N34° 05.250' W116° 54.863'**). Mill Creek Canyon is prone to dangerous floods, mudslides, and avalanches in times of heavy precipitation, and hiking is not recommended on those days.

Follow the trail down into the broad boulder wash of Mill Creek. The path across the creek is washed away almost every spring, so there's no use trying to follow it. Instead, traverse directly across the boulder maze to the north bank, where you will pick up a trail that climbs north onto a low bench. Here your trail turns left (west) and climbs the chaparral-blanketed slope to a junction with the old beginning of the Momyer Creek Trail coming up from Torrey Pines Road. Turn right and follow the well-defined footpath as it switchbacks steeply up the divide between Momyer Creek and Alger Creek, through chaparral and scrub oak. Soon you are climbing through a patchy forest of oak and Jeffrey pine.

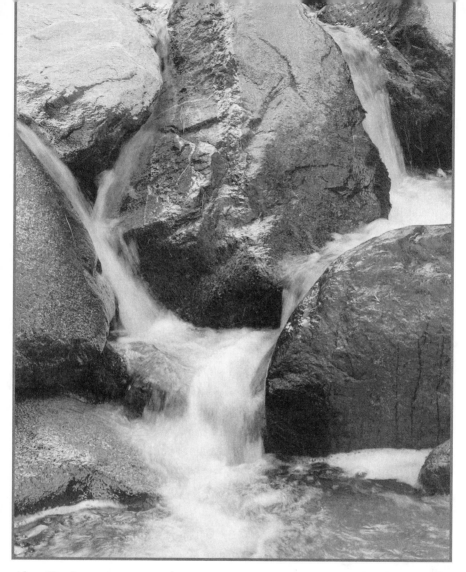

Alger Creek

In 2.6 miles you reach the marked junction with the Alger Creek Trail, branching right (northeast). Turn right and follow this lateral trail, following the line of John Dobbs's old flume, before dropping to Alger Creek Trail Camp, 1 mile. The cedar-shaded trail camp is to your right, just above the tumultuous creek (**GPS N34° 06.198' W116° 54.198'**).

This trail continues 100 yards to the creek, fords it, and continues on to Falls Creek (see next hike). Enjoy the delightful wilderness setting of Alger Creek, and then return the way you came.

■ Hike 52 DOLLAR LAKE SADDLE FROM MILL CREEK 🥾 🐴 🏃

HIKE LENGTH 18 miles out-and-back; 4,700' elevation gain
DIFFICULTY Moderate (2 days), Strenuous (1 day)
SEASON June–October
TOPO MAPS *Forest Falls, San Gorgonio Mtn.* (both 7.5-minute), *San Gorgonio Wilderness* (Tom Harrison)
PERMIT San Gorgonio Wilderness Permit required

■ FEATURES

The Falls Creek Trail, climbing from Mill Creek Canyon to Dollar Lake Saddle atop the main divide, is one of the historic pathways in the San Gorgonio Wilderness. The lower part of it was constructed by John W. Dobbs in 1898, in order to tap the water of Falls Creek and build a flume for a hydroelectric plant in lower Mill Creek. Unfortunately, the Forest Service has closed the lower portion of the trail because of an objection by a property owner in Mill Creek Canyon. Now the only legitimate route into Falls Creek from below is via the Momyer Creek Trail and the Alger Creek Lateral Trail, a roundabout way that adds 6 miles to the round-trip. Nevertheless, this trip is an inviting one, reaching into the geographical center of the wilderness and giving access to three beautiful trail camps—Alger Creek, Dobbs Cabin, and Saxton. You can stay the night at one of these trail camps and return the same way, or you can use the route as a springboard for any of several wilderness loop trips, the best of which are mentioned at the end of this trip.

■ DESCRIPTION

From Redlands, drive east on Highway 38 to its junction with Valley of the Falls Road at the huge switchback 20 yards before mile marker 038 SBD 15.00. Turn right and continue east up Mill Creek Canyon to the large parking area for the Momyer Creek and Falls Creek Trails, on your left 100 yards before the fire station, 2.9 miles (**GPS N34° 05.250' W116° 54.863'**). Mill Creek Canyon is prone to dangerous floods, mudslides, and avalanches in times of heavy precipitation, and hiking is not recommended on those days.

Follow the trail down into the broad boulder wash of Mill Creek. The path across the creek is washed away almost every spring, so there's no use trying to follow it. Instead, traverse directly across the boulder maze to the north bank, where you will pick up a trail that climbs north onto a low bench. Here your trail turns left (west) and climbs the chaparral-blanketed slope to a junction with the old beginning of the Momyer Creek Trail coming up from Torrey Pines Road. Turn

Dobbs Cabin, circa 1910

right and follow the well-defined footpath as it switchbacks steeply up the divide between Momyer Creek and Alger Creek, through chaparral and scrub oak. Soon you are climbing through a patchy forest of oak and Jeffrey pine.

In 2.6 miles you reach the marked junction with the Alger Creek Trail, branching right (northeast). Turn right and follow this lateral trail, following the line of John Dobbs's old flume, before dropping to Alger Creek Trail Camp, 1 mile. The cedar-shaded trail camp is to your right, just above the tumultuous creek.

Cross the creek and continue east on the Alger Creek Lateral Trail as it climbs, then contours around the steep mountainside to a junction with the Falls Creek Trail, 1 mile. Turn left (northeast) onto the latter. In 100 yards you pass the San Gorgonio Wilderness boundary sign, then climb east through a lush forest of Jeffrey pine and white fir to the ridge just west of Falls Creek. Here is another trail junction. To visit Dobbs Cabin Trail Camp, go right and steeply down to Falls Creek 0.25 mile ahead. Just across the creek is the trail camp, set on little flats and shaded by tall cedars, firs, and pines. Dobbs's old cabin site is at the lower edge of the camp; only log foundations remain. To continue up the main trail, go left at the junction. The trail climbs through open forest along the west slope of Falls Creek, fords the west fork, and reaches Saxton Trail Camp, 2 more miles. Water is available from the west fork, 0.2 mile down the trail. Your trail now climbs northeastward, passes the sloping bog of Plummer Meadow (where camping is no longer permitted), fords the east fork of Falls Creek, and climbs steeply up through a lodgepole forest to Dollar Lake Saddle, 9 miles from the start (**GPS N34° 07.096' W116° 51.624'**). Two small trail camps are just west of the saddle: Red Rock Flat (no water) and, 0.5 mile farther west, just south of the main divide trail, High Meadow Springs (always water).

You now have a number of options. You can return the way you came. You can turn right (southeast) and ascend San Gorgonio Mountain (see Hike 42, page 107), then descend via the Vivian Creek Trail (see Hike 54, page 134). You can turn left (northwest) and follow the San Bernardino Peak Divide Trail (see Hike 48, page 121), then descend either the Momyer Creek Trail back to Mill Creek Canyon (see Hike 50, page 126) or continue on to Angelus Oaks (Hikes 45 and 48, pages 115 and 121). Or you can turn northeast and descend to South Fork Meadows and Jenks Lake Road (see Hike 42).

■ Hike 53 BIG FALLS 🥾 🐕 👫

HIKE LENGTH 0.6 mile out-and-back; 200' elevation gain

DIFFICULTY Easy

SEASON April–October

TOPO MAPS *Forest Falls* (7.5-minute), *San Gorgonio Wilderness* (Tom Harrison)

■ FEATURES

Falls Creek churns and somersaults from high on the shoulders of San Bernardino Peak Divide into a narrow hanging valley, then plunges headlong into the canyon of Mill Creek. The place where it makes this final drop is known as Big Falls. Author and naturalist Charles Francis Saunders described it best: "Looking upward, you see the little creek, a couple of hundred feet above, leap out of a patch of blue sky and drop by a succession of precipitous pitches down a narrow, shadowy gorge, to be shattered at the bottom into a series of musical cascades." Waterfalls are infrequent in the San Bernardinos; it seems a slight upon the beauty of this one that it should have been given no more fanciful name than Big Falls.

These spectacular falls are but a short walk from the road. Visit them in springtime, when the melting mountain snowpack is filling Falls Creek, and canyonsides are aroar with the thunder of plunging waters. Bring sandals and a swimsuit.

■ DESCRIPTION

From Redlands, drive east on Highway 38 to its junction with Valley of the Falls Drive at the huge switchback 20 yards before mile marker 038 SBD 15.00. Take

Big Falls tumbles down dangerously unstable rock.

this road east up Mill Creek Canyon to the Big Falls parking area on your left, 4.3 miles (**GPS N34° 05.954' W116° 49.495'**).

Follow the trail down across the broad boulder wash of Mill Creek, where it disappears among the boulders. The creek crossing may be difficult in times of high water; bring sandals or wading shoes and exercise caution. The trail then climbs into the lower end of Falls Creek to a viewpoint some 200 yards below the falls (**GPS N34° 04.944' W116° 53.595'**). Hikers have been injured almost every year trying to climb the falls, so do not venture beyond the trail's end.

■ Hike 54 SAN GORGONIO MOUNTAIN VIA VIVIAN CREEK 🥾 🐕 🏃

HIKE LENGTH 17 miles out-and-back; 5,500' elevation gain

DIFFICULTY Moderate (2 days), Very Strenuous (1 day)

SEASON June–October

TOPO MAPS *Forest Falls, San Gorgonio Mtn.* (both 7.5-minute), *San Gorgonio Wilderness* (Tom Harrison)

PERMIT San Gorgonio Wilderness Permit required

■ FEATURES

The Vivian Creek Trail is the shortest way to climb San Gorgonio Mountain, but also one of the steepest. You start from near the head of Mill Creek Canyon, climb into the verdant hanging valley of Vivian Creek, cross a high ridge into High Creek, and finally ascend gravelly slopes to the barren summit. En route you pass three beautiful trail camps—Vivian Creek, Halfway Camp, and High Creek. Any one of the three makes a pleasant overnight stop if you are doing the mountain in two days.

The Vivian Creek Trail was the first one up the mountain, built shortly after the creation of the San Bernardino Forest Reserve in 1893. For years it was known as "The Government Trail" and was the only one to San Gorgonio's summit. Today it is just one of many but, in the opinion of many hikers, it remains one of the best.

Vivian Creek is a good way to climb San Gorgonio in the winter or spring. An ice axe and snowshoes or crampons are usually necessary. This is a serious route when covered in snow.

■ DESCRIPTION

From Redlands, drive east on Highway 38 to its junction with Valley of the Falls Drive at the huge switchback 20 yards before mile marker 038 SBD 15.00. Take this road east up Mill Creek Canyon to a parking area on your left, just before reaching closed Big Falls Campground, 4.5 miles. Park at the Vivian Creek Trail sign (**GPS N34° 04.927' W116° 53.466'**).

Walk on up the dirt road, through the closed campground, to the old trailhead parking area, 0.6 mile. Follow the trail down across the boulder wash of Mill Creek, then up the mountainside. The first mile is a sharp pull through oak woodlands—unpleasant going if the day is hot—to the secluded hanging recess of Vivian Creek. Here, nestled in a green forest of cedar, fir, and pine, is Vivian Creek Trail Camp, 2.3 miles from the start. The campsites are spread out for several hundred yards near the bubbling creek. Camp at least 200 feet from the water. Beyond, the trail follows the creek, switching from bank to bank, for another 1.2 miles through

The wind-beaten summit plateau of San Gorgonio Mountain

miniature meadows spotted with wildflowers and shaded by tall ponderosa pines and incense-cedars to Halfway Camp, 3.2 miles out. This trail camp has year-round water and many little flats for sleeping. Beyond, your trail climbs across a ridge to a high-perched, grassy cienega threaded by a small stream of cold, tumbling water. Here is High Creek Trail Camp, 5.2 miles out, a favorite with backpackers, but the altitude is 9,000 feet and nights are apt to be cold. The pines, cedars, and firs have been left below, and the slopes are covered with almost pure stands of weather-resistant lodgepole pines. The view across the head of Mill Creek Canyon to the saw-toothed wall of Yucaipa Ridge is reminiscent of the Sierra Nevada. Above High Creek, the trail winds up through silent lodgepoles to timberline at about 11,000 feet. Ahead looms the massive crown of San Gorgonio, stark against the deep blue sky. Just below the summit you meet the main trail from Dollar Lake Saddle; turn right (east) and cross gravelly slopes, passing a few wind-flattened limber pines and diminutive alpine flowers, to the 11,502-foot summit, 8 miles from the start (**GPS N34° 05.954' W116° 49.495'**).

Return the way you came. A popular variation is to take the trail west to Dollar Lake Saddle, then descend the Falls Creek Trail back to Mill Creek Canyon (see Hike 52, page 130).

■ Hike 55 GALENA PEAK 🏃 🐐

HIKE LENGTH 8 miles out-and-back; 3,200' elevation gain

DIFFICULTY Strenuous

SEASON May–October

TOPO MAPS *Forest Falls, San Gorgonio Mtn.* (both 7.5-minute), *San Gorgonio Wilderness* (Tom Harrison)

■ FEATURES

Galena Peak at 9,324 feet rises precipitously above the head of Mill Creek Canyon. It is the most rugged-appearing peak in the San Bernardinos, standing in marked contrast to the higher but rounded summits of the nearby San Gorgonio Wilderness. No trails approach its rugged upper ramparts, and you must scramble high over loose boulders and steep rock slopes to stand on its crown.

Part of the Mill Creek headwall has slid away recently, making the trip more tedious than it was a few years ago. You must make a trailless, loose uphill scramble from the head of Mill Creek to the saddle that divides the headwaters of Mill Creek from those of the Whitewater River—known by the curious name of Mill Creek Jumpoff. You need cross-country experience and will appreciate boots with good tread.

■ DESCRIPTION

From Redlands, drive east on Highway 38 to its junction with Valley of the Falls Drive at the huge switchback 20 yards before mile marker 038 SBD 15.00. Take this road east up Mill Creek Canyon to a parking area on your left, just before reaching closed Big Falls Campground, 4.5 miles. Park at the Vivian Creek Trail sign (**GPS N34° 04.927' W116° 53.466'**). Walk on up the dirt road, through the closed campground, to the old trailhead parking area, 0.6 mile.

Hike up the poor dirt road that heads east up-canyon. When it ends, continue up the streambed to the headwall at the end of Mill Creek. Climb a small

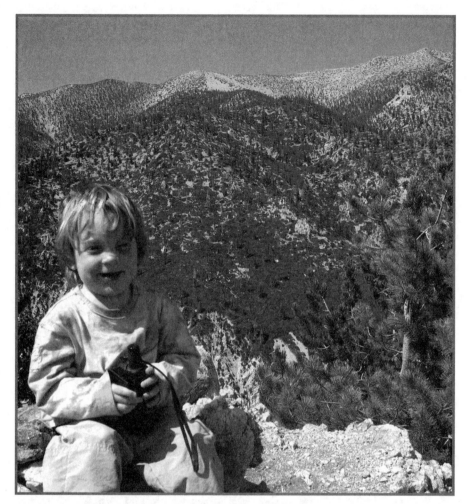

San Bernardino Wilderness from Galena Peak

ridge just left of center; then bear right across loose rock slopes to Mill Creek Jumpoff, 3.2 miles from the start. Turn right (south) and climb up the steep ridge, following a faint climbers' trail partway. Where the trail gets too close to the crumbling headwall, veer left and work your way through manzanita. Approaching the ridgetop, your route veers south-west and divides. The left path climbs to the eastern summit—Galena Peak (**GPS N34° 04.266' W116° 50.780'**). The right path climbs to the western summit, slightly higher but unnamed.

Return the same way. Do *not* try to descend directly into Mill Creek Canyon; it is steep, loose, and dangerous.

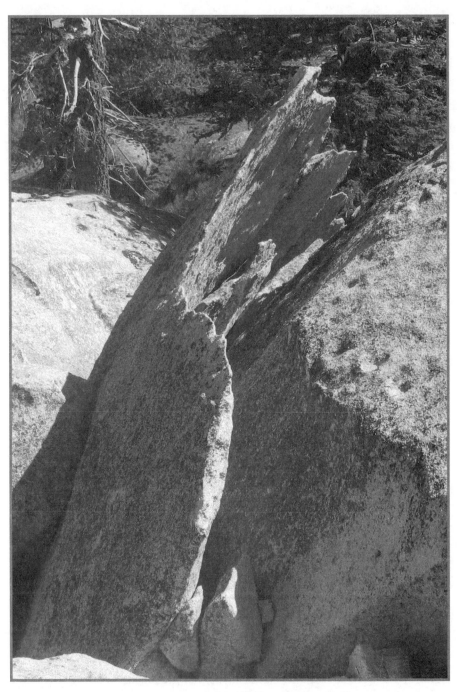

Exfoliating granite on Black Mountain (see Hike 56, page 157)

PART 2

■ The San Jacinto ■ Mountains

Natural History of the San Jacinto Mountains

LAY OF THE LAND

On clear days, travelers driving through San Gorgonio Pass (also called Banning Pass) toward the desert are treated to an awesome panorama. To the left, dominating the northern skyline, is the abrupt south slope of the San Bernardinos, crowned by the long gray hogback of San Gorgonio Mountain. To the right, and ahead, towers a stupendous rock escarpment, soaring in jagged ridgelines and scoured avalanche troughs almost 10,000 vertical feet in 5 horizontal miles. This mountain wall is the northeast face of 10,804-foot San Jacinto Peak, as rugged a precipice as exists in the United States. Somber gray in summer and fall, gleaming white in winter, snow-streaked by late spring, San Jacinto's vaulting desert face has fired the imagination and artistry of many a painter and photographer, and awed thousands of desert visitors.

San Jacinto, as is true with most mountains, has its gentle as well as its rugged features. The southwest side of the mountain is made up of rolling hills that rise from the San Jacinto Valley and become progressively higher and steeper until they culminate at the summit. Scenic paved highways traverse this gentle slope, winding through verdant woods and crossing streams that here and there are dammed to provide fishing lakes, giving access to rustic resorts. Idyllwild is the largest and best known of these resort communities, nestled in secluded, mile-high Strawberry Valley.

But it is the summit country of the San Jacintos that is most alluring. Here, well above the highways and byways that penetrate the lower slopes, is a sky island of delectable alpine wilderness, unsurpassed in Southern California. Under white granite summits and boulder-stacked ridges lie little hanging valleys and tapered benches lush with forest and meadow. A multitude of bubbling springs nourishes icy-cold streams that tumble and cascade down the mountain. In season, alpine wildflowers add a beautiful dash of color. The thin atmosphere is cool, clean, and refreshing.

Those who confine their mountain exploration to places they can reach by automobile will never see this unspoiled mountain roof-garden. Riders of the spectacular Palm Springs Aerial Tramway can witness a small portion of it. But it is only the hiker or horseback rider who can really know the San Jacinto high country. Summer and fall weekends find hundreds of these outing enthusiasts following the wilderness trails that lace the region, lingering overnight at one of the many secluded trail camps, and climbing to the summit of "San Jack" for a view that is unsurpassed in magnificence. Their numbers are increasing every year.

The top of the San Jacintos are protected from civilization's encroachment by two adjacent wild areas. The heart of the region, including San Jacinto Peak, is included within Mount San Jacinto State Wilderness, under the jurisdiction of the state of California. On both sides of it, north and south, is the San Jacinto Wilderness, part of the San Bernardino National Forest. The Santa Rosa and San Jacinto Mountains National Monument safeguards most of the precipitous desert face of the range.

Geographers disagree over the extent of the San Jacinto Mountains. Some include only the great bulk of San Jacinto Peak and its surrounding ridges and valleys. Others say the San Jacintos take in the whole mountain mass from, roughly speaking, Highway 79, south of Beaumont, southeast some 40 miles to the Palms to Pines Scenic Byway (Highway 74), beyond which are the Santa Rosas. Most do not include the isolated ridges of Thomas and Cahuilla Mountains, southwest of the main mountain mass, although both of these regions are part of the San Jacinto Mountain District of San Bernardino National Forest. For the purposes of this book, all of the areas mentioned above (except the Santa Rosas) are included in the San Jacinto Mountains.

The geologist looks at the San Jacintos and sees a strong resemblance to the Sierra Nevada. Both are uplifted, westward-tilting blocks, essentially granitic in composition, bounded by major fault zones. He places the San Jacintos in the Peninsular Ranges province, a line of mountain ranges extending from the Santa Ana Mountains southward to the tip of Baja California. The Peninsular Ranges are generally low mountains, seldom topping 6,000 feet in elevation. Only the San Jacintos and the Sierra de San Pedro Mártir in Baja California rise above 10,000 feet. San Jacinto Peak is the loftiest summit in the entire 800-mile-long province. The San Jacintos are bounded on the west by the San Jacinto Fault, one of the most active in California, the source of many earthquakes in recent years. North and east of the range is a complicated network of relatively short-length faults, offshoots of the great San Andreas Fault. Although not all these desert-side faults have been charted, the stupendous mountain escarpment on this flank bears obvious testimony to their existence.

PLANT LIFE

The botanist studies the San Jacintos and is amazed at the varieties and extremes of plant life. According to Harvey Monroe Hall, whose 1902 botanical survey is still an authoritative source on the flora of the range, "There is probably no place in North America where the alpine and Sonoran floras are in such proximity as they are on San Jacinto Mountain." Between the palm-lined desert canyons at the mountain base and the top of San Jacinto Peak, a horizontal distance of 5 miles, are stacked all the

Columbine (Aquilegia formosa)

climatic and vegetation changes one would encounter on a journey from northern Mexico to Canada. Within this short distance are six distinctive life zones, five of which completely encircle the mountain.

At the northeast base, part of the Colorado Desert, is Lower Sonoran vegetation, the most common plants being creosote bush, burro brush, desert willow, and ironwood tree. Above this, in a wide belt extending completely around the mountain, is the Upper Sonoran zone, the principal shrubs being chamise, manzanita, several species of ceanothus and scrub oak, and the main trees being canyon live oak, interior live oak, Palmer oak on the seaward side, and pinyon pine and California juniper on the desert side. The Transition zone embraces the main mountain forest of the San Jacintos, the principal trees being ponderosa pine, Jeffrey pine, Coulter pine, sugar pine, incense-cedar, California black oak, and, higher up, white fir. The Canadian and Hudsonian zones form narrow belts around the higher summits, and are so intermixed that the line between them cannot be definitely drawn. The principal trees—in fact the only trees—of these two zones are lodgepole pine and limber pine, and the main shrub is chinquapin. On the summit of San Jacinto Peak is a small island of Arctic–Alpine flora, the

Rangers button (Sphenosciadium capitellatum)

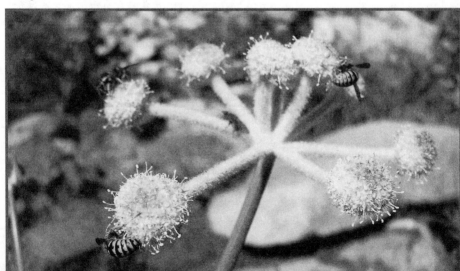

southernmost limit of this zone in the United States. There are some who question whether the summit is truly Arctic–Alpine because of the handful of stunted limber pines, Hudsonian zone trees, just below the top. But botanist Hall found several small plants here that definitely are Arctic–Alpine species. Most notable is alpine sorrel, which grows along snowbanks just north of the summit.

The climatic extremes are most striking to those living in the Coachella Valley just below the mountain. Winter storms often rage on the cloud-enveloped heights while desert foothills are bathed in sunlight. In early summer, it is not at all uncommon to look up from the sweltering valley floor, with temperatures well over 100 degrees, to see the long fingers of snow glistening in the upper ravines. From the opposite perspective, one can stand high on the northeastern escarpment, shivering from icy blasts of alpine wind, and gaze down on shimmering heat waves rising from the sun-scorched desert.

WILDLIFE

The wildlife of the San Jacintos is similar to that of the San Bernardinos, and just as timid. Here, too, humans have preempted most of the range. The most common large mammal is the California mule deer, which summers on the higher slopes and winters at lower elevations. A handful of mountain lions prowl the eastern high country. Bighorn sheep wander on the southern, desert-facing slopes. Bears, once abundant here, are never seen now. On rare occasions, the fortunate hiker glimpses a golden eagle soaring over San Jacinto Peak or a high ridge.

Bighorn mountain sheep

PHOTO: BONNER BLONG

Every hiker has a favorite mountain range that never wears out its appeal. To a great many Southern Californians, the San Jacintos are such a range. There are those who return time and time again to sample the rich wilderness offerings of this granite-ribbed island in the sky. And nothing will cure an aggravated case of urbanitis more quickly or thoroughly than a weekend dose of the San Jacintos.

Human History of the San Jacinto Mountains

LURE OF THE MOUNTAINS

From this day Ramona never knew an instant's peace or rest till she stood on the rim of the refuge valley, high on San Jacinto. Then, gazing around, looking up at the lofty pinnacles above, which seemed to pierce the sky, . . . feeling that infinite unspeakable sense of nearness to heaven, remoteness from earth which comes only on mountain heights, she drew in a long breath of delight, and cried; "At last! At last, Alessandro! Here we are safe!"

—Helen Hunt Jackson, *Ramona* (1884)

This passage, from Jackson's wondrous California classic of romance and tragedy, reflects the aurora of reverence and mysticism that has so often been a part of humans' relationship with the San Jacintos. In the novel, the San Jacintos served as a foreboding last refuge for Ramona and Alessandro, Native American lovers, fleeing from the European Americans' callousness and greed. Jackson was not the only famous author to see in these mountains something awesome, enchanting, and mysterious. George Wharton James, Charles Francis Saunders, and J. Smeaton Chase all treated the San Jacintos with a degree of reverence unaccorded any other mountains in the Southwest. From their widely read works—and particularly from Helen Hunt Jackson's *Ramona*—the San Jacintos have achieved worldwide fame.

ORIGINAL INHABITANTS

In recent geological history, the Gulf of California reached far into the Coachella Valley to points north of Palm Springs. The Colorado River emptied into the gulf from the east at about the location of the Salton Sea. Eventually sediment from the Colorado River formed a delta that cut off the north end of the gulf and formed a lake. This was ancient Lake Cahuilla. Geological evidence of the ancient lake exists today in the form of pebble beach strands and travertine deposits (calcium) on rock outcrops that mark the various shore levels of the lake.

PHOTO: CHARLES VAN FLEET

Earliest known photograph of San Jacinto summit, 1885

During the existence of Lake Cahuilla, the Colorado River changed course several times, alternately emptying into the lake or the Gulf of California. This and the drier climate caused the lake to alternately dry up and then be refilled. The lake existed from 700 AD to 1400, 1430 to 1530 AD, and 1600 to 1700 AD. The Salton Sea was formed in 1905 when the flooding Colorado River overtopped human-made irrigation canals and flowed into Lake Cahuilla's basin.

Around 1,000 years ago the first humans migrated into the area and inhabited areas along the shores of ancient Lake Cahuilla. These were the Cahuilla Indians and are believed to have migrated from northern Mexico. The Cahuilla survived on an abundance of fish and other sources of nutrition. Archeological evidence of this are the fire rings and stone weirs (fish traps) along the north and northwest shorelines of the ancient lake. After 1700 the Cahuilla moved into the nearby mountains and canyons where there was a continuing abundance of water and food. Today, the Cahuilla live on the flanks of the San Jacinto and Santa Rosa Mountains. The present-day tribes of the Cahuilla consist of the Morongo at the north end of the San Jacintos, the Agua Caliente in the Palm Springs area, and the Santa Rosa in the Santa Rosa Mountains. Other tribes in the area are the Cabazon, Torres Martinez, Ramona, Los Coyotes, and Augustine.

Forster's terns (Sterna forsteri*) over the Salton Sea*

The primary concern of these peoples was the search for food, which took them far and wide. From the desert came such staples as mesquite and screwbean; slightly higher, agave and yucca were collected; and on mountain slopes, acorns and pinyon nuts provided a dependable source of food. Animals hunted by the Cahuillas included the rabbit, wood rat, quail, antelope, mountain sheep, and deer. It was the abundance of deer on the San Jacintos that lured the Western Cahuillas into the high country. Strong hunters climbed the desert face of the mountain to the area where the deer were grazing, killed and dressed them on the spot, and descended with their kill slung over their shoulders.

The Cahuilla Indians were the first to weave a web of mythical lore around the mountains. To the Cahuillas, the San Jacinto Mountains were a sacred place, the home of Dakush, a large, low-flying meteor, legendary founder of the Cahuilla people. They were also the dwelling place of Tahquitz, an evil and powerful demon with an insatiable appetite for beautiful maidens and human flesh. The tales about Tahquitz are many and they vary greatly, but all of them agree that he was a terror to the Native Americans. Hunters and food-gatherers who disappeared in the mountains were said to have been carried off by the evil demon to his lair underneath Tahquitz Peak and eaten. When thunder and lightning rumbled across the mountains, it was said that Tahquitz was angry. At such times, no Native American would dare venture onto the mountain. The Tahquitz legend was known not just to the Cahuillas; it was part of the folklore of almost every Native American people in Southern California.

FIRST EXPLORERS

It was through the Cahuilla Valley and Bautista Canyon, below the southwestern foothills of the San Jacintos, that the early explorers came. The Spanish soldier Pedro Fages was first on the scene, pursuing army deserters from San Diego. Not much is known about the Fages trip, and he left us no descriptions of the San Jacinto country. Two years later, in 1774, came Captain Juan Bautista de Anza, leading a party of 34 from Mexico to Monterey in the most famous overland expedition in California history.

Anza had set out from Tubac, Sonora, to find a route across the desert to California. He and his men almost perished in the burning sands of the Colorado and Borrego Deserts, but on their second attempt they managed to find water and locate a gap in the mountain barrier—today's Coyote Canyon. Up this boulder-strewn canyon they struggled until they reached the broad Cahuilla Valley. "Right here there is a pass which I named the Royal Pass of San Carlos. From it are seen most beautiful green and flower-strewn prairies, and snow-covered mountains with pines, oaks, and other trees which grow in cold countries," Anza wrote in his diary. This is the earliest description of the San Jacinto Mountains we have. In the Cahuilla Valley, Anza met 200 peaceful Native Americans—his first encounter with the Cahuillas. Then he descended Bautista Canyon, crossed the San Jacinto Valley, "keeping on our right a high, snow-covered mountain," and continued on to Monterey. Anza passed this way once again in 1776.

EARLY SETTLERS, SURVEYORS, AND PROSPECTORS

The Spaniards or their Mexican Californio successors did not settle in the San Jacinto country for many years. Just when they did come to stay is unknown—sometime before 1821 is as close as historians can pin it down. Around this time Mission San Luis Rey established an outlying cattle ranch in the flatlands west of the mountains. This they named Rancho San Jacinto, in honor of Saint Hyacinth of Silesia (1185–1231), a Dominican missionary credited with many conversions in Tibet and China. Thus the name *San Jacinto* was born, first used for the stock rancho and later extended to the San Jacinto Valley, the San Jacinto River, and finally the San Jacinto Mountains.

Except for occasional ventures to search for strayed stock or to hunt grizzlies, the early Spaniards and Californios stayed clear of the mountains. Even with their thick leather chaps, the rancheros found the dense chaparral that coated the lower slopes of the San Jacintos uninviting. There was enough feed for cattle on the plains. The mountains existed mainly as a source of water. There is no evidence that these early Californians ever reached the high country.

With the coming of American and immigrant settlers from the eastern United States—from the 1840s onward—the San Jacintos began to receive more attention. The first believed to have left his mark on the mountains was Tennessee-born Paulino Weaver. Weaver had come to California, perhaps with the Ewing Young trapping party, in the early 1830s. He apparently became a Mexican citizen, for he was granted land in the area of San Gorgonio Pass by Governor Pio Pico in 1845. According to Banning historian Tom Hughes, Weaver was cutting timber from both sides of San Gorgonio Pass—including the northern foothills of the San Jacintos—as early as 1846. He also is said to have hunted bear and deer in the mountains. Weaver later served as a US Army scout during the Civil War, and moved to Arizona, where he died in 1867.

Lieutenant Robert S. Williamson's Pacific Railroad Survey party came through San Gorgonio Pass in 1853. William Blake, geologist of the expedition, crossed to the south side of the pass to investigate the rocks of San Jacinto Peak (which he mistakenly called "San Gorgonio"). His report contains the first scientific description of the mountain.

Lieutenant Williamson's official map, published by the War Department, showed San Jacinto Peak as "San Gorgonio" and San Gorgonio Mountain as "San Bernardino," which for a short time caused confusion among surveyors and new settlers.[1]

However, the mistake was rectified two years later (1855) when Lieutenant John G. Parke's Pacific Railroad Survey party passed through the area. Dr. Thomas Antisell, geologist of the Parke expedition, correctly labeled the mountain south of the pass as "San Jacinto," and it has been known singularly by this name ever since.

The 1860s saw pioneer settlers establish isolated homes in the San Jacinto Mountains. Most historians give Charles Thomas credit for being first. Thomas ran away from his New York home at the age of 12, sailed around Cape Horn,

---

1 Some writers claim that at the same time San Jacinto Peak was called "San Gorgonio," San Gorgonio Mountain was known as "San Jacinto." After extensive research, I was unable to find any evidence of this. As far as can be documented, San Gorgonio Mountain was never known as "San Jacinto."

landed in San Francisco, and drifted south in the 1850s. He took a young Californio bride at Santa Barbara and settled on a ranch near Temecula to raise cattle. The story goes that he was led into the beautiful Garner Valley (then unnamed), high on the south slope of the San Jacintos, by his Cahuilla friends. Thomas fell in love with the mountain-rimmed basin and decided to make it his home. In 1861 he filed on 480 acres in the heart of the valley, brought up his wife and children, and began raising Mexican longhorn cattle there. In 1876 Thomas purchased 4,300 more acres of surrounding mountain land from the Southern Pacific Company. In later years, besides raising cattle, he bred racehorses in partnership with Lucky Baldwin. The Thomas Ranch became a well-known Southern California landmark.

To obtain lumber for the ranch buildings and fences, he sent his ranch hands high into the lush forests of the San Jacintos—probably as far as Strawberry Valley—to cut and haul timber. Bears, grizzly and otherwise, abounded in the mountains then. A man named Herkey, cutting timber for Thomas, was attacked and severely mauled while drinking from a creek; he made it back to the ranch, where he died from his wounds. Herkey Creek (sometimes spelled Hurkey) commemorates him today. Deer were thick in the mountains, too. Thomas and his men frequently made hunting trips into the high country. One story tells of deer coming into camp in Round Valley "so tame that six were shot before the herd took fright." Thomas and his family remained on the ranch until 1905, when they sold out to San Bernardino stockman Robert F. Garner.

Others followed Thomas into the San Jacintos—ranchers, herders, hunters, prospectors, and lumbermen. As early as 1875, sheepmen and cattlemen herded their hungry livestock into the lush mountain grasslands around Strawberry Valley, some even climbing over the difficult Devils Slide into upper Tahquitz Valley. Hunters soon decimated the large herds of deer. Prospectors searched for mineral wealth in the mountains, but found little to reward their efforts. Henry Hamilton discovered a few valuable tourmaline gemstones on Thomas Mountain in 1872. An Englishman named Harold Kenworthy poured a fortune into a gold-mining operation near the southern end of Garner Valley in the 1880s, but no great amounts of gold were ever uncovered. Emil Chilsen developed the Hemet Belle Mine near Kenworthy around the turn of the 20th century. No one ever made much off the Hemet Belle, and it changed hands so often that it became known as the "Grubstake Mine." Salting mines with gold became a regular procedure: "All you did was load up a shotgun with gold dust, fire it into the rock, and you had a mine for sale," mountain pioneer Lincoln Hamilton recalled.

TIMBER AND WATER SEEKERS

It was the commercial loggers who really opened up the San Jacintos. Rich stands of sugar and ponderosa pine had long been known to exist in the mountains, but the difficulty of hauling out timber over rugged slopes had prevented all but insignificant logging efforts by local settlers. To bring out this timber, wagon roads would need to be hacked up the steep mountainsides. Two such projects were begun in 1875–76: one up the north slopes from San Gorgonio Pass, the other up the west side from the San Jacinto Valley.

The Southern Pacific Railroad got things started on the north side. The Southern Pacific was constructing its main east–west line through San Gorgonio Pass and needed lumber for construction camps and railroad ties. To obtain this timber, Colonel Milton S. Hall, a promoter and grading contractor who was commissioned by the Southern Pacific to grade the right-of-way between Spadra and Indio, built a very steep wagon road—known as Hall's Grade—up the mountainside from "Hall City" (near today's Cabazon) to a point above the present Lake Fulmor. Here he had a man named Fuller set up a small sawmill. Shortly afterward, Fuller moved the sawmill over the ridge and down to a new site above the present Fuller Mill Creek. The enterprise was none too successful. For one thing, the road was too precipitous for heavy loads, and at least two men were killed and several teams and loaded wagons smashed when they broke loose on the grade. After a

Snow Creek from San Jacinto Peak

frustrating year, the road was abandoned and the sawmill machinery hauled piece by piece down into lower Snow Creek Canyon. Here, at the bottom end of a dizzy skidway, it was set up to await the logs that never reached it. They either jumped the track or broke into splinters in their mad rush from high on the mountain. By 1877 the Southern Pacific had its railroad through the pass and the costly logging efforts were abandoned. But Hall's Grade remained, later to become the spring-board for other road-making projects in the mountains.

Much more successful were the logging enterprises on the west slope of the San Jacintos. In 1875, Joseph Crawford, Union Army veteran and home-steader at Oak Cliff in the San Jacinto Valley, secured a 50-year franchise from the San Diego County Board of Supervisors (San Diego County included the San Jacintos until 1893) to build a toll road from Oak Cliff up the west side of the mountains to Alvin Meadow and Strawberry Valley. Crawford spent $5,500 building his road into the timber belt, and even before it was finished loggers swarmed into the mountains. The road was narrow and just about as precipitous as Hall's Grade, and it elicited comments such as, "Steep? Why in places it leans over backwards!" There was a welcome water stop at Halfway House Spring, where teamsters and animals often collapsed.

Shortly after Crawford finished his toll road, large-scale logging efforts began on the western slopes. A number of sawmills were built along the North Fork of the San Jacinto River, in the vicinity of Dutch Flat, and in Strawberry Valley. Who built the first mill is not known for certain. Bradley and Stafford are believed to have erected the pioneer sawmill in Strawberry Valley, then sold out around 1881 to Amasa Saunders, who built a spectacular overhead flume leading to a large water-wheel to operate his saws. Saunders Meadow near Idyllwild honors him today. Anton Scherman had a number of mills in and around Strawberry Valley, and at the peak of his operations was said to have cut 25,000 board feet per day. George B. Hannahs purchased 4,500 acres of timberland from the Southern Pacific Railroad[2] and erected two mills—one at Dutch Flat, the other in Strawberry Valley. Hannahs is credited with starting the first settlement in Strawberry Valley, which he named Raynetta after his infant son, Raymond. His store was the focal point for "outers, ranchers, cowboys, lumbermen, and everyone else attached to the mountains by either business or pleasure." Here also was the first post office in the San Jacinto Mountains, established in 1893. Hannahs was an explorer, too, and knew every foot

---

2   In 1876, the Southern Pacific Railroad was given every other section of land for 11 miles on both sides of their right-of-way, part of the federal government's huge subsidy program for American big business during the later decades of the 19th century. Most of the San Jacinto Mountains fell within this checkerboard pattern.

of the mountains. He is credited with having named Round Valley and Long Valley and with discovering Hidden Lake, which he called "Lake Surprise."

By the early 1890s, the timberlands of the western San Jacintos vibrated to the thunder of falling trees, the swearing of tough woodsmen, the creaking of wagons, and the whine of steel saws. Tall pines were cut from the mountainside, hauled to mill by "bull teams," sliced into lumber, then wagoned down Crawford's toll road—the toll-keeper collected 75¢ per wagon load —to San Jacinto. Most of the lumber was sold and used in the San Jacinto Valley; some was shipped to San Bernardino and Los Angeles.

Water seekers came into the mountains, too. Ranchers in the San Jacinto Valley needed water for their lands and saw in the San Jacinto Mountains a ready source. In 1887, E. L. Mayberry, W. F. Whittier, and other valley pioneers formed the Lake Hemet Water Company to bring water down from the mountains. A site was selected at the northwest end of Garner Valley, where the South Fork of the San Jacinto River drops into a deep gorge. At the top of this narrow canyon, a masonry dam was constructed. When the dam was completed in 1893, it rose 122 feet above the canyon floor and formed a lake of 600 acres. It was said to have been, at the time, the largest masonry dam in the world. Water from the reservoir was carried to valley farms via a network of large wooden flumes.

SAVING THE SAN JACINTOS

Acre by acre, the lumber monster was eating away at the mountain forest, each year relentlessly cutting farther up the western slopes of the San Jacintos. Sheep and cattle by the thousands were being herded to summer pasture in the high-country meadows, stripping them of their rich green cover. Wagon roads were being hacked higher and higher into the mountains. As with the San Gabriel and San Bernardino Mountains, even those with myopic vision could see that reckless land-use practices were destroying both the beauty of the mountains and— more important to the practically minded—the mountain watershed. Federal protection was called for. As a result of strong pressure from those who wanted the mountains saved, for either aesthetic or practical reasons, President Grover Cleveland signed a bill creating the San Jacinto Forest Reserve on February 22, 1897. At first it was a forest reserve in name only, and not much was done to stop the continuing depredation. As with the San Bernardinos, much of the mountain lands were already in private hands—particularly the hands of the Southern Pacific Railroad—and outside Forest Service jurisdiction. In 1898 the first forest rangers were assigned to the reserve and a patrol system established. These early

Tahquitz Peak and Lily Rock

rangers of the old San Jacinto Forest Reserve—Charley Vandeventer, Theodore Olds, John Oloan, "Sulphur Springs" Thompson—did their job zealously, guarding against further timber cutting on public lands, chasing herders and their herds out of the high country, fighting brush fires, locating lost and injured persons. They set the standards followed by today's Forest Service in the San Jacintos. In 1907 the name was changed to San Jacinto National Forest, and the following year the San Jacinto was joined with the smaller Trabuco to create Cleveland National Forest. In 1925, the San Jacinto district was cut from the Cleveland and joined to San Bernardino National Forest. So it remains today.

Around the turn of the 20th century, recreation replaced logging as the major activity in the San Jacinto Mountains. In 1893 or thereabouts, John and Mary Keen built their one-story Strawberry Valley Hotel, and a few years later started Keen Camp. In 1898 a group of Los Angeles doctors, headed by Dr. Walter Lindley and Dr. W. W. Becket, formed the California Health Resort Company and purchased 3,500 acres in Strawberry Valley. Here they built a three-story hotel and surrounding cottages for the treatment of tuberculosis patients. Around this sanitarium hotel a small resort community grew. In 1899 the federal government decided to relocate the post office in the hotel, at the time managed by Mrs. Laura Rutledge and her husband. Mrs. Rutledge suggested the name "Idyllwild" for the new post office and community. So it is known today. The first hotel, known as the Idyllwild Sanitarium, burned to the ground in 1904 and was replaced a few years later by the Idyllwild Inn, which became a popular summer resort. The Idyllwild Inn burned in 1945 and was replaced by the present structure. Through the years, particularly after World War II, Idyllwild has grown into a well-known resort community with a population today of more than 3,000. It stands at the gateway to the San Jacinto Wilderness.

With the people came new roads. Crawford's old toll road was superseded in 1891 by the Mayberry Road, which basically followed today's Highway 74 from the San Jacinto Valley to Keen Camp. Built by C. L. Mayberry, its original function was to transport materials for the construction of Hemet Dam. From Keen Camp, Charles Thomas's old cattle trail to Strawberry Valley was improved into a road to Idyllwild. In 1909 the famous Idyllwild Control Road—one-way traffic only, alternating up and down every two hours—was constructed approximately along the route of Crawford's 1876 road. In 1911 the first primitive road from Banning to Idyllwild was constructed. In recent years, many of these roads have been improved and new ones built, allowing easy, high-gear access to the mountain communities.

Visiting the spectacular and beautiful San Jacinto high country—on foot or horseback—has long been a favorite pastime of outdoor-minded Southern Californians. As early as 1885, parties camped in Round Valley and climbed to the top of San Jacinto Peak. After 1900, visits became much more frequent. Many of these early mountain visitors realized the need for safeguarding this unique alpine

Stone cabin built by the CCC in 1936, just below San Jacinto Peak

PHOTO: UNKNOWN PHOTOGRAPHER (from an old postcard)

wilderness from the perils of unrestricted overuse and possible exploitation. First with a concrete proposal was A. C. Lovekin of Riverside, who in 1919 advocated setting aside the higher altitudes of the San Jacintos as a great wilderness memorial park in memory of those who gave their lives in World War I. Lovekin's plan met with general public approval, but nothing came of it for eight years. Then, in 1927, the California legislature created the state park system, and attention was once again focused on the Mount San Jacinto wilderness park proposal. In 1928 the San Jacinto State Park Association was formed, Lovekin serving as president, with the express purpose of including San Jacinto Peak and the surrounding high country in the state park system. At the time, the main stumbling block was land ownership: the odd-numbered sections of land, including San Jacinto Peak itself, were owned by the Southern Pacific Company, while the even-numbered sections were federally owned lands administered by the Forest Service. The State Park Bond Act, passed by the California voters in 1928, and the pledge of matching funds from the Riverside County Board of Supervisors and private citizens, along with land purchase and exchange proposals acceptable to all involved parties, overcame this hurdle. In 1929 the State Park Commission formally adopted plans to acquire the lands and create Mount San Jacinto State Park, and by 1935 all the land atop the range was in state ownership. The valuation of the 12,695 acres within the park, acquired in a three-way deal with the Southern Pacific Land Company, the Forest Service, and the State of California, was $84,218.75. Half of this sum was contributed by Riverside County and friends of the park project. The federal government aided greatly in the development of the park through the Civilian Conservation Corps (CCC) program. In 1935–36, gangs of young CCC workers camped in Round Valley, Tahquitz Valley, and near Idyllwild, built 26 miles of trail, developed 29 campsites, and erected the stone refuge cabin on San Jacinto Peak. June 19, 1937, was a memorable day to conservationists and lovers of the San Jacinto high country; Mount San Jacinto State Park was formally dedicated.

In 1931 the Forest Service designated the mountain regions immediately north and south of the state park as the San Jacinto Wild Area. In 1964 the name was changed to San Jacinto Wilderness. The entire top country of the range, from Fuller Ridge on the north side to the Desert Divide south of Tahquitz Peak, is now protected by the state and federal wilderness systems.

CAUGHT OFF-GUARD

The story of the San Jacinto high country would end here if it were not for the determined efforts of two Palm Springs businessmen. In 1935 Francis F. Crocker of the California Electric Power Company and Carl Barkow of the *Desert Sun* newspaper presented the idea of a tramway (from Palm Springs up the north face of San Jacinto Mountain) to the Palm Springs Chamber of Commerce. The idea quickly caught on, particularly because it was felt that a spectacular mountain tramway would be a boon to the Palm Springs tourist industry. In 1939 a bill was introduced in the state legislature to establish a "Palm Springs Winter Parks Authority" to build the tramway. It passed the legislature but was vetoed by Governor Culbert Olson. Similar bills, slightly changed, were introduced in 1941 and 1943, but both met the same fate. In 1945 a fourth bill was drawn up, this time with considerable change of language. The proposed agency was now called the "Mount San Jacinto Winter Park Authority" and benefits to all Californians, including skiers, were advertised. The appeal to skiers was a brazen smokescreen: the Far West Ski Association pointed out that, because of the craggy nature of the mountain, skiing here was highly unsuitable. But conservationists were caught with their guard down, and the bill sailed through the legislature and was signed by Governor Earl Warren. The undisguised purpose of the Winter Park Authority was to build a tramway up the north wall of the mountain for the benefit of Palm Springs, and it quickly set about to achieve this goal. But it was a long time reaching it.

For the next 15 years—until actual construction began in 1961—one of the most bitter battles between conservationists and business developers ever fought in California raged over the tramway proposal. Charges and counter-charges flew back and forth, and both sides used every weapon in their legal arsenal to advance or defeat the project. A residue of bitterness remains to this day. Finally the last legal obstruction was batted down, $7,700,000 in revenue bonds to finance construction were sold, construction commenced, and the spectacular aerial tramway became a reality in 1963. The Mount San Jacinto Winter Park Authority threw off any vestige of disguise for its true motive when it named the completed project the "Palm Springs Aerial Tramway." From Valley Station in Chino Canyon at an elevation of 2,643 feet, two gondolas suspended on wires supported by five towers whisk visitors more than a mile in elevation gain to Mountain Station, located at 8,516 feet on the edge of Long Valley. It is a steep and breathtaking rise for the 80 passengers on each gondola. And it gives almost instant access to a part of the high wilderness that once required several hours of strenuous hiking to reach. Such is the form of "progress."

The San Jacinto high country is a priceless heirloom of the people of Southern California. Sheer numbers of visitors, increasing every year, constitute what is perhaps the biggest threat to the wilderness character of the mountains (unless you take seriously the hare-brained schemes, voiced now and then, to build an extension of the tramway to the top of San Jacinto Peak). To counter the weight of numbers, the state and the Forest Service instituted the wilderness permit system in 1971, which developed the present quotas for overnight use. Only with wisdom and restraint will Southern California's best mountain wilderness be preserved.

Just below the high country, too, battles are being fought. In a landmark citizen-action campaign in the 1970s, the San Jacinto Mountain Conservation League defeated a developer's proposal to urbanize Garner Valley before a land-use plan and zoning regulations were worked out. With zoning now accomplished, the league's next aim is to get the valley preserved as national forest through federal land exchanges. Some land exchanges have been made, but much remains to be done.

In recent years, development has crept forward in Garner Valley and around the fringes of the San Jacinto Wilderness and State Park. But fortunately, the high country has remained inviolate, and the desert side of the mountains is now protected by the Santa Rosa and San Jacinto Mountains National Monument, established by Congress in 2000. The future of the San Jacinto Mountains requires constant vigilance.

■ Hike 56 BLACK MOUNTAIN 🥾 🐕 🚶

HIKE LENGTH 7.5 miles out-and-back; 2,700' elevation gain
DIFFICULTY Moderate
SEASON All year
TOPO MAP *Lake Fulmor* (7.5-minute), *San Jacinto Wilderness* (Tom Harrison)

■ FEATURES

Black Mountain at 7,772 feet dominates the northern end of the San Jacintos. From the fire lookout on the summit, you are rewarded with a superb vista over miles of mountain, valley, and desert country, with the jagged ramparts of San Jacinto Peak looming in the southeast.

■ DESCRIPTION

From Banning, drive southeast on Highway 243 1 mile beyond Vista Grande Ranger Station to the beginning of the Black Mountain Trail (2E35) marked by a large wooden sign at mile marker 243 RIV 16.75. Turn left and drive 100 yards on a dirt road to the parking area (**GPS N33° 49.643' W116° 47.725'**).

Proceed up the trail through Jeffrey pine, oak, and chaparral. The trail climbs 2.5 miles up the bouldery ridge, crosses a divide, and contours into a shady forest to fern-filled Indian Creek (water in spring only). You then climb steeply up to

Black Mountain Lookout

a pine-shaded flat on the ridgetop known as Shake Camp (no overnight camping) and switchback up the forested slope to a spur of the Black Mountain lookout road, 3.5 miles out. Turn right and walk past a water tank; then follow a faint use trail steeply up the short distance to the summit lookout tower (**GPS N33° 49.440' W116° 45.470'**). If you lose the path, pick your own route upward, weaving among the giant boulders. Alternatively, descend the spur road to Boulder Basin Campground, and then turn right and hike 0.5 mile up a gated dirt road to the lookout.

The fire lookout is open to the public from 9 a.m. to 5 p.m. as long as the access road is passable (usually Memorial Day through the first winter snows). The volunteer fire spotters are happy to share their knowledge of the San Jacinto Mountains.

Return the same way. An option, with a 9-mile car shuttle, is to descend the lookout road (4S68), passing Boulder Basin Campground, to Black Mountain Road (4S01), 1 mile. To reach this junction, drive up Highway 243, passing Lake Fulmor, to Black Mountain Road, 4.2 miles from the Black Mountain Trailhead. Turn left (north) and drive up Black Mountain Road to its junction with the side road to Boulder Basin Campground, 4.8 miles. Park here (**GPS N33° 49.591' W116° 45.025'**), or pay the campground fee at Boulder Basin, 0.4 mile farther.

■ Hike 57 SAN JACINTO PEAK VIA FULLER RIDGE TRAIL ✦ 🚶

HIKE LENGTH 15 miles out-and-back; 4,100' elevation gain

DIFFICULTY Strenuous (1 day), Moderate (2 days)

SEASON June–October

TOPO MAPS *Lake Fulmor, San Jacinto Peak* (both 7.5-minute), *San Jacinto Wilderness* (Tom Harrison)

PERMIT San Jacinto Wilderness Permit required

■ FEATURES

From Black Mountain, the craggy spine of Fuller Ridge dips downward and then soars upward, like a long kite string, to Folly Peak. Broken gendarmes and huge granite outcroppings make it one of the most rugged mountain backbones in Southern California. Weather-toughened pines and firs cling to its precipitous slopes.

The Fuller Ridge Trail threads its way around these gray-white gendarmes, first on the north side of the ridge, then on the south, from the Black Mountain Road to the Deer Springs Trail below San Jacinto Peak. Views are magnificent, particularly down into the wild and beautiful gorge of upper Snow Creek and beyond to the desert. Much less traveled than the heavily used trails out of Idyllwild and the Palm Springs Aerial Tramway, this ranks as one of the best trips in the San Jacintos.

This trip takes the Pacific Crest Trail to Deer Springs, then uses the Deer Springs Trail to ascend San Jacinto Peak (10,804 feet). You can do it in one very long day, or make it more leisurely by staying the night at Little Round Valley Trail Camp. (*Note:* Deer Springs Trail Camp and the summit camping area have been closed because of overuse.)

Although the summit is only 3,100 feet above the trailhead, the trail dips and climbs several times to bypass rock obstacles on the ridge, adding a bonus 500 feet of elevation on the ascent, then again on the weary descent.

■ DESCRIPTION

From Highway 243, 0.5 mile east of mile marker 243 RIV 13.00, turn northeast up the good dirt Black Mountain Road. After 4.8 miles, pass a side road on your left to Black Mountain Campground and fire lookout. Your road winds through spectacular open forest with giant granite boulders. It passes the entrance of the Black Mountain Group Campground after 1 mile, then a rocky outcropping on the left in another 0.8 mile featuring spectacular views of San Gorgonio Mountain and the pass below. In another 0.7 mile, turn right up a hill at a sign for

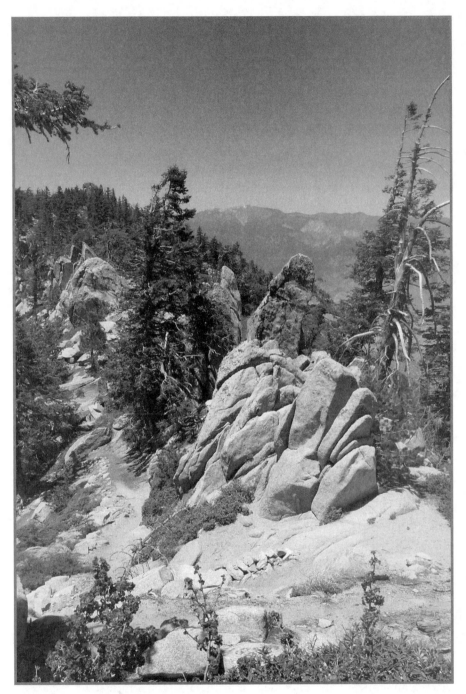

Pacific Crest Trail on Fuller Ridge

the Fuller Ridge Trailhead. Climb 0.2 mile and park in the clearing (**GPS N33° 50.341' W116° 44.174'**).

The trail, which is a segment of the Pacific Crest Trail (PCT), rounds the north side of the slope and climbs through pine, cedar, and fir to a notch in Fuller Ridge, 2 miles. Along the way, you will find gooseberries and huge bushes of red and blue currants. You then drop, climb, and contour around granite outcroppings on both sides of the ridge, with spectacular views through "windows" in the rocky spine. You can peer down into the extremely rugged upper reaches of Snow Creek's west fork, where there are the remains of the flume in which Colonel Hall tried to drop timber from the mountain forest to the desert in 1876. Southward, you look down into the forested bowl of Fuller Mill Creek, once the scene of large-scale logging. After another mile you begin to contour, then climb along the southwest slope of the San Jacinto massif, passing two small creeks of icy-cold water, to a junction with the Deer Springs Trail, 4.5 miles from the start.

Go left (northeast) up the slope, and follow the Deer Springs Trail past small Boggy Meadow to Little Round Valley Trail Camp, 1.3 miles above the junction (see Hike 65, page 172, for a full description of the Deer Springs Trail). You are in lodgepole forest now. From Little Round Valley, continue up the trail to a junction with the San Jacinto Peak Trail, 1.2 miles. Turn left and climb past the stone shelter cabin to the summit, 300 yards (**GPS N33° 48.881' W116° 40.764'**). Camping is not allowed on the peak.

Return the same way—or, with a car shuttle, take one of the numerous options that are open to you (see Hikes 60, 61, 65, and 67). Alternatively, climbers can cross-country over to Folly Peak, then down the brush-spotted ridge to the Fuller Ridge/Pacific Crest Trail halfway between the Deer Springs Trail junction and the road-head, but don't attempt this unless you are experienced in cross-country travel. Rock-hopping along the crest of the ridge can be fun and keeps you clear of the worst of the brush until the last 400 feet, where wading through chinquapin and brushing aside sappy trees become inevitable. The final 100 yards cross a flat of dense chaparral to pick up the PCT just left of a rocky outcrop at 8,700 feet.

■ Hike 58 INDIAN MOUNTAIN 🡕 🐕 ⊕

HIKE LENGTH 5.5 miles out-and-back; 1,300' elevation gain

DIFFICULTY Moderate

SEASON November–June

TOPO MAP *Lake Fulmor* (7.5-minute), *San Jacinto Wilderness* (Tom Harrison)

San Jacinto from Indian Mountain

▓ FEATURES

Indian Mountain rises to 5,790 feet over the western foothills of the range, offering a splendid panorama over chaparral-coated hillsides and the flat expanse of San Jacinto Valley. This trip is a fire-road walk most of the way, best done on a cool, clear winter or spring day.

▓ DESCRIPTION

From Banning, drive southeast on Highway 243 to the Indian Vista overlook parking area 0.6 mile past the Lake Fulmor picnic area and just past mile marker 243 RIV 14.00 (**GPS N33° 47.820' W116° 46.624'**). The Indian Mountain fire road (4S21) begins just northwest of the overlook parking area.

Walk through the gate (usually open for recreational vehicles) and down the fire road to a saddle, then up and around the east and south slopes of Indian Mountain—mostly through chaparral country, with clumps of Jeffrey pine and oak offering occasional shade. The fire road climbs almost to the summit on the southwest side before beginning its 6-mile descent to Highway 74. When it reaches its high point, turn right and follow the old, partly overgrown firebreak to the boulder-strewn summit (**GPS N33° 46.922' W116° 47.307'**).

Return the same way.

■ Hike 59 NORTH FORK SAN JACINTO RIVER 🏃 👫

HIKE LENGTH 1.4 miles out-and-back; 400' elevation gain
DIFFICULTY Easy to moderate
SEASON May–October
TOPO MAP *San Jacinto Peak* (7.5-minute), *San Jacinto Wilderness* (Tom Harrison)

■ FEATURES

There is no better place to experience the riparian delights of the San Jacintos than along the North Fork of the San Jacinto River. The musical waters of the creek exhibit a delightful variety of moods—now splashing merrily over boulders, now pausing in limpid pools, only to plunge headlong over miniature waterfalls and cascades. Along its banks sprout western azalea, its sweet-smelling gold and white flowers often growing under western dogwood, splendid in spring with flowerlike clusters of white bracts and just as glorious in fall when its leaves turn burgundy-red. Scarlet monkeyflower and pale columbine cheer these shady thickets with colorful blooms, all under a verdant canopy of alder, willow, and bay. On the slopes above is a mixed forest of live oak, incense-cedar, and ponderosa and Jeffrey pine, all contributing to nature's soft picture of elegance.

This trip is more of a saunter than a hike, a place to contemplate the gifts of the natural world and briefly forget civilization's tribulations. The area is of special biological interest as well since it is one of the last remaining populated habitats in the San Bernardino National Forest for the federally endangered mountain yellow-legged frog. This frog was historically one of the most common frogs in Southern California and used to be found in virtually every year-round stream in the mountains, but has declined in 99% of its range in the last couple of decades. Due to the presence of this sensitive species and others, the Forest Service asks visitors to avoid wading, rock hopping, fishing, and engaging in other water play within 10 feet of the creek edge. Watch for posted signs in the area with the latest information or check with the Idyllwild Ranger Station. Wear boots with good tread and ankle support.

■ DESCRIPTION

From Banning, drive southeast on Highway 243 to its crossing of the signed North Fork of the San Jacinto River at mile marker 243 RIV 11.25, 0.7 mile past Fuller Mill Creek picnic area (**GPS N33° 47.779' W116° 44.447'**). There are numerous turnouts for parking near the river.

Just south of the highway bridge, on the east side, find the unmarked start of the trail. The trail forks often with most side paths leading down toward the

Thimbleberry flowers

stream, but there is a main path that continues weaving around boulders and logs along the southeast side of the creek. Farther up, there are a few places where you must scramble to get around rock obstructions. If you are a beginner, a half mile is about as far as you should go. It is possible to follow the North Fork another quarter mile up to Dark Canyon Campground (**GPS N33° 48.146' W116° 43.949'**), but this is for experienced hikers only as slopes near the end become steep and slippery. Once at the campground, the creek flows under a bridge and the use trails continue along the northwest side of the creek up to the state wilderness boundary and Seven Pines Trail crossing.

■ Hike 60 SEVEN PINES TRAIL 🡵 🚶

HIKE LENGTH 7 miles out-and-back; 2,400' elevation gain
DIFFICULTY Moderate
SEASON June–October
TOPO MAPS *San Jacinto Peak* (7.5-minute), *San Jacinto Wilderness* (Tom Harrison)
PERMIT San Jacinto Wilderness Permit required

■ FEATURES

The Seven Pines Trail climbs the ridge between Fuller Mill Creek and Dark Canyon and continues up to Deer Springs. You wind through granite outcroppings and beautiful forest country, with views now and then toward the rugged headwall of Fuller Ridge. It is a steep but pleasant walk on a good trail, crossing and recrossing tumbling North Fork, and you have several options for the return.

■ DESCRIPTION

Drive 200 yards east of the Alandale Ranger Station on Highway 243 (near mile marker 243 RIV 9.75, 19 miles from Banning and 6 miles from Idyllwild), then head up the paved Marion Mountain Road (4S02), going left at a junction in 100 yards and left again in 0.8 mile, to Dark Canyon Campground. Follow the one-way loop road right through the campground to rejoin 4S02 as a fair dirt road just past the top of

Seven Pines Trail junction

the loop. Turn right and follow 4S02, passing the Azalea Trails Girl Scout Camp, to the signed Seven Pines 2E13 trailhead, on your right, 4.3 miles out (**GPS N33° 48.595' W116° 44.038'**).

Follow the trail as it climbs up the boulder-stacked, forested ridge between Fuller Mill Creek and Dark Canyon. In 1.25 miles you cross the ridgecrest and drop to the North Fork, where you enter Mount San Jacinto State Park Wilderness. The trail fords the creek and climbs east, crossing and recrossing the North Fork, to a junction with Deer Springs Trail, 3.5 miles from the start. Turn left (east) and follow the latter to Deer Springs, 0.25 mile. There is water here, but overnight camping is not allowed.

Return the way you came. Options are to descend the Marion Mountain Trail (see next hike), the Deer Springs Trail to Idyllwild (Hike 65, page 172), or the Fuller Ridge Trail to Black Mountain Road (Hike 57, page 159). All require shuttles.

■ Hike 61 SAN JACINTO PEAK VIA MARION MOUNTAIN TRAIL 🡵 🚶

HIKE LENGTH 13 miles out-and-back; 4,600' elevation gain
DIFFICULTY Strenuous (1 day), Moderate (2 days)
SEASON June–October
TOPO MAP *San Jacinto Peak* (7.5-minute), *San Jacinto Wilderness* (Tom Harrison)
PERMIT San Jacinto Wilderness Permit required

■ FEATURES

This is the shortest way to climb San Jacinto Peak from the southwest slope. The first 2.25 miles are the most strenuous; you gain 2,200 feet from the trailhead just below Marion Mountain Campground to Deer Springs. The remainder of the route is only slightly less precipitous—2,400 feet more gain in 3.25 miles via the Deer Springs Trail. You can do it in one exhausting pull or make it more enjoyable by spending the night at Little Round Valley Trail Camp. This trip is a living demonstration of forest change with altitude—you start up in Jeffrey pine and oak, climb through a belt of sugar pine and white fir, then into lodgepole pine interspersed with thickets of manzanita, snowbrush, and chinquapin, and finally emerge above timberline at the summit.

■ DESCRIPTION

From 200 yards east of Alandale Ranger Station on Highway 243 (near mile marker 243 RIV 9.75, 19 miles from Banning or 6 miles from Idyllwild), drive up the paved Marion Mountain Road (4S02), going left at a junction in 100 yards, to a junction with Marion Mountain Campground Road (4S71) in 0.8 mile. Go right and follow the latter for 0.6 mile, passing the entrance to Fern Basin Campground, to the Marion Mountain Trailhead (**GPS N33° 47.476' W116° 44.128'**), just short of Marion Mountain Campground. The parking area on your left has space for 10–12 vehicles.

Cross 4S71 to the signed Marion Mountain Trail (2E14). Pass a short access trail coming up from Marion Mountain Campground, then steeply ascend the northwest flank of Marion Ridge to a junction with the Deer Springs Trail, 2.8 miles. Turn left and follow the latter footpath 0.25 mile to Deer Springs. Water is available here but no camping. Continue up the Deer Springs Trail past Boggy Meadows to Little Round Valley Trail Camp, just below the peak. Water is available here through late summer but should be purified before drinking. Continue up the trail to a junction with the short San Jacinto Peak Trail, 1.2 miles. Turn left and climb the latter, passing the stone shelter cabin built by the Civilian Conservation Corps in 1936, to the 10,804-foot summit, 0.3 mile (**GPS N33° 48.881' W116° 40.764'**). Camping is not allowed in the summit area.

Return the same way. Another way down, requiring a 3-mile car or bike shuttle, is via the Seven Pines Trail (see previous hike). With much longer car shuttles, you can descend the Fuller Ridge/Pacific Crest Trail to Black Mountain Road (Hike 57, page 159), the Deer Springs Trail to Idyllwild (Hike 65, page 172), the San Jacinto Peak and Pacific Crest Trails via Wellman Cienega to Humber Park (Hike 67, page 176), or via Round and Long Valleys to the Palm Springs Aerial Tramway (Hike 84, page 208).

■ Hike 62 WEBSTER TRAIL 🥾 🐎

HIKE LENGTH 5 miles out-and-back; 1,900' elevation loss and gain
DIFFICULTY Moderate
SEASON October–June
TOPO MAP *Lake Fulmor, San Jacinto Peak* (both 7.5-minute), *San Jacinto Wilderness* (Tom Harrison)

■ FEATURES

The North Fork of the San Jacinto River cuts a deep swath down the west slope of the range. Melting snows and gushing springs high on the western ramparts of San Jacinto Peak nourish the several streams that join to become the North Fork; then the united waters tumble down the broad, V-shaped chasm to join with the South Fork, just above the San Jacinto Valley. A green canopy of fir, pine, cedar, and oak shades the stream for most of its length. This trip drops into the lonely middle reaches of the North Fork via the old Webster Trail, named for David G. Webster, pioneer rancher at Valle Vista in the San Jacinto Valley, who drove cattle up to high pasture on this path in the 1870s and '80s. Helen Hunt Jackson patterned her character Merrill in *Ramona* after Webster, whom she met while researching conditions of Native Americans in the San Jacinto Valley.

This is an ideal outing for a cool winter or spring day. You start under Jeffrey pines and live oaks, drop down slopes covered with chaparral swiftly growing back after a fire, and reach a secluded part of the creek spotted with tall pines, oaks, and alders. Try it after a rain, when the streams run full and the aroma of damp chaparral perfumes the air. Allow plenty of time for the return trip—it's all uphill. The trail is steep and gravelly, so boots with good tread are recommended.

■ DESCRIPTION

From Pine Cove at the Shell station on Highway 243, 3 miles from Idyllwild and just north of mile marker 247 RIV 7.25, turn west on Pine Cove Road and follow it for 0.8 mile as it curves north to a junction with Forest Roads 5S09 and 5S10. Turn sharp left (southwest) on 5S10 and continue 0.5 mile to a junction at the Lia Hona Lodge. Turn right and descend 0.9 mile on a fair dirt road to the beginning of the Webster Trail, indicated by a wooden sign on the right. Park in the adjacent clearing (**GPS N33° 45.105' W116° 45.542'**).

Follow the trail west as it descends the ridge, first through an open forest of Jeffrey pine and oak, then through dense chaparral. Your view is superb if the day is clear—across velvet-coated foothills to the flat expanse of the San Jacinto Valley. The dirt road you see climbing the next ridge south is part of the old Hemet–Idyllwild control road, used from 1910 to 1929, one-way traffic only. Where the slope begins to descend more steeply as it nears the gorge, the trail makes one long switchback south and reaches the cool waters of the North Fork, 2.5 miles from the start (**GPS N33° 45.259' W116° 47.204'**).

After you take a streamside rest amid sylvan greenery, return the way you came—all uphill now.

■ Hike 63 SUICIDE ROCK 🏃 🐕

HIKE LENGTH 7 miles out-and-back; 1,900' elevation gain

DIFFICULTY Moderate

SEASON May–October

TOPO MAP *San Jacinto Peak* (7.5-minute), *San Jacinto Wilderness* (Tom Harrison)

PERMIT San Jacinto Wilderness Permit required

■ FEATURES

Suicide Rock (7,528 feet) is an outcropping of white granite that juts from the south slope of Marion Ridge, high above Strawberry Valley. Legend says that Suicide Rock was so named after a Native American maiden and her lover jumped to their deaths from its rim rather than live without each other as had been decreed by the tribal chief. A splendid panorama of the valley floor covered with dense forest, the village of Idyllwild, and the rugged granite cliffs of Lily Rock and Tahquitz Peak awaits the hiker who reaches this viewpoint. This relatively short trip takes the Deer Springs Trail to Suicide Junction, then a side trail over to the rock.

■ DESCRIPTION

From Idyllwild Ranger Station, drive west 1 mile on Highway 243. Park on the north side of the road just above the Idyllwild Nature Center and past a sign pointing to Deer Springs Trailhead parking (**GPS N33° 45.180' W116° 43.379'**). The

Suicide Rock

Deer Springs Trail itself (3E17) starts 50 yards down the road. Alternatively, walk up a steep unmarked path above the parking area for 150 yards to a junction with the Deer Springs Trail near some power lines. Turn left and proceed uphill.

Your trail follows an abandoned dirt road about 200 yards, then turns right (north) and climbs steadily through an open forest of oak, Jeffrey pine, and king-sized manzanita to the ridgetop. You switchback up the ridge to a signed junction with the Suicide Rock Trail, 2.1 miles from the start. Here you leave the Deer Springs Trail and turn east, following the lateral trail as it contours across slopes clothed with pine and fir, crosses the trickle of Marion Creek, and climbs the back side of Suicide Rock to the abrupt rim overlooking Strawberry Valley, 1.2 miles from the junction (**GPS N33° 46.202' W116° 41.803'**). The white dome you see directly across the valley is Lily Rock; the steepled granite summit on the skyline is Tahquitz Peak.

Return the same way.

■ Hike 64 STRAWBERRY–SADDLE LOOP🥾 🐕 🥾

HIKE LENGTH 10 miles one-way; 3,400' elevation gain

DIFFICULTY Moderate

SEASON June–October

TOPO MAP *San Jacinto Peak* (7.5-minute), *San Jacinto Wilderness* (Tom Harrison)

PERMIT San Jacinto Wilderness Permit required

■ FEATURES

Although bordered by desert and semi-arid hill country, the San Jacintos are a particularly lush mountain range. Nowhere is this more evident than at the numerous springs and marshy cienegas that dot the upper slopes. The abundant rain and snow that fall at the high elevations seep into the porous granite, which acts as a natural storage reservoir. Water from this rock reservoir flows out at many points high in the mountains, forming emerald-green and flowery marshes threaded by clear, gurgling streamlets. One of the lushest of these sloping mountainside gardens is Strawberry Cienega, high on the south face of Marion Mountain.

This loop trip—requiring a short car shuttle between Idyllwild and Humber Park—climbs the Deer Springs Trail to Strawberry Junction, turns east on the Pacific Crest Trail (PCT) and contours across the steep south slope of Marion Mountain past Strawberry Cienega, and then descends the PCT to Saddle Junction and the Devils Slide to Humber Park. It is a delightful daylong hike on good trail all

California mountain king snake

the way, passing through rich forest and meadow country, with continuous views of the Yosemite-like cliffs and ridges of Tahquitz Peak and Lily Rock.

◼ DESCRIPTION

Leave a getaway car or bicycle at Humber Park. From the Idyllwild Ranger Station on Highway 243, take Pine Crest Avenue northeast. In 0.6 mile, veer right onto South Circle Drive. In 0.1 mile, turn left onto Fern Valley Road. After 1.7 miles, reach a small parking area for the Ernie Maxwell Scenic Trail. Continue 0.1 mile up the hill to the outhouse and larger parking area of Humber Park (**GPS N33° 45.880' W116° 41.143'**).

Return to the ranger station and go west 1 mile on Highway 243. Park on the north side of the road just above the Idyllwild Nature Center and past a sign pointing to Deer Springs Trailhead parking (**GPS N33° 45.180' W116° 43.379'**). The Deer Springs Trail itself (3E17) starts 50 yards down the road.

Follow the Deer Springs Trail as it climbs northward to Strawberry Junction, where you meet the PCT, 3.7 miles from the start (1.6 miles beyond the Suicide Rock Trail junction). Good camping can be found here; a permit from the state park is required. Turn right (east) and follow the PCT across the south face of Marion Mountain, through open stands of lodgepole pine and white fir, to Strawberry Cienega. Your view across the valley to the rugged spurs of Tahquitz Peak is breathtaking.

Continue east along the trail to a junction where the PCT turns south, 2.2 miles from the Deer Springs Trail. Turn right (south) and descend the boulder-stacked ridge, through scattered Jeffrey pines, to the five-way Saddle Junction, 1.7 miles. Turn right again (west) and descend the Devils Slide Trail to Humber Park, 2.5 miles (see Hike 66, page 174, for full description).

An easier option, with 700 feet less elevation gain, is to do the trip in reverse, starting at Humber Park and ending at Deer Springs Trailhead.

Another option is to start or end the hike at the Suicide Rock climbers' trail rather than Deer Springs, avoiding the car shuttle. This is recommended only for those experienced in cross-country travel. The climbers' trail begins at a small marker 1.4 miles up Fern Valley Road and 0.4 mile below Humber Park (**GPS N33° 46.004' W116° 41.395'**). The trail reaches the top of Suicide Rock, where it joins a path to the Deer Springs Trail (see Hike 63, page 168). This trail passes through private property with permission of the owners. Please respect their land and do not stray from the trail. The upper portion of the climbers' trail climbs a steep, rocky, and loose slope around the north side of Suicide Rock and can be difficult to follow in places.

■ Hike 65 SAN JACINTO PEAK FROM IDYLLWILD

HIKE LENGTH 18 miles out-and-back; 5,200' elevation gain

DIFFICULTY Very Strenuous (1 day), Moderate (2 days)

SEASON June–October

TOPO MAP *San Jacinto Peak* (7.5-minute), *San Jacinto Wilderness* (Tom Harrison)

PERMIT San Jacinto Wilderness Permit required

■ FEATURES

The western slopes of San Jacinto Peak and the long, sinuous ridge of Marion Mountain are blanketed with dense stands of pine, fir, and cedar, interspaced here and there with manzanita and chinquapin thickets and, where water seeps to the surface, verdant meadows. The Deer Springs Trail, a popular hiking route built by the Civilian Conservation Corps during the 1930s, threads most of the length of this slope, then climbs steeply to within a stone's throw of the summit.

This trip makes use of the Deer Springs Trail to ascend San Jacinto Peak, then loops around and back through Wellman and Strawberry Cienegas on the return. En route you pass two trail camps—Strawberry Junction, 3.7 miles up the trail where the Pacific Crest Trail (PCT) meets your route, and Little Round Valley,

Delightful Jeffrey pines along the Deer Springs Trail

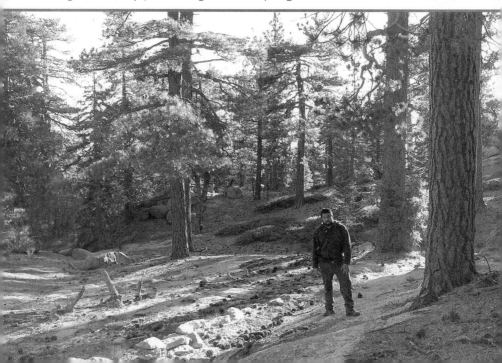

high on a lodgepole pine–shaded bench under San Jacinto Peak. There is water at Little Round Valley until late summer. Choose one for your overnight stay; the next day, climb to the summit for a panorama unsurpassed in Southern California, and circle back via the two cienegas.

DESCRIPTION

From Idyllwild Ranger Station, drive west 1 mile on Highway 243. Park on the north side of the road just above the Idyllwild Nature Center and past a sign pointing to Deer Springs Trailhead parking (**GPS N33° 45.180' W116° 43.379'**). The Deer Springs Trail itself (3E17) starts 50 yards down the road. Alternatively, walk 150 yards up a steep unmarked path above the parking area to a junction with the Deer Springs Trail near some power lines.

Proceed northward up the Deer Springs Trail, through alternating stands of canyon live oak, Jeffrey pine, and manzanita, passing a junction with the Suicide Rock Trail. At Strawberry Junction Trail Camp in 3.7 miles, the Deer Springs Trail merges with the northbound PCT. Water is available from Stone Creek about 100 yards up the PCT.

Your path now continues up the PCT to the top of Marion Ridge and then contours and climbs through a gorgeous forest of pine and fir, crossing several trickling streamlets of icy-cold water. You pass junctions with the Marion Mountain Trail (Hike 61, page 166) and the Seven Pines Trail (Hike 60, page 164), both leading down to your left, and continue to where reliable Deer Springs flows across the trail, 5.9 miles from the start. From Deer Springs, the trail climbs 200 yards to a junction where the Deer Springs Trail diverges from the PCT. Take the Deer Springs Trail right (northeast), up a steep slope covered with manzanita, snowbrush, and chinquapin, across a marshy bench known as Boggy Meadows, and up to Little Round Valley, 1.3 miles from Deer Springs. Here also are plentiful campsites amid lodgepole pine under granite spurs. You'll find water here until late summer, but you should purify it before drinking. From Little Round Valley, the trail climbs steeply through lodgepoles to a junction with the San Jacinto Peak Trail, 1.2 miles. Turn left and climb past the stone shelter building to the boulder-stacked summit, 300 yards (**GPS N33° 48.881' W116° 40.764'**).

After taking in the fabulous view, return to the before-mentioned junction. Turn left (southeast) and descend the main trail (see Hike 67, page 176, for a full description) past Wellman Divide and Wellman Cienega to a junction with the PCT, 3 miles. Turn right (west) on the latter and follow it 2.2 miles through Strawberry Cienega (see previous hike) back to Strawberry Junction. Turn left (south) and descend the Deer Springs Trail to Idyllwild.

■ Hike 66 SKUNK CABBAGE MEADOW ⤢ 🐕 🚶

HIKE LENGTH 6.5 miles out-and-back; 1,700' elevation gain

DIFFICULTY Moderate

SEASON June–October

TOPO MAPS *San Jacinto Peak* (7.5-minute), *San Jacinto Wilderness* (Tom Harrison)

PERMIT San Jacinto Wilderness Permit required

This area burned in the 2013 Mountain Fire. As of 2016, the trail remains closed east of Saddle Junction. Check with the Idyllwild Ranger Station at 909-382-2921 to determine if the trail has reopened.

■ FEATURES

The Devils Slide Trail is the hiker's main gateway into the San Jacinto Wilderness. The trail climbs the steep mountain wall above the head of Strawberry Valley in long, easy-graded switchbacks, then abruptly crosses the crest to Saddle Junction, the locus of footpaths leading in five directions. En route you pass through beautiful stands of oak, pine, cedar, and fir, with patches of manzanita and snowbrush just below the top. Three trickling rills—Jolley Spring, Middle Spring, and Powderbox Spring—offer trailside refreshment in early season, but dry up one by one as summer fades into fall.

The Devils Slide Trail today is a gradual uphill climb, certainly undeserving of its notorious name. But once it was quite different. In pioneer days, when Charles Thomas and later Frank Wellman drove cattle up the mountain to feed on the rich grasses of Tahquitz Valley, it was a frightful climb. No switchbacks then—just right up the mountainside, over loose boulders and fallen trees, through thorny chaparral thickets. Many a cow and even a few cowboys took a neck-breaking spill on this treacherous slope, and anyone who knew the Devils Slide then always remembered it. Since then, the Devils Slide Trail has been worked and reworked many times, until it in no way resembles its historical namesake. In fact, it has become so gentle that one wiseacre has suggested the name be changed to "Angels Walk."

This rather short trip uses the Devils Slide Trail to offer a small sampling of the beautiful San Jacinto Wilderness. You climb to Saddle Junction, then continue a slight distance to Skunk Cabbage Meadow, an emerald-green oasis set amid the dark forest. An overnight stay in the Skunk Cabbage Zone is guaranteed to please.

■ DESCRIPTION

From the Idyllwild Ranger Station on Highway 243, head northeast on Pine Crest Avenue. In 0.6 mile, veer right onto South Circle Drive. In 0.1 mile, turn left onto

Fern Valley Road. After 1.7 miles, reach a small parking area for the Ernie Maxwell Scenic Trail. Continue 0.1 mile up the hill to the outhouse and larger parking area of Humber Park (**GPS N33° 45.880' W116° 41.143'**).

The Devils Slide Trail starts from the top of the parking area, under the shadow of towering Lily Rock. You zigzag up the mountainside through a varied forest of Jeffrey pine, incense-cedar, white fir, and several species of oak. As you gain elevation, the views south over Strawberry Valley and north across the canyon to the precipitous south slope of Marion Mountain become impressive. In 1.25 miles, you will pass a small rivulet coming down from Jolley Spring. The trail then makes a long switchback out across oak- and manzanita-covered slopes and passes Middle Spring (often flowing long into the summer). The trail then reenters the pine and fir forest, passes Powderbox Spring, and crosses a low point in the rim to Saddle Junction, 2.5 miles. Here, on the heavily forested tableland, is a five-way trail fork (see Hikes 67, 69, 71, and 72 for particulars). The Willow Creek Trail to the northeast leads to Skunk Cabbage Meadow. Proceed this way, through a lush forest of tall Jeffrey pines with ferns matting the floor, to another junction, 0.5 mile. Turn right (south) as indicated by the sign and walk 0.25 mile farther to the verdant clearing of Skunk Cabbage Meadow.

From Skunk Cabbage Meadow, short exploratory trips are possible to Willow Creek (see Hike 69, page 101), Tahquitz Valley, and Tahquitz Creek (see Hike 70, page 183). Longer side trips are possible to points too numerous to mention here (see Hikes 67, 71, and 72). Because of its central location, the Skunk Cabbage Zone makes an ideal campsite.

Return the way you came.

San Jacinto Wilderness

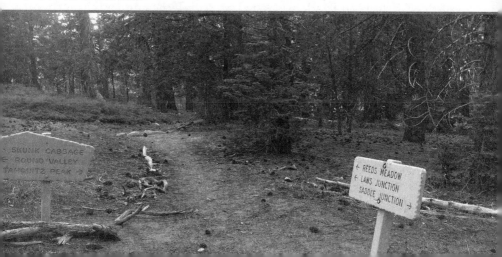

■ Hike 67 SAN JACINTO PEAK FROM HUMBER PARK 🥾 🧗

HIKE LENGTH 14 miles out-and-back; 4,400' elevation gain
DIFFICULTY Moderate (2 days), Strenuous (1 day)
SEASON June–October
TOPO MAP *San Jacinto Peak* (7.5-minute), *San Jacinto Wilderness* (Tom Harrison)
PERMIT San Jacinto Wilderness Permit required

■ FEATURES

When naturalist John Muir stood on the summit and watched the sunrise in 1896, he is said to have exclaimed, "The view from San Jacinto is the most sublime spectacle to be found anywhere on this earth!"[3] Since then, countless others have experienced Muir's inspiration. The vista is utterly magnificent, extending over hundreds of square miles of mountains, foothills, valleys, and desert. On the western horizon, beyond row after row of misty-purple ranges, is the glimmering Pacific. Northwest, the gray hogback of San Gorgonio rises grandly across the deep trough of San Gorgonio Pass. Eastward sprawls the drab tawniness of the Colorado Desert and its debris-strewn hills. Southeast lies the shining platter of the Salton Sea, and beyond, in the distant haze, is Mexico. But what gives the panorama a final touch of grandeur is the gigantic north rampart, plunging in sheer cliffs and castellated ridges to Coachella Valley, nearly 2 miles below. It is truly the altar of the gods!

To the early Native Americans of Southern California, San Jacinto was a sacred mountain. The Cahuillas knew it as "Aya Kaich," meaning "smooth cliffs," the home of the meteor Dakush, legendary founder of the Cahuilla people. The Luisenos called it "Yamiwa," the Serranos "Sovovo." Even the faraway Gabrielinos revered it as "Jamiwu." The Spanish padres supposedly gave it the name "San Jacinto" after an outlying stock ranch of Mission San Luis Rey, which in turn was named for the 15th-century martyr Saint Hyacinth of Silesia. Lieutenant Robert S. Williamson's Pacific Railroad Survey party passed under its towering face in 1853, mistakenly calling it "San Gorgonio" and misjudging its heights as 6,000–7,000 feet. Two years later, Dr. Thomas Antisell of Lieutenant John G. Parke's railroad survey party corrected Williamson's error. Antisell's report of 1855 contains the first written reference to the peak as "San Jacinto."

Who made the first ascent of San Jacinto Peak will probably never be known. Most likely it was a Cahuilla hunter, centuries before the arrival of the Europeans. The earliest climb on record was made in 1874 by a person identified

---

3   The quote is good, but the author could find no evidence that Muir ever climbed San Jacinto Peak.

only as "F. of Riverside" (story in *San Diego Union* of September 16, 1874), who rode a horse up most of the way and scrambled the last 1,000 feet on foot. In 1878, the peak was climbed by Lieutenant George M. Wheeler's US Army survey party, which used the summit for a triangulation station and calculated its height at 10,987 feet above sea level.

In 1897, Edmund T. Perkins of the US Geological Survey lugged a 60-pound plane table and theodolite to the top without benefit of trail, and corrected the elevation to 10,805 feet. Perkins's work was amazingly accurate—today's official height, determined by instruments far superior to those he used, is 10,804 feet. The first trail to the summit was forged by the US Coast and Geodetic Survey in 1898 in order to install a heliograph for signaling to parties on other Southern California peaks. This trail was the forerunner of the present Devils Slide–Round Valley–San Jacinto Peak route. Since then, thousands have made the ascent via this trail and other footpaths constructed by the Civilian Conservation Corps (CCC) during the mid-1930s. The stone shelter cabin just below the summit was built by the CCC in 1936.

This trip takes the most direct and the most traveled route from Idyllwild to the summit. It is an arduous 7-mile pull, but one of the most scenic and rewarding mountain paths in Southern California. You climb rock-ribbed slopes, cross chaparral thickets, pass through dense forest, and pause at bubbling springs. The higher you climb, the more glorious the vista. Halfway up, high on the mountainside, you pass a spot of lush grasses ribboned with trickling rills of icy water. This is Wellman Cienega, named for Frank Wellman, a part-Irish and part-English character who herded cattle on the

Unusual snow-free December day atop Mount San Jacinto

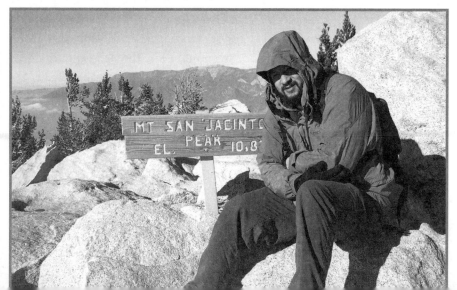

mountain in the 1890s. Beyond Wellman Cienega, you enter a world of weather-toughened lodgepole, sky-piercing granite crests, and thin, cold air: the alpine roof-top of Southern California.

■ DESCRIPTION

From the Idyllwild Ranger Station on Highway 243, head northeast on Pine Crest Avenue. In 0.6 mile, veer right onto South Circle Drive. In 0.1 mile, turn left on Fern Valley Road. After 1.7 miles, reach a small parking area for the Ernie Maxwell Scenic Trail. Continue 0.1 mile up the hill to the outhouse and larger parking area of Humber Park (**GPS N33° 45.880' W116° 41.143'**).

Climb the Devils Slide Trail, which starts at the top of the parking area, to Saddle Junction, 2.5 miles (see Hike 66, page 174, for details). At Saddle Junction, take the leftmost trail, leading north and marked by a sign indicating SAN JACINTO PEAK. You climb, through a forest of Jeffrey pine and white fir, up the bouldered ridge that forms the northeast wall of the Strawberry Valley amphitheater. Views into the valley and across to Lily Rock and Tahquitz Peak are impressive. The trail then winds along the mountainside to a junction with the lateral trail to Strawberry Cienega (see Hike 64, page 170), 1.7 miles from Saddle Junction.

Continue straight ahead (north), through lodgepole pine and white fir. The footpath rounds the head of Willow Creek to the grassy patch of Wellman Cienega, 0.7 mile. Here is the last running water before the summit. Beyond Wellman's, you climb through thickets of manzanita and chinquapin to Wellman Divide, 0.5 mile, high on the ridge between Round and Tahquitz Valleys. Here is a trail junction—left to the summit, right to Round Valley. If you're doing the climb in one day, go left. (If it's a two-day venture, your best overnight camp is in Round Valley—go right and descend to Round Valley Trail Camp, 1 mile.) Going the summit route (left), the trail climbs through a silent forest of lodgepole pine, then makes a long switchback up the southeast slope of San Jacinto Peak, through dense chinqua-pin and manzanita, to the ridgetop between Jean and San Jacinto Peaks, 1.7 mile. Here you meet the San Jacinto Peak Trail. (The main trail continues down to Little Round Valley and Deer Springs—see Hike 65.) Turn right and climb 0.2 mile through an open lodgepole forest, past the stone shelter cabin, to the boul-der-strewn summit (**GPS N33° 48.881' W116° 40.764'**).

Return the same way. Or take the roundabout route back through Round Valley and across Hidden Lake Divide (see Hike 69, page 181). With a 3.5-mile car or bicycle shuttle, descend the Deer Springs Trail to Idyllwild (see Hike 65, page 172). Or take the aerial tramway down to Palm Springs with an across-the-range car shuttle (see Hike 84, page 208).

■ Hike 68 JEAN PEAK AND MARION MOUNTAIN 🥾🚶

HIKE LENGTH 16 miles one-way; 4,600' elevation gain
DIFFICULTY Strenuous
SEASON June–October
TOPO MAP *San Jacinto Peak* (7.5-minute), *San Jacinto Wilderness* (Tom Harrison)
PERMIT San Jacinto Wilderness Permit required

■ FEATURES

Edmund Taylor Perkins had a special way of immortalizing the women in his life. He named mountains for them. When the tall, good-looking topographer came into the San Jacintos in 1897 to map the range for the US Geological Survey, he met a young schoolteacher camped with friends near today's Pine Cove. She was Marion Kelly of White Cloud, Michigan, described as "a wonderful woman, blue eyes, and a gentle nature." She was employed by the Indian Bureau at the Morongo Valley Reservation. The story goes that Miss Kelly fell deeply in love with Perkins, but he kept putting her off by saying he was married to his work. But he did think enough of the young woman to place her name on a nearby mountain peak— Marion Mountain. Another young lady was in Perkins's mind, too, one he had met previously while surveying in Northern California. She was Jean Waters of

San Jacinto from Marion Mountain

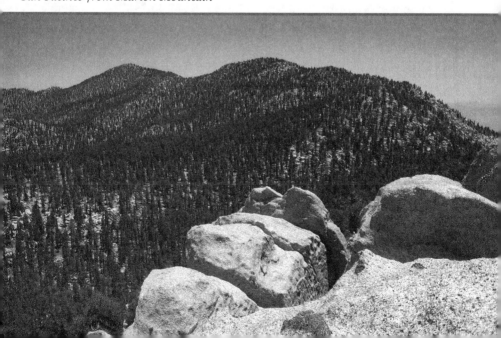

Plumas County, California. He put her name on the neighboring mountain—Jean Peak. Marion was destined to be disappointed. Jean was more fortunate: she and Edmund Perkins were married in 1903.

No trails reach to the twin summits of white granite that eternalize the memory of these two women. To reach them, you must scramble across jumbo boulders and, in the case of Marion, climb a short but rather precipitous summit block. This loop trip is only for those in top condition and experienced in cross-country travel.

■ DESCRIPTION

From Idyllwild Ranger Station, drive west 1 mile on Highway 243. Leave a car on the north side of the road just above the Idyllwild Nature Center and past a sign pointing to Deer Springs Trailhead parking (**GPS N33° 45.180' W116° 43.3794'**). Drive the other car to Humber Park: Return to the ranger station and take Pine Crest Avenue northeast. In 0.6 mile, veer right onto South Circle Drive. In 0.1 mile, turn left onto Fern Valley Road. After 1.7 miles, reach a small parking area for the Ernie Maxwell Scenic Trail. Continue 0.1 mile up the hill to the outhouse and larger parking area of Humber Park (**GPS N33° 45.880' W116° 41.143'**).

Take the Devils Slide Trail to Saddle Junction, then the San Jacinto Peak Trail to the point where it reaches the ridgetop just south of San Jacinto Peak, 7 miles (see previous hike for details). Leave the trail here and scramble across boulders south along the ridge through an open lodgepole forest. You drop 100 feet to a saddle, then ascend 300 feet to the pile of white granite that marks the 10,670-foot summit of Jean Peak (**GPS N33° 48.366' W116° 40.746'**). After signing the Sierra Club summit register, continue down the ridge, south, then southwest, over an intermediate unnamed bump to the granite outcropping that is the summit of 10,362-foot Marion Mountain (**GPS N33° 47.755' W116° 41.328'**). The granite block is not difficult, but climb with care. After signing in here, continue down the ridge, curving west, through some brush, to the Deer Springs Trail. (*Note:* do not try to descend southeast to Wellman Cienega or south to the Strawberry Cienega Trail from Marion Mountain—you will become tangled in dense, thorny chaparral.) Follow the Deer Springs Trail 4 miles south to the trailhead.

To avoid a car shuttle, you can take the Strawberry Cienega lateral trail (see Hike 64, page 170) back to the San Jacinto Peak Trail below Wellman Cienega. This adds 2.5 miles to the total hiking mileage.

■ Hike 69 HUMBER PARK–ROUND VALLEY LOOP ○ 🥾

HIKE LENGTH 14 miles semiloop; 3,600' elevation gain

DIFFICULTY Strenuous (1 day), Moderate (2 days)

SEASON June–October

TOPO MAP *San Jacinto Peak* (7.5-minute), *San Jacinto Wilderness* (Tom Harrison)

PERMIT San Jacinto Wilderness Permit required

This area burned in the 2013 Mountain Fire. As of 2016, the Willow Creek Trail remains closed. Check with the Idyllwild Ranger Station at 909-382-2921 to determine if the trail has reopened.

■ FEATURES

Southeast from San Jacinto's lofty crown, nestled in high hanging valleys ringed by jagged spurs of white granite, is an enchanting wonderland of green. Here, suspended 8,000 feet above the desert, pines and firs grow tall and sturdy, lush meadows are waist-high with fern and azalea, lupines spot hillsides in their late-summer

Cornell Peak overlooks Round Valley.

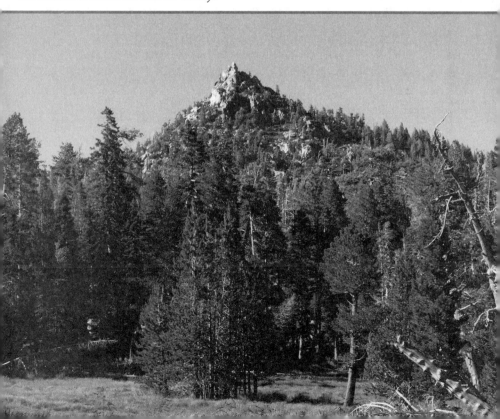

bloom of purple and pale mauve, and little singing streams flow clear and cold. In the heart of this high sylvan wilderness is Round Valley, an oval meadow of verdant grass, threaded by an icy-cold brook, surrounded by a dense forest of lodgepole pine. Here is the most popular trail camp in the San Jacinto high country, frequented by dozens of backpackers almost every summer and early fall weekend.

This trip makes a broad loop through this inviting wilderness beneath the high peaks, with an overnight stop in Round Valley. The entire hike is on good trail and can be done in one long day, if you're in a monumental hurry. But it's a much more enjoyable trip if you take the full two days and savor this superb bit of sylvan grandeur high on the rugged shoulder of the San Jacintos.

■ DESCRIPTION

From the Idyllwild Ranger Station on Highway 243, head northeast on Pine Crest Avenue. In 0.6 mile, veer right onto South Circle Drive. In 0.1 mile, turn left onto Fern Valley Road. After 1.7 miles, reach a small parking area for the Ernie Maxwell Scenic Trail. Continue 0.1 mile up the hill to the outhouse and larger parking area of Humber Park (**GPS N33° 45.880' W116° 41.143'**).

Climb the Devils Slide Trail, which starts at the top of the parking area, to Saddle Junction, 2.5 miles (see Hike 66, page 174, for details). At Saddle Junction take the trail fork leading northeast, marked WILLOW CREEK and LONG VALLEY. The 1.5-mile walk to Willow Creek passes through a forest garden of ferns shaded by tall Jeffrey pines, passing a side trail leading south to Skunk Cabbage Meadow. Willow Creek itself flows reliably all year. Good camping can be found anywhere along the Willow Creek Trail, as long as you are at least 200 feet from the trail and water. The north side of the trail is the North Rim Zone, and the south side is in the Skunk Cabbage Zone.

Beyond, the trail starts climbing northeastward, and in 0.5 mile it reaches a junction with a trail on the right to Laws Junction. Continue straight ahead and within minutes you will arrive at the boundary of Mount San Jacinto State Park Wilderness, marked by a handsome sign.

The trail continues to climb higher on the south slope of the rocky divide overlooking Tahquitz Creek, with splendid vistas over the latter and beyond to the desert and the Santa Rosa Mountains. In 2.2 miles from Willow Creek, the trail makes several switchbacks and reaches Hidden Lake Divide. Just beyond, leading east, is the presently closed lateral trail to Hidden Lake and Desert View. The little vernal pool, just above the escarpment, has suffered from overuse and needs time to recuperate, so please do not visit it. Continue north on the main trail. In 0.25 mile you reach a junction with the trail leading northeast to Long Valley and the upper tramway terminal, 1 mile. Go left (northwest)—the sign indicates ROUND VALLEY 2 MILES. The trail contours through lodgepole pines, along the north slope of the divide overlooking Long Valley, passes a junction with the other end of the loop trail from Long Valley and the tramway, and reaches the lush green meadow of Round Valley. Here, on both sides of the valley, are many lodgepole-shaded camping spots.

For the return trip, take the trail that leads west, upstream; a sign indicates WELLMAN JUNCTION 1 MILE. You climb 1 mile through lodgepoles, verdant grasses, and lupine to a junction with the San Jacinto Peak Trail. Turn left (southwest) and descend the trail through Wellman Cienega to Saddle Junction, 3 miles (see Hike 67, page 176, for details). Then take the Devils Slide Trail down to Humber Park.

■ Hike 70 TAHQUITZ VALLEY 🥾 🐕 🚶

HIKE LENGTH 6 miles out-and-back; 1,700' elevation gain

DIFFICULTY Moderate

SEASON June–October

TOPO MAPS *San Jacinto Peak, Palm Springs* (both 7.5-minute), *San Jacinto Wilderness* (Tom Harrison)

PERMIT San Jacinto Wilderness Permit required

This area burned in the 2013 Mountain Fire. As of 2016, the trail remains closed east of Saddle Junction. Check with the Idyllwild Ranger Station at 909-382-2921 to determine if the trail has reopened.

▨ FEATURES

Close under the granite spurs of Tahquitz Peak, nestled in a shallow bowl floored with forest and lush green meadow, is Tahquitz Valley. For the lover of pure sylvan beauty, this is the best the San Jacintos have to offer. Ferns and azaleas grow waist-high amid emerald grassland. Lemon lilies, crimson penstemon, purple lupine, and creamy buttercups add an enchanting dash of brilliance during early-summer bloom. Cool, clear water bubbles up from springs, and a musical creek threads the valley floor. Surrounding this mountain garden are dense stands of pine and fir.

Years ago, cowboys herded cattle up the notorious Devils Slide and into Tahquitz Valley to feed on the rich grasses. Frank Wellman is said to have built the first cabin here back in the 1890s. But the cattle have been gone for more than 70

Campsite in Tahquitz Valley

years and the old cabin has been removed, and nature's pristine beauty once again reigns in this lovely mountain basin.

This trip climbs the Devils Slide Trail and drops into this sylvan sanctuary. You can do it in one day, picnicking in the green, flower-bedecked turf, or make it a leisurely two-day jaunt, staying the night in the Tahquitz or Chinquapin Camping Zones.

■ DESCRIPTION

From the Idyllwild Ranger Station on Highway 243, head northeast on Pine Crest Avenue. In 0.6 mile, veer right onto South Circle Drive. In 0.1 mile, turn left onto Fern Valley Road. After 1.7 miles, reach a small parking area for the Ernie Maxwell Scenic Trail. Continue 0.1 mile up the hill to the outhouse and larger parking area of Humber Park (**GPS N33° 45.880' W116° 41.143'**).

Climb the Devils Slide Trail, which starts at the top of the parking area, to Saddle Junction, 2.5 miles (see Hike 66, page 174 for details). At Saddle Junction, take the Caramba Trail leading right (southeast) toward Tahquitz Valley. Proceed 0.6 mile through the forest of Jeffrey pine and white fir to Tahquitz Valley. Here is the Tahquitz Camping Zone, with brown posts indicating where large groups may camp. Water is available here except during severe drought. Stop here or proceed

Penstemon (Penstemon labrosus)

0.25 mile farther south, going right at a trail fork, to Little Tahquitz Valley, where you can find seasonal water and more camping. Staying straight at the before-mentioned junction takes you to Reeds Meadow, with water from the stream. The water will need to be purified before drinking.

If you're making Tahquitz Valley your base camp and staying awhile, several interesting side trips are possible. Climb by good trail to Tahquitz Peak Lookout (see Hike 72, page 187). Descend Tahquitz Creek to Laws Camp and Caramba (see next hike), also on good trail. Walk a short distance north to Skunk Cabbage Meadow (see Hike 66, page 174). Or scramble cross-country up Red Tahquitz for a breathtaking view of the Desert Divide country (see Hike 74, page 191).

Return the same way. An option is to take the South Ridge Trail to the road-head above Saunders Meadow (see Hike 76, page 195).

■ Hike 71 CARAMBA 🥾 🐕 🚶

HIKE LENGTH 14 miles out-and-back; 3,300' elevation gain

DIFFICULTY Strenuous (1 day), Moderate (2 days)

SEASON June–October

TOPO MAPS *San Jacinto Peak, Palm Springs* (both 7.5-minute), *San Jacinto Wilderness* (Tom Harrison)

PERMIT San Jacinto Wilderness Permit required

This area burned in the 2013 Mountain Fire. As of 2016, the trail remains closed east of Saddle Junction. Check with the Idyllwild Ranger Station at 909-382-2921 to determine if the trail has reopened.

■ FEATURES

Eastward from Tahquitz Valley, Tahquitz Creek descends in little tumbling cascades and swirling rapids for 3 meandering miles, then plunges abruptly off the eastern precipice to die in the thirsty sands of the desert. As the creek loses

elevation, the character of the vegetation changes. Emerald grasses,
ferns, and flowering herbs gradually give way to willow thickets and
clumps of bitter cherry and nettle.
The adjacent forest cover changes,
too, from dense stands of white fir
and Jeffrey pine to sparse Jeffreys
and finally to hardy pinyon pine.

Winding through the Tahquitz
Creek basin, from the Tahquitz Valley
through Laws Camp to the sudden
drop-off just past Caramba, is a well-
beaten trail, a pathway through some
of the wildest high country in the
range.

Laws Camp, near the junc-
tion of Willow and Tahquitz Creeks,
commemorates writer George Law,
who built a cabin of shale rock with
a ramada-type roof near here about
1916. Every summer for years, Law
and his "little donkeys with their tin-
kering bells" would pack in to enjoy
nature's solitude and find inspiration
for his newspaper and magazine arti-

George Law's cabin, now long gone, in Tahquitz Valley, 1921

cles. The remains of his old cabin are almost gone, hidden on a rocky spur several
hundred yards above Willow Creek.

Caramba is a little-used Spanish word meaning strange or unusual. The story
goes that many years ago some cowboys camping here were terrified by weird
sounds during the night and gave the place this unusual name.

This trip climbs over the Devils Slide and drops down parallel to Tahquitz
Creek. Good camping can be found in the Lower Basin Camping Zone east of
Willow Creek. Just beyond Caramba, you are rewarded with a breathtaking vista
over the desert. If you like your mountains primitive and unpeopled, this outing
should suit your taste.

■ DESCRIPTION

From the Idyllwild Ranger Station on Highway 243, head northeast on Pine Crest Avenue. In 0.6 mile, veer right onto South Circle Drive. In 0.1 mile, turn left onto Fern Valley Road. After 1.7 miles, reach a small parking area for the Ernie Maxwell Scenic Trail. Continue 0.1 mile up the hill to the outhouse and larger parking area of Humber Park (**GPS N33° 45.880' W116° 41.143'**).

Climb the Devils Slide Trail, which starts at the top of the parking area, to Saddle Junction, 2.5 miles (see Hike 66, page 174, for details). At Saddle Junction take the trail leading right (southeast), marked TAHQUITZ VALLEY and LAWS-CARAMBA. Proceed 0.6 mile through forests of pine and fir to Tahquitz Valley. In the valley take the trail northeast, marked LAWS and CARAMBA. The trail proceeds above the north bank of Tahquitz Creek, dropping 400 feet in 1.5 miles to a junction. The remains of Laws Cabin lie between the trail and creek just south of here, and camping can be found in this area, part of the Lower Basin Camping Zone.

The Laws/Cedar Trail (3E16) leads north from the junction to connect with the main Humber Park–Long Valley Trail (Hike 69, page 181), 1 mile. But this trip continues along the Caramba Trail on the north slope high above Tahquitz Creek, then drops to Caramba (**GPS N33° 46.870' W116° 37.541'**), just above the eastern precipice—300-foot gain and 1,000-foot loss in 2 miles from Laws. More good camping can be found here, which is still part of the Lower Basin Camping Zone. Just east of Caramba, you can scramble up a faint sandy path onto some large rock outcroppings for superb views over the desert face of the San Jacintos. But do not try to descend the precipice or Tahquitz Creek to the desert—many have become lost or injured trying. The Gordon Trail once went this way, but it has not been maintained for more than 70 years, and is impossible to follow now.

Return the way you came.

■ Hike 72 TAHQUITZ PEAK VIA SADDLE JUNCTION

HIKE LENGTH 8 miles out-and-back; 2,400' elevation gain

DIFFICULTY Moderate

SEASON June–October

TOPO MAPS *San Jacinto Peak* (7.5-minute), *San Jacinto Wilderness* (Tom Harrison)

PERMIT San Jacinto Wilderness Permit required

Tahquitz Peak from the north

■ FEATURES

Tahquitz Peak (8,846 feet) is the southern citadel of the San Jacinto high country. Its granite spurs and steep battlements rise impressively above Strawberry Valley on one side and Tahquitz Valley on the other. From the Forest Service lookout on its summit, you are rewarded with breathtaking panoramas over the southern half of the San Jacintos, with the Santa Rosas on the distant skyline.

Tahquitz Peak is named for the powerful demon of Cahuilla legend who allegedly lived in a cave below the peak and came out at night to terrorize and devour those who ventured too close to his sacred mountain. The summit lookout tower, held up by steel beams, was built in 1938 to replace a more primitive wooden structure built around 1918. It is manned by volunteers during fire season, usually June–November.

■ DESCRIPTION

From the Idyllwild Ranger Station on Highway 243, head northeast on Pine Crest Avenue. In 0.6 mile, veer right onto South Circle Drive. In 0.1 mile, turn left onto Fern Valley Road. After 1.7 miles, reach a small parking area for the Ernie Maxwell

Scenic Trail. Continue 0.1 mile up the hill to the outhouse and larger parking area of Humber Park (**GPS N33° 45.880' W116° 41.143'**).

Climb the Devils Slide Trail 2.5 miles to Saddle Junction (see Hike 66, page 174). At Saddle Junction, take the far-right trail leading south, marked TAHQUITZ PEAK. In 1.2 miles through the forest, you reach Chinquapin Flat junction—covered, as the name implies, with a thick mantle of bush chinquapin. Go right again (southwest) and follow the trail up through chinquapin, lodgepole pine, and a few limber pine to the summit lookout, 0.5 mile (**GPS N33° 45.327' W116° 40.614'**).

Return the same way, or take the South Ridge Trail down (Hike 76, page 195).

■ Hike 73 LILY ROCK ↗

HIKE LENGTH 2 miles out-and-back; 1,600' elevation gain

DIFFICULTY Moderate

SEASON May–October

TOPO MAP *San Jacinto Peak* (7.5-minute), *San Jacinto Wilderness* (Tom Harrison)

■ FEATURES

If you're starting up the Devils Slide Trail some summer weekend, chances are good that you'll hear faint shouts such as "On belay," "Climbing," "Off belay," and sometimes, "Falling." If you glance upward, you may be able to spot tiny, antlike figures clinging to vertical walls, now and then inching ahead with patience and care. These are rock climbers testing their skill on the Yosemite-like dome of Lily Rock. Climbers prefer to call it by the more masculine-sounding name of Tahquitz Rock, but whatever name you use, there is no doubt that this sheer-walled granite monolith offers the best technical climbing in Southern California. Almost every rock climber in this part of the state has, at one time or other, improved his or her skill here.

The front walls of Lily Rock are no place for anyone not trained in climbing techniques. But for hikers who want to climb this striking natural feature, there is an easier route up the back side. This trip follows a very steep trail from Humber Park up and around to a saddle between Lily Rock and the serrated ridge leading to Tahquitz Peak; from here it is a short scramble to the summit. Wear boots with good tread.

■ DESCRIPTION

From the Idyllwild Ranger Station on Highway 243, head northeast on Pine Crest Avenue. In 0.6 mile, veer right onto South Circle Drive. In 0.1 mile, turn left onto

Lily Rock

Fern Valley Road. After 1.7 miles, reach a small parking area for the Ernie Maxwell Scenic Trail (**GPS N33° 45.878' W116° 41.220'**). If you reach the Humber Park parking lot and outhouse, you have gone 0.1 mile too far.

Take the prominent footpath marked ERNIE MAXWELL SCENIC TRAIL that leaves the southeast edge of the parking area and runs directly below Lily Rock. In 0.25 mile, turn left onto a narrow, unmarked trail that leads steeply up the slope toward the rock. The trail zigzags up the hillside, keeping just to the right of the prominent rockslide that extends down from the center of the rock. After 700 feet of climbing, you reach what climbers call Lunch Rock, at the foot of many of the climbing routes. To your right (southeast) notice a worn pathway leading around the bottom of Lily Rock. Follow this trail—used by climbers descending from the rock—around the west face and steeply up the back side to the saddle between Lily Rock and the broken ridge leading up to Tahquitz Peak. From this saddle, scramble up easy granite ledges and slopes to the bald summit (**GPS N33° 45.614' W116° 40.998'**).

After taking in the fabulous view of Strawberry Valley and the high surrounding ridges, descend exactly the same way. Any other route is very dangerous.

■ Hike 74 DESERT DIVIDE ✔ �+ 🎿

HIKE LENGTH 17 miles one-way; 2,800' elevation gain

DIFFICULTY Strenuous (1 day), Moderate (2 days)

SEASON May–October

TOPO MAPS *San Jacinto Peak, Idyllwild, Palm View Peak* (all 7.5-minute), *San Jacinto Wilderness* (Tom Harrison)

PERMIT San Jacinto Wilderness Permit required

This area burned in the 2013 Mountain Fire. As of 2016, the PCT along the Desert Divide remains closed. Check with the Idyllwild Ranger Station at 909-382-2921 to determine if the trail has reopened.

■ FEATURES

South from Red Tahquitz Peak runs an extremely rugged mountain backbone known as the Desert Divide, separating the high basin of Garner Valley from the desert-draining palm canyons to the east. The northern part of this backbone—from Red Tahquitz south to Antsell Rock—contains some of the wildest, most inaccessible mountain terrain in Southern California. Until the Pacific Crest Trail (PCT) was carved through here in 1977, only the crude Sam Fink route penetrated this wall of granite spurs and saddles, brush-choked slopes and forested ledges.

The late Sam Fink, former Santa Ana fire captain whose avocation was mountaineering, was a living legend among Southern California hikers. One of his exploits was to build a trail along this foreboding mountain ridge. In 1967 Fink went up, by himself, with a saw and pruner and spent three days on the ridge, cutting brush and marking a route with red tags. This became known as The Sam Fink Trail and remained a hikers' route until the new stretch of the PCT was cut and blasted through in 1977.

According to the Idyllwild district ranger, this stretch of the PCT over the Desert Divide was the most difficult route to survey and construct in all of Southern California. Parts of it had to literally be carved out of granite walls by tedious drilling and blasting. The job required three years of strenuous effort.

The result is one of the best-engineered trails in California. A broad pathway and gentle switchbacks take the place of the steep, sometimes exposed, tedious scrambling of the old Sam Fink route. This trail trip takes the hiker over the northern, more spectacular section of the footpath, from Tahquitz Valley to the Apache Peak–Spitler Peak saddle.

You can do it in one long, strenuous day or, better, stay the night in Tahquitz or Little Tahquitz Valley and enjoy two days in this premier mountain wilderness country.

■ DESCRIPTION

The trip requires a car shuttle. Drive one car to the Humber Park parking area: From the Idyllwild Ranger Station on Highway 243, head northeast on Pine Crest Avenue. In 0.6 mile, veer right onto South Circle Drive. In 0.1 mile, turn left onto Fern Valley Road. After 1.7 miles, reach a small parking area for the Ernie Maxwell Scenic Trail. Continue 0.1 mile up the hill to the outhouse and larger parking area of Humber Park (**GPS N33° 45.880' W116° 41.143'**). Either park another car or arrange to be picked up at the Spitler Peak Trailhead in Apple Canyon: Head south on Highway 243 to Highway 74; then continue south 3.4 miles to Apple Canyon Road just before mile marker 074 RIV 62.75. Turn left and go 2.6 miles up the paved road to a turnout at the signed Spitler Peak (3E22) Trailhead (**GPS N33° 41.863' W116° 39.150'**). (*Note:* do not continue to the private ranches at road's end.)

From Humber Park, take the Devils Slide Trail to the five-way Saddle Junction (see Hike 66, page 174, for details). Follow the Caramba Trail southeast (second from the right) to the edge of Tahquitz Valley to a second trail junction, then right (south) across Tahquitz Meadow and Creek to Little Tahquitz Valley, 1 mile from Saddle Junction. If you are making this a two-day trip, consider camping in the Tahquitz or Chinquapin Zones. To continue, proceed south up the Little Tahquitz Trail to its junction with the Pacific Crest Trail. Be certain to fill your canteens in Tahquitz Creek; this is the last water until Apache Spring, 8.5 miles south.

Turn left (east) and follow the broad, well-graded PCT as it contours and climbs along the north slope of Red Tahquitz, through an open forest of lodgepole pine and white fir, then abruptly turns south around the east shoulder of the peak. Panoramic views open to the east, down over Andreas and Murray Canyons to the deep trench of Palm Canyon and the desert beyond. Although much of the vegetation here was burned in the 1980 Palm Canyon Fire, it has grown back. Your trail gradually descends southward along the east slope of what is known as the Desert Divide, reaching a saddle between Red Tahquitz and South Peaks, where you pass among the jagged granite crags with alternating views west to Garner Valley and Lake Hemet and east to the desert. The trail then climbs around the east flank of South Peak and drops in long, majestic switchbacks to the precipitous rock ridge north of Antsell Rock. The scenery here is more befitting the Sierra Nevada than Southern California. You pass well below the crags, traverse under the east face of Antsell Rock, and contour through a forest of bigcone Douglas-fir, white fir, and black oak to Apple Canyon Saddle. An old trail drops down Apple Canyon from here to the Zen Center. Staying on the PCT, you climb the open slopes of Apache Peak, traverse around

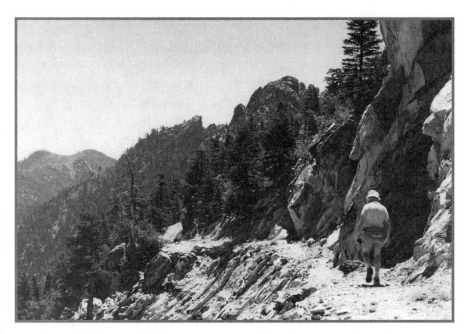

PCT on Desert Divide, looking south to Antsell Rock and Apache Peak

the east flanks a few hundred feet below the bare summit, and reach a junction with the Apache Spring Trail. The spring, which usually has water, is 0.5 mile down to your left (east). Continue south on the PCT down to the saddle between Apache and Spitler Peaks. Here you can leave the PCT and turn west, descending the Spitler Peak Trail to Apple Canyon Road (see Hike 77, page 197, for a full description), where your transportation should be waiting.

An option is to continue south on the PCT to Fobes Saddle, then right, down the Fobes Trail (4E02), to the Fobes Canyon Trailhead (see Hike 79, page 200). This option saves 1 mile compared to the circuitous Spitler Peak Trail.

■ Hike 75 ERNIE MAXWELL SCENIC TRAIL

HIKE LENGTH 2.5 miles one-way; 600' elevation gain

DIFFICULTY Easy

SEASON May–October

TOPO MAPS *Idyllwild, San Jacinto Peak* (both 7.5-minute), *San Jacinto Wilderness* (Tom Harrison)

■ FEATURES

This is an ideal family trip—climbing gently most of the way. The Ernie Maxwell Scenic Trail, named for the late Idyllwild conservationist and former editor of the *Town Crier,* contours along the mountainside above Strawberry Valley from Saunders Meadow to Humber Park. This easygoing footpath lives up to its name, winding through rich stands of pine, fir, and oak, with superb vistas over the densely wooded valley to the granite spurs of Marion Ridge. In spring, wildflowers add a beautiful sprinkling of color. It is a fitting introduction to the Idyllwild country.

■ DESCRIPTION

From Highway 243 on the south edge of Idyllwild next to the Idyllwild School, drive up Saunders Meadow Road for 0.8 mile. Turn left onto Pine Avenue, drive 0.2 mile, and then turn right onto Tahquitz View Drive for 0.5 mile, passing the South Ridge Trail road junction, to the beginning of the ERNIE MAXWELL SCENIC TRAIL, so marked by a small sign to the right of the roads (**GPS N33° 44.415' W116° 42.149'**). Parking is limited to a few wide spots along the road. You finish at Humber Park, so have someone meet you there or employ a car shuttle. To reach Humber Park, return to Highway 243 and turn northeast on North Circle Drive just below the ranger station. Drive 0.7 mile to a four-way intersection; then turn right onto South Circle Drive. Proceed 0.1 mile, and turn left onto Fern Valley Road. After 1.7 miles, reach a small parking area for the Ernie Maxwell Scenic Trail (**GPS N33° 45.878' W116° 41.220'**). If you reach the Humber Park parking lot outhouse, you have gone 0.1 mile too far.

Beautifully forested Ernie Maxwell Trail

Follow the well-built trail as it winds along the slope through beautiful forest. It is mostly level going, with gentle ups and downs here and there. The prominent feature ahead is Lily Rock, which looms more massively as you get nearer. The final 0.5 mile is gentle uphill, with two switchbacks just before reaching Humber Park.

You can do this trail the other way—downhill from Humber Park to Tahquitz View Drive—even more easily.

■ Hike 76 TAHQUITZ PEAK VIA SOUTH RIDGE TRAIL 🐕 🐐 🥾

HIKE LENGTH 7 miles out-and-back; 2,300' elevation gain

DIFFICULTY Moderate

SEASON June–October

TOPO MAPS *Idyllwild, San Jacinto Peak* (both 7.5-minute), *San Jacinto Wilderness* (Tom Harrison)

PERMIT San Jacinto Wilderness Permit required

▓ FEATURES

This trail trip climbs the steep south ridge to Tahquitz Peak, zigzagging up through stands of Jeffrey pine, white fir, and live oak, with chinquapin thickets and lodgepole pine near the top. Various points along the trail offer far-reaching vistas south over the Desert Divide country, and northwest over Strawberry Valley to Marion Mountain and its rocky spurs. Years ago, the route followed an old, steep footpath up from Keen Camp; old-timers would hardly recognize today's well-graded trail.

▓ DESCRIPTION

From Highway 243 on the south edge of Idyllwild next to the Idyllwild School, drive up Saunders Meadow Road for 0.8 mile. Turn left onto Pine Avenue, drive 0.2 mile, and turn right onto Tahquitz View Drive for 0.3 mile. Just before the road becomes dirt, turn right onto South Ridge Road (5S11). Proceed 0.9 mile, passing several minor side roads, to the signed South Ridge Trail (3E08) parking area (**GPS N33° 44.126' W116° 41.761'**).

Follow the trail as it climbs to the ridgecrest, then zigzags up the divide through rich forest. In 1.4 miles, pass a curious "window" in the rock framing a splendid view to the east. Continue through a field of jumbo boulders for 0.3 mile to a flat clearing—this makes a good rest stop at the halfway point. Beyond, you climb steeply on the west face below the rocky ridge. Pass through chinquapin thickets and scattered lodgepoles, between granite gendarmes. The views continue to open up, with Lily Rock and the San Jacinto massif to the north, Suicide Rock and the San Gabriel Mountains to the northwest, Idyllwild and Santiago Peak to the west, and the Garner Valley, Desert Divide, and Toro Peak to the south. Just below the summit, reach a trail junction with the trail from Devils Slide. Turn right

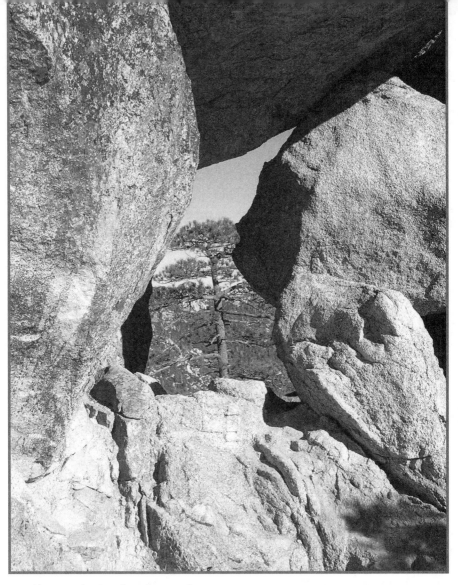

Window on the South Ridge Trail

and walk a short distance to the summit lookout, 3.6 miles from the start (**GPS N33° 45.327' W116° 40.614'**).

After taking in the fabulous panorama over the southern half of the San Jacintos, descend the way you came. An option, with car shuttle, is to descend the Pacific Crest Trail north to Saddle Junction, then go down the Devils Slide Trail to Humber Park (see Hike 72, page 187).

■ Hike 77 ANTSELL ROCK 🥾 🧍

HIKE LENGTH 15 miles out-and-back; 4,000' elevation gain

DIFFICULTY Strenuous

SEASON All year

TOPO MAPS *Idyllwild, Palm View Peak* (both 7.5-minute), *San Jacinto Wilderness* (Tom Harrison)

PERMIT San Jacinto Wilderness Permit required

This area burned in the 2013 Mountain Fire. As of 2016, the trail remains closed. Check with the Idyllwild Ranger Station at 909-382-2921 to determine if the trail has reopened.

■ FEATURES

At 7,679 feet, Antsell Rock is the crowning feature of the Desert Divide. Its impos-ing knob of multicolored rock can be seen from almost anywhere in Garner Valley. Antsell Rock is one of the very few peaks in the San Jacintos whose ascent involves more than a plodding walk up. Its nearly vertical upper ramparts give you a taste of the alpinist's exhilaration. It's what climbers call a "fun peak."

The peak was named by USGS topographer Edmund Perkins in 1897–98. The story goes that Perkins ran across an artist painting mountain scenes at Keen Camp, an early-day resort just east of Mountain Center. The artist's name was Antsell and the mountain he was painting was this imposing rock knob, so Perkins labeled the knob "Antsell Rock" on his survey map.

The climb is not particularly difficult for those in good physical condition who have had experience on Class 3 rock. Boots with deep tread for traction on rock are recommended. Take extra care on the descent, for that is when most acci-dents occur.

The Desert Divide has made a remarkable recovery from the great Palm Canyon Fire of 1980, which burned right up Andreas and Murray Canyons to the crest. The chaparral has grown back as green as ever, and only a few blackened tree trunks remind you of the former devastation.

■ DESCRIPTION

Drive south on Highway 74 for 3.4 miles from Mountain Center to Apple Can-yon Road just before mile marker 074 RIV 62.75. Turn left and go 2.6 miles up the paved road to a turnout at the signed Spitler Peak (3E22) Trailhead (**GPS N33° 41.863' W116° 39.150'**). (*Note:* do not continue to the private ranches at road's end.)

Follow the rerouted trail east, through oak and high chaparral, then northeast up the rock-ribbed slopes of Apple Canyon's east fork. You pass through open groves of Jeffrey and Coulter pine and the ubiquitous live oak as you climb steadily to the Apache Peak–Spitler Peak saddle on the Desert Divide and a junction with the Pacific Crest Trail (PCT), 4.6 miles.

Turn left (north) and follow the PCT up and around the east and north flanks of bare Apache Peak, passing a side trail that drops down the desert slope to Apache Spring, and then down 200 vertical feet to Apple Canyon saddle. (The old trail down Apple Canyon joins the PCT here.) Continue north on the PCT through a forest of black oak, white fir, and Jeffrey pine until it traverses the slope almost directly underneath and east of Antsell Rock. Here you must look carefully for a small duck and a climber's rough path leading steeply up the gully to your left. Leave the PCT and follow this route up unstable slopes to the top of the divide immediately southeast of Antsell Rock's summit block. The final 100 feet to the top is Class 3 and recommended only for those comfortable with heights. To continue, scramble to the top of the large rock outcropping to your right; then step across and friction-climb the sloping granite to a steep, narrow gully. Follow the gully to the summit ridge, and on to the summit (**GPS N33° 43.812' W116° 38.484'**). Some may desire a rope belay on these final pitches. Return the same way.

Antsell Rock

■ Hike 78 APACHE PEAK 🥾 🐕 🏃

HIKE LENGTH 11 miles out-and-back; 2,600' elevation gain

DIFFICULTY Moderate

SEASON All year

TOPO MAPS *Idyllwild, Palm View Peak* (both 7.5-minute), *San Jacinto Wilderness*
(Tom Harrison)

PERMIT San Jacinto Wilderness Permit required

This area burned in the 2013 Mountain Fire. As of 2016, the trail remains closed. Check with the Idyllwild Ranger Station at 909-382-2921 to determine if the trail has reopened.

■ FEATURES

This trip climbs Apache Peak (7,567 feet) for a superb vista over the southern end of the San Jacintos and the desert canyons, then drops over the desert side to secluded Apache Spring. You follow the rerouted Spitler Peak Trail to the Desert Divide, then ascend the Pacific Crest Trail (PCT) to the southeast slope of Apache Peak. Steep but clearly discernible lateral trails take you first up to the summit of Apache Peak and then down to Apache Spring.

■ DESCRIPTION

Drive south on Highway 74 for 3.4 miles from Mountain Center to Apple Canyon Road just before mile marker 074 RIV 62.75. Turn left and go 2.6 miles up the paved road to a turnout at the signed Spitler Peak Trailhead (**GPS N33° 41.863' W116° 39.150'**). (*Note:* do not continue to the private ranches at road's end.)

Take the Spitler Peak Trail (3E22) from lower Apple Canyon up to the Desert Divide and a junction with the PCT (see the previous hike for details). Turn left (north) and follow the PCT up to an unmarked but clearly discernible trail junction, 0.75 mile. Here you leave the PCT and scramble up a steep, rocky path to the bare summit of Apache Peak and its far-reaching vistas, 0.25 mile (**GPS N33° 43.120' W116° 37.618'**). Return the same way to the PCT. If you wish to camp, consider taking the lateral trail leading east and then northeast 500 vertical feet down the desert slope to Apache Spring. The little wooded spring always flows cold and clear, although in dry months it dwindles to a trickle.

■ Hike 79 PALM VIEW PEAK 🡕 🐕 🥾

HIKE LENGTH 8 miles out-and-back; 2,100' elevation gain
DIFFICULTY Moderate
SEASON All year
TOPO MAP *Palm View Peak* (7.5-minute)

▥ FEATURES

South from Apache Peak, the Desert Divide gradually descends and loses its rugged character. The Pacific Crest Trail (PCT) follows along the crest of the long backbone, a hiker's avenue through waist-high chaparral and occasional clusters of fir and oak, with far-reaching views in all directions.

The Desert Divide country, particularly the southern half, is not well known to hikers. But it offers great opportunities for hiking trips, particularly in the fall–winter–spring season, when the high country to the north is closed by snow. Sample it sometime; you won't be disappointed.

This trip accesses the PCT along the Desert Divide from Fobes Canyon. The trail (4E02) lies just east of the Fobes Ranch boundary and offers easy access to Fobes Saddle, a low gap on the long Desert Divide. From the saddle, you climb southeast on the view-rich PCT to Palm View Peak. The panoramas are magnificent in all directions—the tawny Coachella Valley to the east, Garner and Anza Valleys to the west, and on the northern skyline the San Jacinto high country, covered by its snowy mantle through spring.

■ DESCRIPTION

From Highway 74, 6.8 miles southeast of Mountain Center and just past mile marker 074 RIV 66.00, turn left (northeast) onto the fair dirt Fobes Ranch Road (6S05). Stay left at a fork in 0.4 mile; then follow it across the Garner Valley for 3.2 miles to another junction. The main road goes north to Fobes Ranch (private); you turn right and proceed 0.4 mile to the signed Fobes Trailhead (**GPS N33° 40.766' W116° 36.849'**). Parking is limited to three or four vehicles; you may have to park a short distance below the trailhead.

Proceed up the gently graded Fobes Trail (4E02), through chaparral and, higher up, through a small open grove of Jeffrey pines to a junction with the PCT at Fobes Saddle, 1.5 miles. Turn right (southeast) and follow the PCT as it climbs to a grassy bench, 2 miles from the low saddle. Halfway across the grassy area, veer left, off trail, through a grove of black oak and white fir, to the hidden summit of Palm View Peak (7,162 feet; **GPS N33° 40.749' W116° 35.448'**). (The peak is misnamed—there are no palms nearby and the view from the wooded top is nonexistent.)

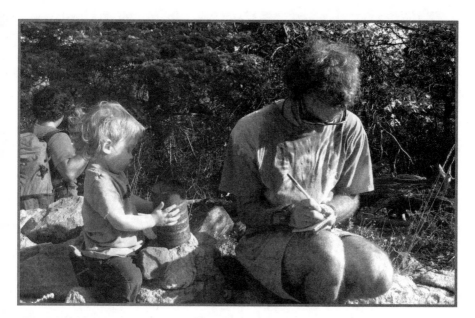

Signing the summit register on Palm View Peak

Return the same way. Or, you have several options. If your desire is to bag more peaks, you can follow the PCT north from Fobes Saddle and scramble to the summit of Spitler Peak (7,440 feet) and/or Apache Peak (7,567 feet), adding 4 and 6 miles respectively to the round-trip. With a car shuttle, you can descend via the Spitler Peak Trail to Apple Canyon (see previous hike) or the Morris Trail to Morris Ranch Road. Any way you do it, you're bound to enjoy this sample of the scenic Desert Divide country.

■ Hike 80 CEDAR SPRING 🡕 🐕 🚶

HIKE LENGTH 6 miles out-and-back; 1,700' elevation gain

DIFFICULTY Moderate

SEASON All year

TOPO MAPS *Palm View Peak, Butterfly Peak* (both 7.5-minute)

This area burned in the 2013 Mountain Fire. As of 2016, the Cedar Springs Trail remains closed east of the Pacific Crest Trail. Check with the Idyllwild Ranger Station at 909-382-2921 to determine if the trail has reopened.

■ FEATURES

On both sides of the Desert Divide are a number of little springs trickling cold water. Cedar Spring, on the desert slope of the ridge, shaded by incense-cedars and

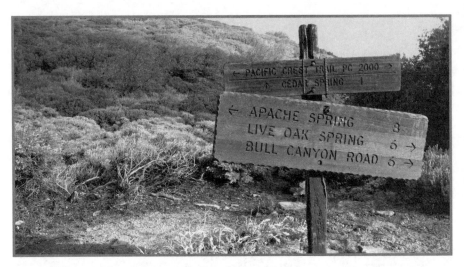

Pacific Crest Trail junction on the Desert Divide

black oaks, is one of the nicest of these water sources. Just below the spring, in a shaded recess, is a small campsite much favored by hunters and Boy Scout groups.

This short trail trip climbs over the Desert Divide from Morris Ranch Road and drops into this little sylvan sanctuary with its ribbon of running water. It's best as a spring trip, when the water flows abundantly and the hillside is damp from spring rains.

■ DESCRIPTION

From Highway 74, 8.6 miles south of Mountain Center in the Garner Valley and just beyond mile marker 074 RIV 67.75, turn left (northeast) onto the paved Morris Ranch Road (6S53). Follow it up 3.7 miles, passing Camp Scherman Girl Scout camp, to the signed Cedar Springs Trailhead (4E17) on the right (**GPS N33° 39.251' W116° 35.373'**). (If you reach Morris Ranch, you've driven 0.25 mile too far.)

Proceed on foot up the trail to an oak-dotted valley, 0.5 mile. At the head of the miniature valley, pick up a trail that switchbacks up the chaparral-coated slope to a saddle on the Desert Divide, 2.3 miles. Here is a four-way junction. Go northeast on a trail marked CEDAR SPRING and drop down the desert-facing slope 0.9 mile through chaparral to Cedar Spring, located in a forested crease in the mountainside. There is an unimproved campsite 100 feet below the spring, on a small shaded bench (**GPS N33° 40.606' W116° 34.686'**).

Return the same way. Or, from the four-way trail junction, follow the Pacific Crest Trail north to Palm View Peak and on to the Fobes Canyon Trailhead (see previous hike), adding 3 miles to the trip and requiring a car shuttle.

■ Hike 81 THOMAS MOUNTAIN ↗ 🐕 ◉ 🚶

HIKE LENGTH 12 miles out-and-back; 2,400' elevation gain
DIFFICULTY Moderate
SEASON All year
TOPO MAP *Anza* (7.5-minute)

■ FEATURES

The Ramona Trail climbs from Garner Valley over Thomas Mountain and down to the Ramona Indian Reservation, named, of course, after the beautiful Native American girl in Helen Hunt Jackson's famous novel. This trip takes the Ramona Trail to the crest of the divide, then follows the Thomas Mountain fire road northwest to the summit. En route you climb slopes dense with chaparral (mainly red shank) and reach into Jeffrey pine forest that covers the crown of the mountain, passing little Tool Box Spring and its primitive trail camp. There is usually water here year-round.

■ DESCRIPTION

From Highway 74 in Garner Valley 8.1 miles south of Mountain Center just beyond mile marker 074 RIV 67.25, turn into the Ramona Trail parking area (**GPS N33° 37.261' W116° 38.049'**).

Garner Valley and the Desert Divide from the Ramona Trail

Follow the well-marked trail (3E26) as it switchbacks and climbs the chaparral-coated mountainside. As you climb higher, fine views open up over the Garner Valley, with the San Jacintos and Desert Divide country beyond. After 1.5 miles, you begin encountering Jeffrey pines, a welcome change from the shadeless red shank, manzanita, and mountain mahogany. In 2 miles your trail enters the forest and, a short distance higher, reaches Tool Box Spring and its welcome water seeping from the tank and the protruding pipe. From the spring, continue up the trail to Tool Box Spring Campground, 3.5 miles from the highway. When you reach the crest of Thomas Mountain's long hogback, turn right onto Forest Road 6S13 and follow it northwest to primitive Thomas Mountain Campground and the summit, 6 miles from the start (**GPS N33° 37.178' W116° 40.871'**).

Return the same way. Or you could have someone drive up Thomas Mountain Road (reached from Highway 74, 1 mile south of the Lake Hemet turnoff) to meet you on top. Another option is to descend the other half of the Ramona Trail southwest to the Indian reservation. Obtain permission before doing this.

■ Hike 82 CAHUILLA MOUNTAIN 🏃 🐕 🚶

HIKE LENGTH 6 miles out-and-back; 1,400' elevation gain

DIFFICULTY Moderate

SEASON November–June

TOPO MAP *Cahuilla Mountain* (7.5-minute)

■ FEATURES

Cahuilla Mountain, its stony battlements facing southward, rises in lonely isolation above Cahuilla Valley, 10 miles southwest of the San Jacintos proper. The mountain is seldom visited nowadays, yet it is the setting for the climax of one of the most famous novels of early-day California. The novel, of course, is Helen Hunt Jackson's *Ramona*, published in 1884.

Jackson's book is based on actual people and events. High on the mountain, on a small flat between the summits of Cahuilla and Little Cahuilla, once lived Juan Diego, his wife, Ramona Lubo, and their small child. Juan Diego, a mountain Cahuilla who often did odd jobs for nearby white settlers, had fashioned a small cabin, a garden, and a few fruit trees alongside a spring here. He was known to those in the valley as friendly but *loco*, with occasional mental lapses that caused him to do erratic things.

One day he returned home from sheep shearing in the San Jacinto Valley riding a strange horse. His wife, afraid he would be accused of stealing the horse,

Sunset from Cahuilla Mountain

urged him to return it at once and get his own, which he had apparently left in the valley. Juan replied that he would, as soon as he had rested, and then he fell asleep. Awakened a short time later by the barking of dogs, he ran out to see what was causing the noise. A white man, Sam Temple, the owner of the horse that Juan had ridden home, rode up, and on seeing Juan poured out a volley of oaths, leveled his gun and shot him to death. After firing three more shots into the prostrate body, Temple took his horse and rode away. Ramona, who had witnessed the killing, ran with her baby on her back to the Cahuilla village and told what had happened. The next day the Cahuilla went up to the flat, brought Juan Diego's body to the village, and buried it. Sam Temple was later tried for murder in the court of Judge Samuel V. Tripp and acquitted.

Here the story would have ended, soon forgotten, if Helen Hunt Jackson had not heard of it. Jackson was concerned with the plight of Native Americans in the United States. In 1881 she had written *A Century of Dishonor,* a factual chronicle of white settlers' cruelty to Native Americans, but this book had not really stirred the public conscience. Now, in 1883, she was investigating Native American conditions in California for the federal government, and in the back of her mind was an idea for a novel to dramatize the sad situation. In the course of her work, Jackson came to San Jacinto and learned of the tragic killing of Juan Diego. Here at last was the long-looked-for episode around which she could crystallize the experiences and facts she had picked up in her studies. *Ramona* was conceived.

In the novel, the character Alessandro is patterned after Juan Diego. Jim Farrar is Sam Temple. (However, the beautiful Ramona of Jackson's pen is in no way similar to Juan Diego's wife, Ramona Lubo.) Although many of the episodes are pure fiction, the tragic climax in which Farrar shoots down Alessandro with Ramona looking on is very close to what actually happened.

Ramona was an overnight success, and it achieved astounding popularity that has lasted to this day. The spotlight of public attention turned to the Cahuillas, and travelers came by the wagon load into the Cahuilla Valley, some journeying up to lonely Juan Diego Flat, others seeking out Ramona Lubo. The plight of the Cahuillas, brought in sharp focus by *Ramona*, was lessened as the federal government stepped in to take a more active role in achieving justice for Native Americans.

Ramona Lubo died in 1922 and was buried beside her husband, Juan Diego, in the old Cahuilla cemetery that lies in the shadow of Cahuilla Mountain. Juan Diego Flat has been almost forgotten and sees few visitors nowadays. The access road, a small section of which crosses private property, is now open to the public.

This trip relives these stirring events of the past as it visits Juan Diego Flat and climbs to the top of Cahuilla Mountain for a breathtaking view over the country of Ramona and the Cahuillas.

■ DESCRIPTION

West of the town of Anza on Highway 371 near mile marker 371 RIV 68.0 at the sign for Cahuilla Mountain Trail (2E45), turn right (north) onto Cary Road. Cary Road eventually changes name to Tripp Flats Road. At a signed junction in 3.6 miles, turn left onto the dirt Forest Road 6S22. Drive up to Juan Diego Flat, 2.4 miles, to the beginning of the Cahuilla Mountain Trail (2E45), on your left, close to phone lines overhead (**GPS N33° 35.783' W116° 46.823'**). A sign on your left indicates the trailhead. Park in the small clearing on your right.

Follow the distinct, well-graded trail up the northeast slope of the mountain, through an elfin forest of ribbonwood, chamise, manzanita, scrub oak, and mountain mahogany. The trail then crosses to the west side of the mountain and undulates through a lovely open forest of black oak and Coulter pine on the summit ridge. The trail ends at the 5,635-foot high point of Cahuilla Mountain (**GPS N33° 34.427' W116° 46.968'**). Half a mile before the summit, a sign indicates a side trail leading 0.1 mile down a steep gully to a seasonal spring.

After enjoying the superb vista east over the Anza Valley—the route taken by the great pathfinder Juan Bautista de Anza two centuries ago, and the long hogback of Palomar Mountain to the southwest—return the way you came.

■ Hike 83 LONG, ROUND, AND TAMARACK VALLEYS 🡕 👫 🎒

HIKE LENGTH 5 miles out-and-back; 800' elevation gain

DIFFICULTY Easy

SEASON May–October

TOPO MAP *San Jacinto Peak* (7.5-minute), *San Jacinto Wilderness* (Tom Harrison)

PERMIT San Jacinto Wilderness Permit required

■ FEATURES

From lower Chino Canyon, just above Palm Springs, the spectacular Palm Springs Aerial Tramway hauls visitors from palms to pines in a few short minutes. For hikers, this is the easy way to enter Mount San Jacinto State Park. From 8,516-foot Mountain Station, the tramway's upper terminus, trails lead into the heart of the high wilderness.

This pleasant trip takes a wooded trail through upper Long Valley to the beautiful, though overused, green oasis of Round Valley. You can enjoy a picnic lunch along the crystal stream in Round Valley or under the tamarack (really lodgepole pines) in Tamarack Valley.

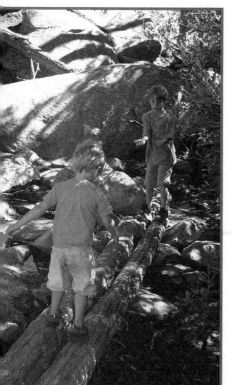

Kid-friendly creek crossing

■ DESCRIPTION

From Highway 111, 8.5 miles south of Interstate 10 at the northern edge of Palm Springs, turn west up Tramway Road and drive 2 miles to Valley Station, the lower terminus of the tramway (**GPS N33° 50.232' W116° 36.834'**). The tramway operates daily, starting at 10 a.m. Monday–Friday and 8 a.m. Saturday, Sunday, and holidays. At the time this guide was written, the last return is 9:45 p.m. Ride the tramway to Mountain Station, the upper terminus just above Long Valley. Round-trip tickets are $24.95. Visit pstramway.com or call 888-515-TRAM for more information.

From Mountain Station, proceed down the cement walkway into the Long Valley picnic area; then take the trail leading west, next to the ranger station, marked ROUND VALLEY 2 MILES. Follow the well-graded footpath as it leads up Long Valley Creek, through a rich forest of sugar pine and white fir. After a mile the trail veers left (southwest) and climbs into a lodgepole forest. In another 0.75 mile, you reach a trail cutting back east toward the Willow Creek Trail (see Hike 69, page 181); this trip continues west 0.25 mile to Round Valley. Here is a well-used campground and a three-way trail junction. Turn right (north); the sign indicates TAMARACK VALLEY. You pass the trail camp and wind through a lodgepole forest to the grassy clearing of Tamarack Valley and its small trail camp, 0.5 mile (**GPS N33° 48.559' W116° 39.622'**). Across the valley, dominating the skyline, is the needlelike summit of Cornell Peak (named for Cornell University of Ithaca, New York, alma mater of Robert T. Hill, geologist for the USGS mapping party of 1897–98). Only experienced mountaineers should attempt this peak.

Return the way you came.

■ Hike 84 SAN JACINTO PEAK FROM THE TRAMWAY

HIKE LENGTH 10 miles out-and-back; 2,600' elevation gain

DIFFICULTY Moderate

SEASON June–October

TOPO MAP *San Jacinto Peak* (7.5-minute), *San Jacinto Wilderness* (Tom Harrison)

PERMIT San Jacinto Wilderness Permit required

■ FEATURES

The Palm Springs Aerial Tramway gives the hiker an 8000-foot head start on this desert-side route to San Jacinto Peak. This route climbs through some of the most verdant and inviting high country in the range—all on good, well-marked trail. You visit lush Round Valley, then ascend granite slopes dotted with lodgepole pines to the summit with the best view in southern California.

■ DESCRIPTION

From State Highway 111, 8.5 miles south of Interstate 10 at the northern edge of Palm Springs, turn west up Tramway Road and drive 2 miles to Valley Station,

View of Palm Springs from the Aerial Tramway observation deck
PHOTO: LARRY B. VAN DYKE

the lower terminus of the tramway (**GPS N33° 50.232' W116° 36.834'**). The tramway operates daily, starting at 10 a.m. Monday–Friday; 8 a.m. Saturday, Sunday, and holidays. At the time this guide was written, last return is 9:45 p.m. Ride the tramway to Mountain Station, the upper terminus just above Long Valley. Round-trip tickets are $24.95. Visit pstramway.com or call 888-515-TRAM for more information.

From Mountain Station, proceed to Round Valley, 2 miles (see previous hike for details). From Round Valley, your last dependable water, ascend the trail west—the sign indicates SAN JACINTO PEAK. You climb steadily through an open lodgepole forest to a junction with the Saddle Junction–San Jacinto Peak Trail, 1 mile. Turn right (north) and follow the well-used trail through the silent lodgepoles, then up a long switchback through dense manzanita and chinquapin, to the south ridge of San Jacinto Peak. Here you intersect the summit trail. Go right (north) and climb past the stone shelter building to the top, 300 yards (**GPS N33° 48.881' W116° 40.764'**).

Return the same way.

■ Hike 85 LYKKEN LOOP ⟲

HIKE LENGTH 3.3-mile loop; 1,000' elevation gain

DIFFICULTY Moderate

SEASON October–May

TOPO MAPS *Palm Springs* (7.5-minute), *Santa Rosa and San Jacinto Mountains National Monument*

■ FEATURES

The Lykken Trail is named after Carl Lykken, Palm Springs's first postmaster. This trip leaves the western boundary of Palm Springs and heads up the east flank of the San Jacinto Mountains. It features a 180-degree view from north to south. All of Palm Springs is laid out before you. To the north and across the Coachella Valley, you can see the Little San Bernardino Mountains and the south end of Joshua Tree National Park. To the east you can see Palm Springs and the airport. You can watch airplanes take off and fly beneath you! To the southeast you see other cities of the Coachella Valley: Cathedral City, Rancho Mirage, and Palm Desert. To the south you see the Indian Canyons and Palm Canyon almost to its beginnings.

An added benefit at the end of the trip is that you can walk a few blocks to Palm Canyon Drive and have a bite to eat and something to drink at one of the outdoor restaurants.

■ DESCRIPTION

Take Interstate 10 east over San Gorgonio Pass to Highway 111. Follow the highway south toward Palm Springs for 11.1 miles to Tahquitz Canyon Way. Make a right, go 0.2 mile, and turn right onto Museum Drive.

The easiest way to do this trip is to start early in the morning and park on the street across from the Palm Springs Art Museum (**GPS N33° 49.515' W116° 33.032'**).

Walk south to Tahquitz Canyon Way, and then jog left to Cahuilla Road and continue south to its end at Ramon Road (0.6 mile). There is also limited public parking along Cahuilla Road. Turn right (west) and hike along Ramon Road for 0.4 mile to its end and the trailhead. There is no parking here, but there is limited public parking on Camino Calidad for those who want to hike up the Lykken Trail and then return the same way.

Walk up the dirt road/trail for 50 yards to a fork. Turn left onto the Lykken Trail, which immediately makes steep switchbacks up the slope. The trail is well traveled and marked with white dots periodically painted on the rocks to help night hikers. Lizards scurry to and fro, and you may startle a jackrabbit. Follow the trail up the ridges and then along the east flank of the San Jacinto Mountains enjoying the spectacular views. The trail passes through a field of barrel cactus. At a large cairn in 1.3 miles, turn right and drop to the picnic area. Stop to take in the views and have a snack if you brought one.

From the picnic tables, head east and switchback down the steep trail to the museum. At one point, the trail goes uphill for 50 yards to bypass a rocky drop. Near the bottom, cross a paved driveway and come out at the signed trailhead at the northwest corner of the museum parking lot.

An arduous trail climbs from the cairn upward to Long Valley at the top of the Aerial Tramway and to the peak of San Jacinto (see next hike).

■ Hike 86 SAN JACINTO VIA SKYLINE TRAIL 🏃🚶

HIKE LENGTH 20 miles one-way; 10,700' elevation gain

DIFFICULTY Very Strenuous

SEASON October–November

TOPO MAPS *San Jacinto Peak, Palm Springs* (7.5-minute), *Santa Rosa and San Jacinto Mountains National Monument*

PERMIT San Jacinto Wilderness Permit required

■ FEATURES

After the San Gorgonio massif, San Jacinto is the second tallest peak overlooking the Los Angeles Basin. This hike offers the greatest continuous elevation gain of any trail in the United States. It starts near sea level in Palm Springs and ends on the summit of San Jacinto. It is one of the test pieces for serious Southern California day hikers.

The Skyline Trail is not on most maps and is not officially maintained, but it's in good condition and generally easy to follow unless covered in ice. The trail begins behind the Palm Springs Art Museum and switchbacks up the ridge south of Chino Canyon to Long Valley near the Palm Springs Aerial Tramway, gaining 8,000 feet. In Long Valley, it joins Hike 84 to the summit of San Jacinto. Most hikers descend the tramway and take a taxi or car shuttle back to the trailhead.

The Skyline Trail was originally a Native American footpath. It was improved by the Civilian Conservation Corps (CCC) in the 1930s. The middle portion became overgrown with brush, but has been restored to good condition and now sees a good deal of foot traffic.

Upper reaches of the Skyline Trail. Note Coffman's Crag just right of center—the trail stays left of the crag.

The trip is best done in late fall. Even in October, daytime temperatures in Palm Springs can exceed 100°. Most of the trail is exposed to the sun. Start before dawn and carry at least 5 quarts of water. Wear sunscreen and a suitable hat. Bring salty food to restore your electrolytes. Watch for rattlesnakes, and don't get snagged by cactus. In winter and spring, the upper gully is icy and requires an ice axe and crampons.

Three other routes on the desert faces of San Jacinto are of historical interest: Tahquitz Creek, the Gordon Trail, and Snow Creek.

The Tahquitz Creek route climbs from Palm Springs up the extremely rugged gorge of Tahquitz Creek 6,000 feet to Caramba Camp. It requires technical climbing around waterfalls and nasty bushwhacking. The lower canyon is on the Agua Caliente Indian reservation and is now closed to public access.

The Gordon Trail is another ancient Cahuilla footpath, improved by Dr. M. S. Gordon of Palm Springs in 1915–16 and the CCC in the 1930s. It has not been touched since and has disappeared beneath dense brush. It climbed from the mouth of Andreas Canon northwest up and over the ridge to Caramba Camp.

Snow Creek ascends the great north face of San Jacinto. It starts in the town of Snow Creek and ascends the creek canyon directly to the summit of San Jacinto. The route involves Class 4 climbing around waterfalls and a huge chockstone in the canyon. The canyon is ravaged by avalanches after each snowstorm and accumulates a deep pack of snow. When the snow in the upper canyon is well consolidated, typically in April, the last 6,000 feet are the longest snow couloir climb in Southern California. Unfortunately, the lower portion of the creek is on land owned by the Desert Water Agency, which has ceased issuing permits. Unless their policy changes, legal access requires a circuitous detour around their land.

■ DESCRIPTION

Take Interstate 10 east over San Gorgonio Pass to Highway 111. Follow the highway south toward Palm Springs. After 8.5 miles, you will pass Tramway Road on the right, leading 4 miles west to the Palm Springs Aerial Tramway, where you may wish to leave a car (**GPS N33° 50.232' W116° 36.834'**). At the time this guide was written, the last ride down from Mountain Station is 9:45 p.m. Visit pstramway.com or call 888-515-TRAM for more information.

Continue south on Highway 111 for 2.6 miles to Tahquitz Canyon Way. Make a right, go 0.2 mile, and turn right onto Museum Drive, where you can park across from the Palm Springs Art Museum.

If you intend to drive to Palm Springs the previous night and get an early start, several inexpensive motels and a wide range of dining options are located on Palm Canyon Drive near the trailhead.

The Skyline Trail (signed Museum Trail) starts in the northwest corner of the museum's north parking lot at 480 feet (**GPS N33° 49.515' W116° 33.032'**). It switchbacks steeply up the hill and is clearly marked with white paint dots. After 1 mile, you will pass a four-way trail junction; continue upward (west) for 8.4 more miles. Although it is not shown on maps, the trail is in good condition and is easy to follow. The Skyline Trail picks up the top of the shallow ridge between Tahquitz and Tachevah Canyons and follows this ridge through multiple desert ecosystems to a forested area and up a gully between a prominent rock outcropping on the left and Coffman's Crag on the right before topping out in Long Valley at 8,400 feet.

You have just climbed 8,000 arduous feet. You can enjoy the shade and then walk over to the tram station and ride the tram down. If you have robust knees, you can retrace your steps back down the Skyline Trail. Or if time and energy allow, get a wilderness permit at the ranger station and top off water bottles. Then follow Hike 84 to the summit (**GPS N33° 48.881' W116° 40.764'**). After enjoying the view, return to Long Valley.

■ Hike 87 MURRAY CANYON ↗ 🏃

HIKE LENGTH 4 miles out-and-back; 500' elevation gain

DIFFICULTY Easy

SEASON October–April

TOPO MAPS *Santa Rosa and San Jacinto Mountains National Monument*

PERMIT Indian Canyons admission

■ FEATURES

With its palm oasis, pools, and waterfall, Murray Canyon is a justifiably popular hike in the Indian Canyons. Named for Scottish rancher Welwood Murray who established the Palm Springs Hotel in 1887 and popularized the winter resort, the canyon has been home for centuries to the Cahuilla people. The hike is best in winter and spring when the days are mild and the creek runs clear. The trail crosses the creek repeatedly, so a trekking pole is helpful and this hike is not recommended for those with poor balance.

■ DESCRIPTION

From Interstate 10, take Highway 111 south into Palm Springs. The name changes to North Palm Canyon Drive. After passing through downtown, the road forks. Stay right as it becomes South Palm Canyon Drive. Continue to the toll gate at the entrance to the canyon, 15.2 miles from the interstate. At the time of this writing, the canyon is open from 8 a.m. to 5 p.m. From July 8 to October 1, it is open only Friday–Sunday. After paying the entrance fee, immediately turn right and follow Andreas Canyon Road 0.8 mile to the Andreas Canyon picnic area. Turn left, cross a bridge, pass the Bent Palm Picnic Area, and park at the Murray Canyon Trailhead in 0.2 mile (**GPS N33° 45.573' W116° 32.860'**).

The trail leads south across the desert at the base of a ridge. In 0.2 mile, pass the Andreas Canyon South Trail on the left. Continue 0.5 mile, switchbacking down to cross Murray Creek at a palm oasis. On the far side, watch for the West Fork North Trail on the left. Reach the mouth of Murray Canyon in another 0.3 mile.

Follow the trail up the canyon, crisscrossing the creek. In 0.4 mile, the Hoffman Trail forks left. The last half mile of the trail is the most rugged, with steep climbs and slippery rock. The trail ends at the Seven Sisters, a series of stone pools with a 12-foot waterfall (**GPS N33° 44.648' W116° 33.132'**).

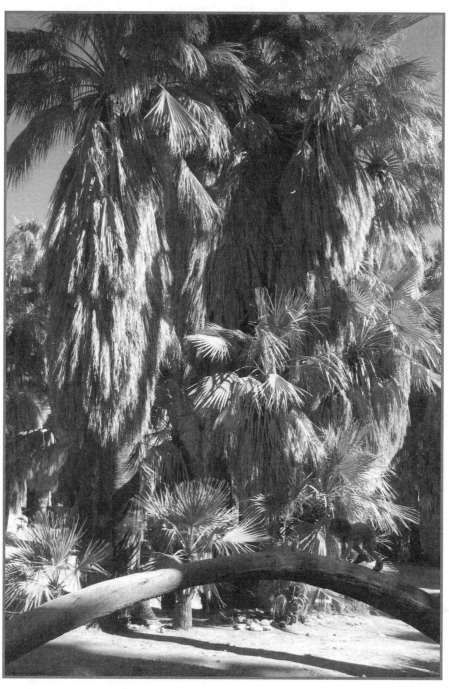

Murray Canyon Trailhead

■ Hike 88 LOWER PALM CANYON ↗ 🚶

HIKE LENGTH 4.5 miles out-and-back; 600' elevation gain

DIFFICULTY Easy

SEASON October–April

TOPO MAPS *Palm View Peak* (7.5-minute), *Santa Rosa and San Jacinto Mountains National Monument*

PERMIT Indian Canyons admission

■ FEATURES

The splendid palm canyons at the desert foot of the San Jacintos and Santa Rosas are a delight to behold. Thousands of California fan palms (*Washingtonia filifera*), their bright green fronds swaying in the breeze, crowd the canyon bottoms, seeking the life-giving water that tumbles down all-year streams. Rushes and other verdant water plants grow dense alongside limpid pools, completing the oasis effect that is all the more striking because the adjacent slopes are bone-dry and drab.

The daddy of all these green oasis canyons is Palm Canyon, running almost due south from Palm Springs to the Palms to Pines Scenic Byway. Somewhere around 3,000 California fan palms grace the lower half of this canyon, extending from just below Hermits Bench almost to Palm Canyon Falls, a distance of 7 miles. Other groves of these palms extend short distances up many of the lower tributaries of Palm Canyon—Andreas Canyon, Murray Canyon, Fern Canyon, and the West and East Forks of Palm Canyon.

For centuries before settlers arrived, the Cahuillas lived in these beautiful canyons. Relics of Native American habitation are still found along the banks and up the dry slopes—grinding holes, stone tools, faint traces of red pictographs. Today, most of Lower Palm Canyon is the property of the Agua Caliente band of Mission Indians. Funds derived from the admission charges collected from visitors at the entrance gate go to maintain the canyons.

This trip follows a well-traveled trail that leads up Palm Canyon from the roadhead on Hermits Bench. It is a streamside walk through lush greenery, with arid canyon walls close on both sides. You have the option of extending the trip by wandering up some of the palm-filled tributary canyons. Do it in leisurely fashion to fully appreciate nature's unique contribution to the desert side of the mountains.

■ DESCRIPTION

From Interstate 10, take Highway 111 south into Palm Springs. The name changes to North Palm Canyon Drive. After passing through downtown, the road forks.

Stay right as it becomes South Palm Canyon Drive. Continue to the toll gate at the entrance to the canyon, 15.2 miles from the interstate. At the time of this writing, the canyon is open from 8 a.m. to 5 p.m. From July 8 to October 1, it is open only Friday–Sunday. Call 760-323-6018 for current information. After paying the entrance fee, proceed south 2.5 miles to the Trading Post at the end of the road on Hermits Bench (**GPS N33° 44.284' W116° 32.305'**).

Walk along the trail that drops into the canyon, then winds through the California fan palms, along the stream, up-canyon for 2.2 miles. Beyond here, the trail follows the east slope before dropping back into the canyon farther up (see Hike 91, page 221). But you stop at the junction with the Indian Potrero Trail (**GPS N33° 42.873' W116° 31.675'**) and saunter back down-canyon to Hermits Bench.

For a change of scenery on the way back, consider veering off to the right onto the Victor Trail at a signed junction 1 mile south of Hermits Bench. Follow the Victor Trail up the ridge along the east side of Palm Canyon for a beautiful overlook of the oasis. The trail drops down to join the Fern Canyon Trail. Turn left (west) and hike 0.1 mile back to Hermits Bench.

If you wish to explore these beautiful palm canyons and oases further, other trails lead up Fern Canyon, east from Hermits Bench, and up the East Fork, east

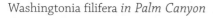

Washingtonia filifera *in Palm Canyon*

from Palm Canyon 0.5 mile south of Hermits Bench. Or you can drive over to Andreas Canyon on your way out and explore the palm greenery there—the road leads west 0.5 mile from just south of the toll gate. Remember that you must be out of the canyons by 5 p.m., when the toll gate closes.

■ Hike 89 FERN CANYON LOOP Ⓠ

HIKE LENGTH 6.5-mile loop; 1,000' elevation gain

DIFFICULTY Moderate

SEASON October–April

TOPO MAPS *Palm View Peak* (7.5-minute), *Santa Rosa and San Jacinto Mountains National Monument*

PERMIT Indian Canyons admission

■ FEATURES

Fern Canyon is noted for its vertical wall dripping with moisture that supports hanging ferns in the midst of the arid desert. This trip explores the canyon and also tours the cactus-studded slopes above, and it offers a great view into the oasis of Palm Canyon.

■ DESCRIPTION

From Interstate 10, take Highway 111 south into Palm Springs. The name changes to North Palm Canyon Drive. After passing through downtown, the road forks. Stay right as it becomes South Palm Canyon Drive. Continue to the toll gate at the entrance to the canyon, 15.2 miles from the interstate. At the time of this writing, the canyon is open from 8 a.m. to 5 p.m. From July 8 to October 1, it is open only Friday–Sunday. Call 760-323-6018 for current information. After paying the entrance fee, proceed south 2.5 miles to the Trading Post, at the end of the road on Hermits Bench (**GPS N33° 44.284' W116° 32.305'**).

The Fern Canyon and Vandeventer Trails are well maintained and well marked. From the Trading Post at Hermits Bench, head east and down through the parking lot. Go to the gated lower parking lot, around the hill, left to the trailhead (at the north end of the lower lot). Follow the signs for the Fern Canyon Trail down to the stream crossing and up into the mouth of the canyon. In a quarter mile, pass the junction of the Alexander and Victor Trails. Follow the Fern Canyon Trail east into the hills, up a steep incline, and then back into Fern Canyon to view the hanging ferns in 1 mile.

Continuing up the canyon half a mile brings you to a marker post indicating the junction with the Wild Horse Trail. The Vandeventer Trail is to the east and

Hermits Bench

south (as indicated by the marker post). While heading south, you will pass the well-marked junctions with the Dunn Road Trail and the Hahn–Buena Vista Trail (which head to the east).

Once you reach the Vandeventer Trail, loop around back to the west and north to return to Hermits Bench. Some of the largest barrel cactus in California grow along these hills.

■ Hike 90 JO POND TRAIL 🏃

HIKE LENGTH 16 miles out-and-back; 6,200' elevation gain

DIFFICULTY Strenuous

SEASON October–November, March–April

TOPO MAP *Palm View Peak* (7.5-minute), *Santa Rosa and San Jacinto Mountains National Monument*

PERMIT Indian Canyons admission

■ FEATURES

The Jo Pond Trail is one of the highlights of the Coachella Valley. Starting in Palm Canyon, it ascends the Garnet Ridge to Cedar Spring, providing astounding views of the Coachella Valley, Salton Sea, and San Jacinto Mountains, especially when the peaks are cloaked in their snowy winter mantle. Parts of the hike are on shady north slopes that hold snow longer than the surrounding hills, so an ice axe and crampons may be necessary in midwinter.

Despite what you might imagine, the Jo Pond Trail does not visit any standing bodies of water. Rather, it was named for a member of the Desert Riders who was a strong proponent of trails in the Coachella Valley. The trail was completed in 1994.

A complication of this trip is that your vehicle must be out of the canyon by 5 p.m. when the gate closes. This is a long hike and you'll be in hot water if you miss the closing time. Watch the time carefully, or park outside the toll gate.

■ DESCRIPTION

From Interstate 10, take Highway 111 south into Palm Springs. The name changes to North Palm Canyon Drive. After passing through downtown, the road forks. Stay right as it becomes South Palm Canyon Drive. Continue to the toll gate at the entrance to the canyon, 15.2 miles from the interstate. At the time of this writing, the canyon is open from 8 a.m. to 5 p.m. From July 8 to October 1, it is open only Friday–Sunday. Call 760-323-6018 for current information. After paying the entrance fee, proceed south 2.5 miles to the Trading Post at the end of the road on Hermits Bench (**GPS N33° 44.284' W116° 32.305'**).

Views of Murray Hill beyond Palm Canyon

Begin hiking on the aptly named West Fork Trail that ascends the west fork of Palm Canyon from Hermits Bench past waterfalls and flowering cacti. In 2.3 miles, it reaches a junction where the Pelton Trail heads northward. The West Fork Trail becomes the Jo Pond Trail. In another mile, it begins switchbacking unrelentingly up Garnet Ridge, then contours to Cedar Spring. Your hike ends at a campsite in a stand of incense-cedar by the spring (**GPS N33° 40.606' W116° 34.686'**).

From here, you can retrace your steps to Hermits Bench. Or, better yet, with a car shuttle, you can continue a mile to the crest of the Desert Divide where you cross the Pacific Crest Trail. Then switchback 2 more miles down the Cedar Springs Trail to the Morris Ranch Trailhead in the Garner Valley (see Hike 80, page 201).

■ Hike 91 PALM CANYON TRAVERSE ↗ 🚶

HIKE LENGTH 15 miles one-way; 3,500' elevation loss
DIFFICULTY Strenuous (1 day), Moderate (2 days)
SEASON October–April
TOPO MAPS *Palm View Peak, Butterfly Peak,* and *Toro Peak* (all 7.5-minute), *Santa Rosa and San Jacinto Mountains National Monument*
PERMIT Indian Canyons admission

■ FEATURES

This trip, best done as an overnight backpack, descends the length of Palm Canyon from Ribbonwood on the Palms to Pines Scenic Byway to Hermits Bench, 15 mostly downhill miles. Besides some spectacular canyon scenery, another highlight is the rich and varied desert flora. You start down through Upper Sonoran vegetation—slopes dense with red shank, mesquite, sage, yucca, and scattered junipers and pinyon pines. As you descend, Lower Sonoran flora becomes predominant—cholla, hedgehog cacti, agave, ocotillo, goat nut, ephedra, and scores of other arid-zone plants. Then, alongside the creek, you meet the startling contrast of lush greenery—California fan palm, of course, supplemented by scattered cottonwoods, rushes, ferns, and grasses. It's a different world from the San Jacinto high country just a few miles above.

A car shuttle is required for this one-way trip, made more complicated by the fact that you cannot leave your car at Hermits Bench or anywhere inside the toll gate (property of the Agua Caliente band of Cahuilla Indians) overnight. Unless someone picks you up at the end, plan on hiking an extra 2.5 miles to the south edge of Palm Springs. But the rewards of this venture are so great that it is worth the extra complications.

Mojave mound cactus, a.k.a. hedgehog cactus (Echinocereus triglochidinatus)

■ DESCRIPTION

From the intersection of Highway 111 and Highway 74 in Palm Desert, drive up Highway 74 to Pinyon Pines. Just past mile marker 074 RIV 77.85, turn north on Pine View Drive and proceed 0.2 mile to the end of the paved road (**GPS N33° 34.331' W116° 30.053'**).

This is the beginning of the Palm Canyon Trail. Before heading down this trail, consider walking out to the clearing at the end of the main dirt road for a spectacular view of Palm Canyon. If you look to the north, you will see the dark green patches of trees and grass of Palm Springs 25 miles away.

Arrange to be picked up at Hermits Bench, between 8 a.m. and 5 p.m. the following day. To reach Hermits Bench return on Highway 111 to Palm Springs. When the road turns right (north), stay left on South Palm Canyon Drive. Continue to the toll gate at the entrance to the canyon, 15.2 miles from the interstate. At the time of this writing, the canyon is open from 8 a.m. to 5 p.m. From July 8 to October 1, it is open only Friday–Sunday. Call 760-323-6018 for current information. After paying the entrance fee, proceed south

2.5 miles to the Trading Post, at the end of the road on Hermits Bench (**GPS N33° 44.284' W116° 32.305'**). Alternatively, you can leave another car at the south edge of Palm Springs, outside tribal lands, on South Palm Canyon Drive, and walk an extra 2.5 miles at the end.

From the end of Pine View Drive, walk north along the dirt road through ribbonwood chaparral. In 150 yards, veer right onto a dirt trail signed Pines to Palms.

In 1.3 miles, reach a junction marked by a weathered wooden sign. At this junction you have the choice of staying on the ridge or descending into the canyon; both trails rejoin in 2.5 miles. The ridge trail is easy walking with fine views, while the washed-out canyon is much slower going with obstacles and occasional bushwhacking.

If you stay on the ridge trail, you will pass a marble quarry; the rock is readily recognized by its white color and sandpapery texture. Eventually you will drop down to Omstott Canyon (this junction is easy to miss in the uphill direction), turn left, and reach the signed junction in Palm Canyon where the canyon and ridge trails rejoin.

For the next 3 miles you mostly follow the canyon bottom, with detours here and there to get around rocky obstructions. You pass the entrances of Live Oak and Oak Canyons, coming down from the Desert Divide country. About 6 miles from the start you pass a junction with the faint and unmaintained Live Oak Springs Trail coming down from the Desert Divide (see Hike 93, page 225). Three hundred yards up the trail, out of sight around a bend, is Hidden Falls. A short, trailless side trip gets you to the foot of the seasonal falls.

Continue north down-canyon for 2 miles to Agua Bonita Spring, shaded by cottonwoods, a good overnight campsite. A short distance below here you enter tribal lands (overnight camping prohibited). Below Agua Bonita, the trail climbs southeast out of the canyon to get around the rocky gorge of Palm Canyon Falls. (There is no trail through this most spectacular section of Palm Canyon; hikers have reached the falls by scrambling up-canyon from below.) For the next 6 miles you follow the cactus-rich slopes above the east wall of the canyon, crossing several small tributary canyons. As you near Hermits Bench, you look down on splendid groves of *Washington filifera* palms, both in the main canyon and in tributary canyons to the west. The lush greenery amid the drab desert offers a scene of striking contrast. Finally you climb to Hermits Bench, where you either pick up your ride or walk 2.5 miles farther to Palm Springs.

■ Hike 92 PINYON TRAIL ↗ ⦿

HIKE LENGTH 8 miles out-and-back; 1,400' elevation gain

DIFFICULTY Strenuous

SEASON October–April

TOPO MAPS *Toro Peak* (7.5-minute), *Santa Rosa and San Jacinto Mountains National Monument*

■ FEATURES

The Pinyon Trail traverses a lush desert garden between Palm Canyon and Pinyon Flats. Go on a cool day to enjoy the ribbonwood, cactus, yucca, agave, nolina, and, of course, pinyon pines.

■ DESCRIPTION

From Highway 74 at mile marker 74 RIV 80.50, turn north onto Pinyon Drive. In 0.1 mile, reach the entrance to the Pinyon Flats Campground. Unless you are staying at the campground, park on the shoulder of Pinyon Drive (**GPS N33° 35.097' W116° 27.331'**).

Pinyon pines silhouetted at dawn

The signed Pinyon Trail starts at the campground entrance and leads north along the west side of Pinyon Drive 0.1 mile before turning west along the fence line marking the edge of the national forest. In 0.6 mile, come to a marked junction where the trail crosses private Palm Canyon Drive. Continue northwest on the signed trail.

Now you descend into the badlands of the Santa Rosa Mountains. The dominant vegetation is ribbonwood, a beautiful cousin of chamise found few places except between the Desert Divide and Warner Springs, and in the Santa Monica Mountains. The trail weaves in and out of minor canyons before switchbacking down to Omstott Creek, climbing out, and then dropping in again to meet the Palm Canyon Trail at an unmarked junction (**GPS N33° 36.306' W116° 29.960'**). Return the way you came.

■ Hike 93 DESERT DIVIDE AND PALM CANYON

HIKE LENGTH 19 miles one-way; 2,900' elevation gain

DIFFICULTY Strenuous (1 day), Moderate (2 days)

SEASON October–May

TOPO MAPS *Butterfly Peak, Palm View Peak, Toro Peak* (all 7.5-minute), *Santa Rosa and San Jacinto Mountains National Monument*

■ FEATURES

This backpack trip traverses the semi-arid southern end of the San Jacintos, climbing from Garner Valley over the Desert Divide, then dropping into upper Palm Canyon and ascending the latter to Ribbonwood. You pass through some rich chaparral country, and enjoy far-reaching vistas of snow-capped high mountains and tawny desert foothills. It makes an ideal winter or early spring outing. The Live Oak Trail is unmaintained and very difficult to follow in places, so this is a trip for adventurous hikers with good GPS or outstanding map-and-compass skills.

■ DESCRIPTION

From Highway 74, 8.6 miles south of Mountain Center in the Garner Valley and just beyond mile marker 074 RIV 67.75, turn left (northeast) onto the paved Morris Ranch Road (6S53). Follow it up 3.7 miles, passing the Camp Scherman Girl Scout camp, to the signed Cedar Springs Trailhead (4E17) on the right (**GPS N33° 39.251' W116° 35.373'**). (If you reach Morris Ranch, you've driven 0.25 mile too far.)

Immense canyon live oak at Live Oak Spring

You will come out at Pine View Drive in Ribbonwood (see Hike 91, page 221; **GPS N33° 34.331' W116° 30.053'**), 10 miles farther down Highway 74, so either shuttle a second car there or arrange to be picked up there upon completing your trip.

Hike east on the Cedar Springs Trail 2.2 miles to a four-way junction on a saddle on the Desert Divide (see Hike 80, page 201). Go right (southeast) and follow the Pacific Crest Trail past Pyramid and Lion Peaks, mostly through chaparral, with scattered groves of pine and oak, to a four-way trail junction, 4.1 more miles. You leave the Pacific Crest Trail here and take a sharp left (northeast), descending the Live Oak Trail (4E03) to Live Oak Spring, 1 mile. There is reliable water running out of a pipe here, and primitive camping facilities under the majestic canyon live oak.

Continue down the lushly vegetated and partially overgrown trail. In 1 mile, watch for a partially burnt wooden post near a dry wash that once marked a fork in the trail. The USGS topographic map shows a maze of trails between the Desert Divide and Palm Canyon, but all except the Jo Pond Trail are now unmaintained and have largely faded due to revegetation and disuse after the 1980 Palm Canyon Fire. From this point, two historic trails dropped to Palm Canyon. The southern was called the Live Oak Canyon Trail and reached Palm Canyon immediately north of Omstott Canyon. Discontinuous sections remain visible and the terrain is open enough that one could still descend along this route, but it is no longer recognizable as a proper trail. The northern was called Oak Canyon Trail, and is now designated as the continuation of the Live Oak Springs Trail (4E03) to Palm Canyon. It no longer has much trail tread, but most segments are marked with cairns. Our trip descends this route to Hidden Falls near the Dutch Charlie Trail.

Do not cross the wash and look for traces of the old Live Oak Canyon Trail, but rather turn north and try to find the Oak Canyon Trail (still 4E03). Your first goal is to reach the Rock House shown on the topographic map. This small but well-built cabin, presumably used by a cattleman, sits on a bench overlooking a spring and cattle pen on Oak Creek. Plenty of unsheltered camping could be found on the bench.

From here, continue north-northeast down the ridge between Oak and Live Oak Creeks, looking for cairns, contour around the south and east sides of a knoll, and then cross to the north side of Oak Creek. When you reach a steep slabby drop overlooking Palm Canyon, watch for more cairns following a handy ledge system southeast, crossing back over Oak Creek. When the trail turns east, watch for a post. From here, a short path leads to a view of the aptly named Hidden Falls, which can be impressive in spring but is usually dry by early summer. Our very faint trail bends north and meets the Palm Canyon Trail north of Dutch Charlie Trail, but you might as well strike out cross-country and intersect Palm Canyon south of Dutch Charlie, 5.7 miles from Live Oak Spring.

Turn south on Palm Canyon and hike 2.2 miles to a signed fork between the Ridge and Canyon Trails. Turn left up Omstott Canyon and head 0.5 mile up the wash to where the unmarked and easily overlooked Ridge Trail turns right and climbs onto the ridge. In 2.2 miles, the Canyon Trail rejoins the Ridge Trail at a signed junction. Continue up the trail 1.4 miles to the end of Pine View Drive.

Live Oak Spring

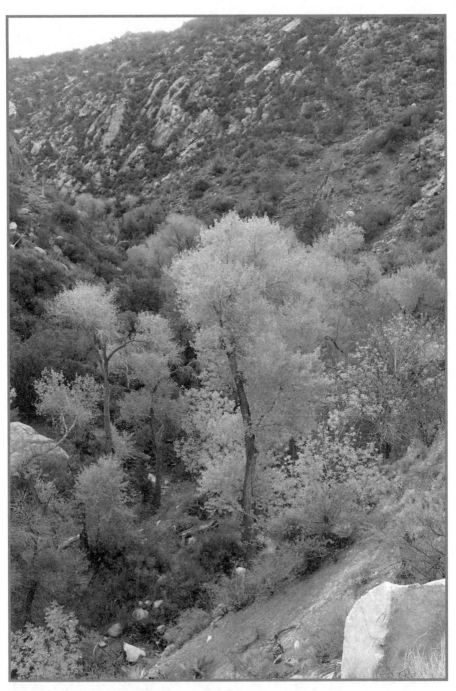

Horsethief Canyon (see Hike 95, page 238)

PART 3

■ The Santa Rosa ■ Mountains

The Santa Rosas

Natural History of the Santa Rosa Mountains

LAY OF THE LAND

South from the Palms to Pines Scenic Byway, the Santa Rosas rise as a sky island out of the desert foothills. Reaching elevations in excess of 8,000 feet at Toro Peak and Santa Rosa Mountain, the high mountain backbone supports a rich forest of Jeffrey and ponderosa pine, white fir, and incense-cedar. A multitude of springs seep cold water down the slopes to the thirsty regions below. In summer, when the surrounding desert country swelters under the burning sun, this green oasis in the sky is cool and refreshing.

PLANT LIFE

There are really two Santa Rosas. South and east from the lofty Santa Rosa Mountain–Toro Peak backbone, the range is lower and shows the strong influence of the desert. Here on the slopes and benches above 4,000 feet, pinyon pine and California juniper are supreme, covering endless miles of mountainous terrain. On the north flank of the range is an ocean of chaparral, primarily shaggy-barked, olive-green red shank (also called ribbonwood). In the desert foothills and canyons to the east, west, and south, Lower Sonoran vegetation takes over—tall and spindly

Fruity yucca on Sawmill Trail

ocotillo, yucca, chamise, barrel and cholla cacti, and waxy-green creosote. In some of the canyons are small oases of *Washingtonia filifera,* arboreal monarchs of the California desert. Except for the high backbone of Santa Rosa Mountain and Toro Peak, the Santa Rosas are primarily a desert range.

WILDLIFE

The desert Santa Rosas are home to the largest herd of bighorn sheep in California, estimated at more than 500 head. These noble masters of the arid crags live mainly in the eastern and southern parts of the range, rocky regions where humans seldom disturb the animals' living habits. Crucial to their survival are the handful of all-year springs that trickle from some of the pinyon flats and desert canyons. The easiest way to see and photograph bighorn sheep is to hide near one of these water holes and await their appearance. (I have seen many in this manner.) Other large mammals common in the Santa Rosas are mule deer and mountain lion. The latter are seldom seen, but their large, unmistakable tracks betray their existence.

Perhaps the greatest appeal of the Santa Rosas is their relative isolation and primitiveness. Except for the forest road climbing to Santa Rosa Mountain and Toro Peak and, at the other end of the range, jeep tracks leading into Rockhouse Canyon, the range is devoid of roads. Trails are few, and most of those that do exist are unmaintained, ancient relics of the Cahuilla. You can have most of these mountains almost to yourself. They make for superb winter outings.

Fortunately, Congress has seen fit to protect most of the Santa Rosas. The Archaeological Resources Protection Act of 1979 makes it illegal to disturb or remove any of the Native American artifacts in these culturally rich mountains. The 20,160-acre Santa Rosa Wilderness, created by the California Wilderness Act of 1984, protects most of the northern Santa Rosas that are within San Bernardino National Forest.

Thanks to the efforts of the Sierra Club and other activists, and with the strong support of Congresswoman Mary Bono (R) of Palm Springs and California Senator Dianne Feinstein (D), the Santa Rosa and San Jacinto Mountains National Monument was established when President Bill Clinton signed the enabling act in October 2000. The 272,000-acre national monument encompasses most of the desert side of the Santa Rosas and San Jacintos and safeguards endangered bighorn sheep and desert tortoises. This is the first congressionally designated national monument under the supervision of the Bureau of Land Management.

A wilderness permit is presently not required to enter the Santa Rosa Wilderness or the Santa Rosa and San Jacinto Mountains National Monument, but may be so in the future if overuse threatens to degrade some of the canyons.

Human History of the Santa Rosa Mountains

A SUBSISTENCE LIFE

Like the San Jacinto country to the north, the Santa Rosas were the ancestral home of numerous Cahuilla peoples. In Deep Canyon, on the northeastern slope of the range, were villages of the Western Cahuilla. Groups of Desert Cahuilla lived in spring-fed oases at the eastern foot of the mountains, above the shoreline of ancient Lake Cahuilla (today's Salton Sea). Mountain Cahuilla villages were numerous on the western slope of the range, particularly in Horse and Rockhouse Canyons and on Vandeventer Flat. The Santa Rosas supplied these hardy people with the necessities of life—pinyon nuts, acorns, agave, yucca fibers, wild game, and water. Footpaths crisscrossed the range, traveling from spring to spring. Many of these ancient trails are still traceable today. In summer, whole villages would migrate into the mountains to gather food and escape the searing desert heat. About the only place in the Santa Rosas avoided by the Cahuilla was Toro Peak; there are stories that this highest mountain in the range was taboo, the dwelling place of evil spirits.

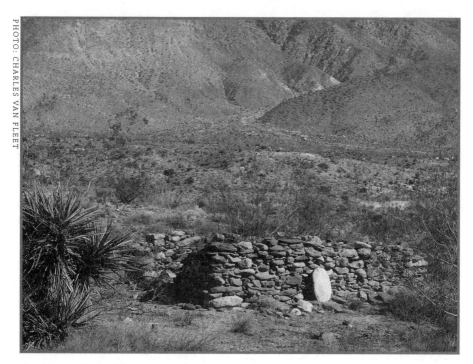

Rockhouse in Rockhouse Canyon

NAMING THE SANTA ROSAS

Spanish trailblazer Juan Bautista de Anza was probably the first of the European explorers to get a good look at the Santa Rosas—in 1774 during his historic overland trek from Mexico to Monterey. Anza and his party rounded the southern tip of the range after crossing the Colorado Desert, then paralleled the Santa Rosas to the west as they ascended Coyote Canyon. There is no record that he took more than perfunctory notice of the range. In fact, the Spaniards and their Mexican Californio successors tended to avoid the mountains of California.

The Californios apparently supplied the name for the mountains, however. "Santa Rosa" was the name given to a Mexican land grant in western Riverside County, dated 1845. This name was evidently later transferred to the mountain range. The reason is a mystery, for the Santa Rosa Mountains lie many miles south of the original land grant. Early maps of San Diego County show the range as an extension of the San Jacintos. Not until 1901, when the US Geological Survey completed its mapping of the mountains, did the name "Santa Rosa Mountains" come into general use.

BLACK GOLD

Gold seekers were probably the first nonnatives to penetrate the desert ramparts of the Santa Rosas. The earliest visitor may have been one-legged Thomas L. "Pegleg" Smith. In 1828 Smith, traveling from Yuma to Los Angeles via Warner's Ranch, left the standard route somewhere near the southern end of the Santa Rosas and sought a shortcut. The story goes that he picked up some black lumps of what he thought was native copper atop "one of three hills." In Los Angeles he showed his rocks to a friend, who suggested he have them assayed. The assayer's report: pure gold coated with "black desert varnish." Smith returned to the region where he found the rocks but was never able to locate the right spot. Ever since, an endless stream of prospectors have sought Pegleg Smith's fabled "black gold." The southern Santa Rosas have been turned inside out in a vain search that has lasted more than a century.

Pegleg's black gold may be nothing more than an elusive fable, but gold in small amounts has been brought out of the Santa Rosas. Around 1900, Nicholas Swartz made a strike in upper Rockhouse Canyon on the southwest slope of the range. It is said that Schwartz took out $18,000 in several years' work. He reportedly built and occupied one of the rock houses that gave the canyon its name. Old Nicholas Canyon, a tributary of Rockhouse Canyon, honors the prospector today. Other prospectors have dug out minute amounts of gold from ledges in the Rockhouse Canyon area, but not enough to make their years of searching worthwhile. And there was Fig Tree John, the colorful Cahuilla who lived above the shores of the Salton Sea and died, some say, at the ripe age of 136. Old Fig Tree often made his purchases with gold dust or small nuggets, giving rise to the belief that he had a secret gold mine somewhere in the Santa Rosas. Even today, an occasional prospector sets out to find the "lost" gold mine of Fig Tree John.

The largest commercial mine in the Santa Rosas was the Garnet Queen, located at 6,000 feet elevation on the northwest slope of the range. Tungsten and garnet were recovered from the Garnet Queen Mine on and off from its development in 1896 into the 1940s. The mine changed hands several times under false premises, and was a marginal success at best.

PRESERVING THE SANTA ROSAS

In 1897, the entire Santa Rosa Mountains were included within the newly created San Jacinto Forest Reserve. Charles Vandeventer, who had a cabin on what is now Vandeventer Flat, was appointed forest ranger and assigned to patrol the Santa Rosas, which, according to all accounts, he did with vigor and relish. In 1908 the old San Jacinto Reserve was cut down in size and joined to the Trabuco Reserve in

PHOTO: JOHN W. ROBINSON

"Desert Steve" Ragsdale's cabin

the Santa Ana Mountains to form Cleveland National Forest. Only the northern end of the Santa Rosas remained as part of the Cleveland. Since 1925, this north section has been in San Bernardino National Forest. The northwestern slope, including the summit of Toro Peak, is within the Santa Rosa Indian Reservation.

Until recent years, only a handful of settlers sought to make their homes in the desert-tempered Santa Rosas. The Vandeventer family built a cattle ranch at the northwestern foot of the range in the 1890s, and herded their stock to high mountain pastures every summer.

Vandeventer was for years a familiar character in these parts. A. H. Nightingale came to Pinyon Flat early in this century and built a hunting cabin at Stump Spring, high on the forested slope of Santa Rosa Mountain. "Desert Steve" Ragsdale, long a gas-station operator at Desert Center and later the best-known dweller of the Santa Rosas, came to the mountains in 1937. He bought 560 acres of timberland atop Santa Rosa Mountain and, right on the summit, built a sturdy log cabin and a spectacular tree ladder. He posted his mountain domain with placards advising visitors that, among other things, "Decent folks are welcome; Enjoy but don't destroy." Ragsdale died in 1971, and his cabin burned down several years after that.

Until the 1940s the Santa Rosa Mountain–Toro Peak high country was reached only by steep trails. Since then, the road built by the Forest Service and Desert Steve

Ragsdale to Santa Rosa Mountain and the later extension to Toro Peak have rendered this sylvan sky island accessible to less-energetic campers and hunters. Public campgrounds have been constructed high in the forest at Santa Rosa Spring, Stump Spring, and Cedar Spring. The summit of Toro Peak is owned by the Santa Rosa Indian Reservation. It is the site of an antenna installation and is closed to the public.

On the lower northern slopes, subdividers are moving in. Pinyon Flat is now honeycombed with roads, and new homes are springing up along the Palms to Pines Scenic Byway. The Santa Rosa and San Jacinto Mountains National Monument aims to safeguard the pristine desert and mountain country adjacent to the new housing tracts from future development.

Most of the range remains as wild as ever. South from Horsethief Creek and Toro Peak, the Santa Rosas are the lonely domain of desert bighorn sheep, coyotes, and rattlesnakes. Here, often within sight of the tourist-infested Salton Sea and Anza-Borrego Desert State Park, you can wander for days, with only the wind, the soft rustle of pinyon needles, and the occasional coyote howl to keep you company.

■ Hike 94 ALTA SECA BENCH ⊕ ↗ 🐕 🚶

HIKE LENGTH 2 miles out-and-back; 800' elevation gain

DIFFICULTY Moderate

SEASON May–November

TOPO MAP *Toro Peak* (7.5-minute), *Santa Rosa and San Jacinto Mountains National Monument*

■ FEATURES

Southeast from Toro Peak, the sky island of the Santa Rosas extends 3 miles before plunging abruptly to desert canyons and foothills. This section of undisturbed high country is known to old-timers as Alta Seca Bench, although it is not so labeled on maps. Little shallow valleys filled with Jeffrey pine lie under rocky outcroppings and gentle, chaparral-spotted slopes. It is a place where you can find natural beauty and solitude and, from its edge, gaze far out over the desert.

No maintained trails reach into the Alta Seca, and about the only visitors nowadays are occasional deer hunters during the fall. But you can find traces of the historic old Cahuilla pathway that climbed out of Horsethief Canyon, crossed the bench, and descended to Old Santa Rosa, a long-abandoned Cahuilla village near the head of Rockhouse Canyon. This trail is too ancient and overgrown to follow with certainty today. You can read about it in Charles Francis Saunders's chapter "Old Santa Rosa" in his *Southern Sierras of California;* in George Wharton James's "Up Martinez Canyon" in *The Wonders of the Colorado Desert,* and, more recently, in Nina Paul Shumway's "Burrowing in the Santa Rosas" in her *Your Desert and Mine.* These books offer delightful introductions to the Santa Rosa high country and the Native American trails that once crisscrossed it.

This cross-country trip leaves Santa Rosa Mountain Road below Toro Peak and drops to Alta Seca Bench, then crosses it to a delightful pine flat at the southeastern end. Here you can look down into Rockhouse Basin and see the route the Cahuilla took to Old Santa Rosa. (Unless you're an experienced mountaineer and are equipped for a two-day trip, don't try to descend the old pathway.) There is no water on Alta Seca (High Dry) Bench, so tote your own if you plan to camp.

■ DESCRIPTION

From Palm Desert, drive up the Palms to Pines Scenic Byway (Highway 74) to a junction with the Santa Rosa Mountain Road (7S02) just west of mile marker 74 RIV 77.00, marked by a large sign. Turn left (south), and proceed via the poor dirt road (high clearance recommended) up the mountainside, passing several beautifully situated campgrounds. At 11.5 miles, pass through a normally open gate. At 12.5 miles, park at a turnout (**GPS N33° 31.359' W116° 25.252'**) beside a hairpin turn below the locked gate leading to the summit of Toro Peak.

Pick up the use trail, descending southeast over rocky terrain spotted with pines and chaparral. The path soon becomes indistinct, but watch for cairns. In 0.4 mile, cross the end of an old jeep road and continue down a shallow gully to Alta Seca Bench, 1 mile (**GPS N33° 30.946' W116° 24.733'**). This would be a good place to stop for a picnic.

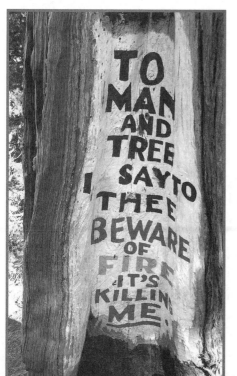

Poetry by Desert Steve

For a longer walk, continue across the bench to Peak 7620, which is most easily climbed from the southwest to avoid thickets of scrub oak. Explore for another mile, staying to the right (southwest) of several boulder outcroppings, to a shallow bowl filled with Jeffrey pines and some live oaks. To look down, climb to the rocky rim immediately south of the shallow valley. The old Native American trail dropped south down a steep ridge to Old Santa Rosa, at the head of the desert basin you see below you. Hikers have continued along the crest of the Santa Rosas all the way to Rabbit Peak and S22, but this 24-mile route, involving severe bushwhacking, is among the most arduous cross-country trips in Southern California.

Return the same way, with an 800-foot gain at the end. Cross-country travel can be deceptive; if you're not certain of your return route, head up for the right (north) shoulder of Toro Peak, which looms high before you. Toro Peak itself is on the Santa Rosa Indian Reservation, and the tribe has requested that hikers do not visit the summit.

■ Hike 95 HORSETHIEF CREEK ↗ 🐕 🥾

HIKE LENGTH 4.5 miles out-and-back; 900' elevation gain
DIFFICULTY Moderate
SEASON October–April
TOPO MAPS *Toro Peak* (7.5-minute), *Santa Rosa and San Jacinto Mountains National Monument*

■ FEATURES

The northeastern end of the Santa Rosas is high desert country, ideal for winter hiking trips. Vast sloping benches and boulder-laced hills are dotted with pinyon pine, juniper, red shank, chamise, yucca, agave, and prickly pear. Shady cottonwoods grow in stream-watered canyons and around seeping springs. The snow-crowned Santa Rosa Mountain–Toro Peak massif dominates the southwestern skyline, while white-capped San Jacinto glimmers on the northern horizon.

This leisurely trip samples a small bit of this delightful high desert region. You follow the Cactus Spring Trail, an old Cahuilla pathway reworked by the Forest Service, from near the Palms to Pines Scenic Byway down into the shady gorge of Horsethief Creek. Here, amid tall cottonwoods and willows, alongside the trickling stream, you can picnic and enjoy the solitude of nature.

Horsethief Creek is wrapped in the lore of the Old West. A century ago, it is said, horse thieves used this canyon as a hideout and a place to rebrand stolen stock. Gangs of rustlers stole the horses in the San Diego region, drove them to

Cottonwoods in Horsethief Canyon

Horsethief Creek where the animals were rebranded, and then herded them to San Bernardino to sell. Before the horses could leave San Bernardino, the story goes, the bandits stole the animals back and went through the entire process in reverse.

▪ DESCRIPTION

From Palm Desert, drive up the Palms to Pines Scenic Byway (Highway 74) to mile marker 74 RIV 80.50 at Pinyon Flat. Opposite the campground road, turn left (south) onto a paved side road (7S09, also labeled Pinon Flats Trans Station Road). A highway sign indicates the Ribbonwood Equestrian Campground and the Sawmill Trail, a footpath leading south. Drive up 7S09 0.3 mile to the vast Sawmill Trail parking area on the left (**GPS N33° 34.798' W116° 27.021'**). A sign at the east end of the lot points to the Cactus Spring Trail (5E01) and the Sawmill Trail (5E03).

Hike east from the lot. Stay right as the road turns to dirt and passes through prickly pear cactus and yucca. Go 0.2 mile and stay right at another fork. Immediately beyond, you will see the signed Cactus Spring Trailhead marker on the left (the road continuing south goes to the Sawmill Trail; see Hike 97, page 242). Sign in at the wilderness box. Follow the Cactus Spring Trail east, up and down over several small gullies, and drop to Horsethief Creek, 2.3 miles (**GPS N33° 34.491' W116° 25.003'**). Here is an all-year stream shaded by magnificent cottonwoods. You can explore up or down Horsethief Creek for quite some distance.

Return the same way.

■ Hike 96 CACTUS SPRING TRAIL 🥾 🐕 🚶

HIKE LENGTH 18 miles out-and-back; 3,000' elevation gain
DIFFICULTY Moderate (2 days), Strenuous (1 day)
SEASON October–April
TOPO MAPS *Toro Peak, Martinez Mountain* (all 7.5-minute), *Santa Rosa and San Jacinto Mountains National Monument*

■ FEATURES

This trip follows the Cactus Spring Trail from near the Palms to Pines Scenic Byway down across Horsethief Creek, then up over miles of rolling plateau country covered by an elfin forest of pinyon and juniper, to Agua Alta Spring. Agua Alta (High Water) Spring, creased into the south slope of Martinez Mountain, flows sparingly over green slime among cat's-claw bushes and bunch grass—not much to look at, but a heaven-sent source of water for the bighorn sheep that roam this region. Keep a sharp lookout; you may spot some of these noble animals climbing the rocky slopes of Martinez Mountain or coming down for water.

On the Cactus Spring Trail

■ DESCRIPTION

From Palm Desert, drive up the Palms to Pines Scenic Byway (Highway 74) to mile marker 74 RIV 80.50 at Pinyon Flat. Opposite the campground road, turn left (south) onto a paved side road (7S09, also labeled Pinon Flats Trans Station Road). A highway sign indicates the Ribbonwood Equestrian Campground and the Sawmill Trail, a footpath leading south. Drive up 7S09 0.3 mile to the vast Sawmill Trail parking area on the left (**GPS N33° 34.798' W116° 27.021'**). A sign at the east end of the lot points to the Cactus Spring Trail (5E01) and the Sawmill Trail (5E03).

Hike east from the lot. Stay right as the road turns to dirt and passes through a field of prickly pear cactus and yucca. Go 0.2 mile and stay right at another fork. Immediately beyond, you will see the signed Cactus Spring Trailhead marker on the left. Take it; the four-wheel-drive road continuing south goes to the Sawmill Trail (see next hike). Sign in at the wilderness box. You follow the Cactus Spring Trail east, up and down over several small north-draining gullies, and drop to Horsethief Creek, 2.3 miles (**GPS N33° 34.491' W116° 25.003'**). Here is an all-year stream shaded by magnificent cottonwoods.

Beyond this point, the trail is less used and requires skilled route-finding to follow. Small cairns mark the path from time to time. The trail crosses the creek, climbs east out of the canyon, follows a dry wash, and climbs through pinyon-dotted terrain to Cactus Spring, 2 miles from Horsethief Creek. The spring, 25 yards north of the trail, is often dry. Your trail continues east, turns left up a sandy wash, curves southeast up a tributary wash, and climbs toward the ridge south of Martinez Mountain. Cross the ridge well above its low point and descend into a series of dry washes leading southeast. The path climbs and descends through rough pinyon-and-juniper terrain to Agua Alta Spring (**GPS N33° 31.781' W116° 20.186'**), marked by a wooden sign, 7 miles from Horsethief Creek. The spring is up the draw to your left. Enough water is almost always available here for drinking and cooking. There are some campsites in the wash as well, but the wash is highly exposed to flash flooding. About 0.5 mile farther on are Pinyon Alta Flat and its campsites.

Return the same way. An option is to scramble north up the long slope to the rocky summit block of Martinez Mountain, 4 miles round-trip from Agua Alta Spring.

A challenging alternative, with a car shuttle, is to descend southeastward, following the Cahuilla footpath, into Martinez Canyon, and then follow the broad canyon around to the northeast all the way out to near Highway 86. The USGS maps show an old trail, but the path across the desert is extremely faint, marked only by an occasional duck. The old jeep road in the upper part of Martinez Canyon above the wilderness boundary has been completely reclaimed by nature and now the canyon is blocked in places with dense reeds. This option requires the Clark Lake NE and Valerie (7.5-minute) quadrangle maps and excellent cross-country navigation skills. The final part of the trail across the desert becomes a four-wheel-drive road and passes between date palm plantations before emerging at the corner of 66th Avenue and Van Buren just west of Highway 86. This option is 23 miles long, though the last 5 miles could be eliminated by driving up the four-wheel-drive road to the wilderness boundary (**GPS N33° 30.779' W116° 13.363'**).

Yet another variation is to descend east from Pinyon Alta Flat into Agua Alta Canyon, then follow this canyon to its junction with Martinez Canyon and on out to the highway.

■ Hike 97 SAWMILL TRAIL 🥾 🐕 ⊚ 🚶

HIKE LENGTH 8 miles one-way; 3,700' elevation gain

DIFFICULTY Strenuous

SEASON March–May, October–November

TOPO MAPS *Toro Peak* (7.5-minute), *Santa Rosa and San Jacinto Mountains National Monument*

■ FEATURES

The Sawmill Trail ascends the north face of the Santa Rosas. It provides excellent views of the northern Santa Rosas, San Jacinto, and the desert from Palm Springs southward. It starts in the desert and ends in the high mountains, so hike in the spring or fall, when it's cool at the trailhead but the Santa Rosa Mountain Road is clear of snow.

■ DESCRIPTION

From Palm Desert, drive up Highway 74 to mile marker 74 RIV 80.50 at Pinyon Flat. Opposite the campground road, turn left (south) onto a paved side road (7S09, also labeled Pinon Flats Trans Station Road). A highway sign indicates Ribbonwood Equestrian Campground and the Sawmill Trail, leading south. Drive up 7S09 0.3 mile to the Sawmill Trail parking area on the left (**GPS N33° 34.798' W116° 27.021'**). A sign at the east end of the lot points to the Cactus Spring Trail (5E01) and the Sawmill Trail (5E03). Leave a second vehicle (or mountain bike) 8.7 miles up the Santa Rosa Mountain Road at the signed 5E03 trail near a bend in the road and a small gate (**GPS N33° 32.559' W116° 27.942'**).

Kiln on Sawmill Trail

From the Cactus Spring parking area, walk east, staying right as the road turns to dirt. Pass through a field of prickly pear cactus and yucca. After 0.1 mile, stay right at another fork. Shortly afterward, you will see the Cactus Spring Trailhead marker 5E01 to the left (see Hike 95, page 238). Stay right on Sawmill Road (7S01) and hike north as it switchbacks up the face of the slope. Watch the flora transition as you climb from desert to mountain.

At 5.6 miles, reach a clearing at 6,250 feet with an old stone charcoal kiln (**GPS N33° 33.010' W116° 26.659'**). From here, the four-wheel-drive road deteriorates into a trail that continues westward. After about 0.5 mile, it forks. Stay left on the connector trail, which climbs southwestward another 2 miles to the Santa Rosa Mountain Road.

Many variations are possible on this hike. To avoid a car shuttle, simply retrace your steps from the kiln or from the top. With a four-wheel-drive vehicle, it is possible to drive up Sawmill Road to the kiln and greatly shorten the hike. From the top of the connector trail, it is also possible to climb all the way to Santa Rosa Mountain.

■ Hike 98 RABBIT PEAK FROM COACHELLA VALLEY

HIKE LENGTH 16 miles out-and-back; 6,700' elevation gain
DIFFICULTY Very Strenuous
SEASON October–December
TOPO MAP *Rabbit Peak* (7.5-minute), *Anza-Borrego Desert Region* (Earthwalk)

▓ FEATURES

Rising high over the southern end of the Santa Rosas, overlooking Anza-Borrego Desert State Park on one side and the Salton Sea on the other, is the 6,640-foot hogback of Rabbit Peak. Pinyon, juniper, and mountain mahogany cover the higher parts of this desert mountain, while the arid lower slopes are spotted with ocotillo, agave, yucca, prickly pear, and other Lower Sonoran types of plants.

Rabbit Peak is a long, tough climb. No trails lead above its desert foothills; to reach its summit you must scramble up steep, cactus-infested slopes and traverse to the north end of its long hogback. Yet it seems to hold a strange attraction to climbers, and there are those who return to this dry, unspectacular mountain time and again. In fact, it seems somehow to inspire the grandest and most touching literary artistry—exemplified in the epic poem "Wild Rabbit," written by Los Angeles Sierra Clubber Chester Versteeg and placed in the summit register in 1948:

You sneak up on him, mile by mile,
Foot by foot, bit by bit.
Four jaws are grim, there's no smile;
Then a final lunge and you've captured it—

THE RABBIT!

For seasoning use sage or wild pea,
And, if you want to pep it up a bit,
Dip the meat yonder in the Salton Sea.
Yum yum, boys and girls, this is it—

THE WILD RABBIT!

Telescope, White Mountain, Boundary or New York Butte,[1]
You bet, we like 'em all a bit.
But today—no steak tough as a climber's boot;
Today, tender and sweet, this is it—

WILD RABBIT!

In 1950, a Sierra Club group led by Jerry Zagorites added the following verse after climbing through clouds and cold rain:

And for flavor add snow and fog,
Even worse than Los Angeles smog.
When it is so cold the fire freezes,
And snow and sleet come on icy breezes—

FROZEN WILD RABBIT!

The latest stanza is a lament by Parker Severson of Los Angeles, written in 1964:

Alas, what prompts we mortals so vain,
To pursue this mighty sore-muscle game.
Plodding with sweat and tears through storm and rain,
To crown these noble summits with our name?

Rabbit Peak can be climbed from almost any direction, a tough haul any way you do it. This trip starts from the Salton Sea side and utilizes an old prospectors' trail to gain the lower slopes. The approach from this side is subject to a seasonal closure to protect the peninsular bighorn sheep and is open only October– December. See Hike 99 for the classic but longer southern approach over Villager

---

1   These are other popular desert peaks.

Peak. Take along a pen or pencil, and add your own stanza to the inspired poetry that this desert mountain seems to generate.

There is *no water* en route; take a plentiful supply. (There is a spring in Sheep Canyon that usually flows into April or May.)

DESCRIPTION

From Indio, drive south on Highway 86 South. Turn right onto 66th Avenue, go 1.1 miles, and then turn left onto Pierce Street. In 5.3 miles, turn left onto Harrison Street. In 0.6 mile, turn right onto 78th Avenue, then left onto Fillmore Street in 1 mile. Drive south on Fillmore Street to its end at a gate and orchard, 0.5 mile (**GPS N33° 28.634' W116° 07.795'**). Familiarize yourself with the landmarks; you may be returning by headlamp.

Observing the NO TRESPASSING signs on the citrus groves, walk south over a levee and down into the wash below it. Turn right and proceed west along the wash (quite sandy in places) to where a road crosses it, 0.5 mile. Turn left (south) on the road and go about 100 yards, passing a lemon grove on your right, to a poor jeep road. Follow this road southwest about a half mile to the beginning of

Rabbit Peak summit

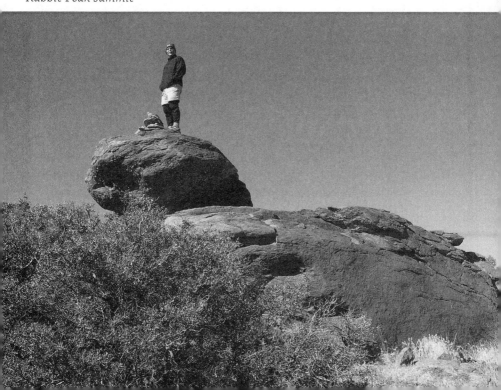

a well-ducked trail that leads across the open desert toward the mountains. (The trail is indistinct in places, so look for the ducks.) Your route climbs steadily southwest to the ridge between Alamo and Barton Canyons, 3.5 miles. You now follow a ducked climbers' path to the left, up to the ridgetop, across a saddle, and on up to a broad, undulating bench just below the steep ridge leading up to Rabbit's hogback, 6 miles and 3,300-foot gain from the start. This is where most parties camp, but it is waterless.

Beyond, it is a steep, trailless climb. Climb up the ridge around several big rock outcrops, to the top of the sloping hogback that is Rabbit Peak. You follow ducks most of the way. The register is in the summit rocks at the far (northwest) end of the plateau (**GPS N33° 25.997' W116° 14.343'**).

Return the same way.

■ Hike 99 VILLAGER AND RABBIT PEAKS 🡕 🚶

HIKE LENGTH 21 miles out-and-back; 7,900' elevation gain

DIFFICULTY Very Strenuous

SEASON October–March

TOPO MAPS *Fonts Point, Rabbit Peak* (both 7.5-minute), *Anza-Borrego Desert Region* (Earthwalk)

■ FEATURES

This ultimate Wild Rabbit experience ascends the long south ridge from the Anza-Borrego Desert, passing over Villager Peak en route. It is one of the test pieces for serious Southern California day hikers. This extremely strenuous hike features a remarkable variety of cactus and yucca. It is best done in late fall or early spring when the temperatures are cool. At this time of year, the hike typically begins before dawn and ends after dark, so a headlamp is essential. Fortunately, route finding is reasonably easy because the hike follows the top of the ridge. A full moon aids walking and makes the trip even more enjoyable.

The hike is completely dry. Bring at least 6 quarts of water, more for a warm day. Because of the plethora of spiky vegetation, long pants are advisable. The trip can be done as an overnight backpack, camping on top of Villager Peak, if you are willing to haul an enormous quantity of water.

■ DESCRIPTION

From Interstate 10 in Indio, turn south onto Highway 86 South toward El Centro and proceed 35 miles to the Borrego-Salton Seaway (S22). Turn right, and drive

The Salton Sea seen from the flank of Rabbit Peak

PHOTO: JOHN W. ROBINSON

14 miles to a parking area on the right at the intersection of the Thimble Trail and Truckhaven Trail dirt roads (**GPS N33° 18.167' W116° 11.879'**). This is just past mile marker 32.0 and adjacent to call box S22-319; it is 13 miles east of Borrego Springs.

From the parking area, identify the ridge leading north on the left side of Rattlesnake Canyon. Wander through a maze of small washes for 1.2 miles, staying right of a small escarpment. At the base of the ridge, identify a good use trail switchbacking up the steep slope through a spectacular cactus garden. Follow this path 5.8 miles all the way to the 5,756-foot summit of Villager Peak.

Villager Peak is a strenuous hike in itself. If you are tired or low on water, Villager Peak is a good place to have lunch and turn around. If time permits, continue northward 3.6 miles over numerous wearisome bumps to the 6,640-foot summit of Rabbit Peak (**GPS N33° 25.997' W116° 14.343'**). The ridge involves 2,000 feet of ascent and 1,100 feet of descent that must be regained on the return journey.

Retrace your steps on the descent. At the 4,400-foot point below Villager, the ridge forks. Stay to the right. The left ridge drops into complicated terrain in Rattlesnake Canyon. Once back to the desert floor, proceed south to S22. There are numerous ducks in the desert, but they are particularly useful at night. You may occasionally see headlights on the road; head for the closest point where the lights pass by you.

■ Hike 100 OLD SANTA ROSA 🥾 🐐 🚶

HIKE LENGTH 20 miles out-and-back; 2,800' elevation gain

DIFFICULTY Moderate (2 days), Strenuous (1 day)

SEASON October–April

TOPO MAPS *Clark Lake, Clark Lake NE, Collins Valley* (all 7.5-minute), *Anza-Borrego Desert Region* (Earthwalk)

■ FEATURES

Charles Francis Saunders, writing in 1923, called Rockhouse Canyon "as wild a region, perhaps, as the Southern California mountains afford, scantily watered, uninhabited and unvisited except by an occasional wandering enthusiast like ourselves or a cowman in search of his strayed stock." Saunders's description holds true today. Only an occasional visitor makes the lonely trip up this narrow desert canyon to the hidden alluvial plain immediately above its head, nestled under the brooding shoulder of the Santa Rosa massif.

Years ago, this naked sloping plain above Rockhouse Canyon was the home of Mountain Cahuillas. Their village, at the northwest edge of the plain, was Old Santa Rosa. They gathered mescal from agave plants, acorns from oaks, and pinyon nuts from pines, and took water from the seeping springs below the mountainside. Although the Cahuillas have long departed and nothing remains of Old Santa Rosa, signs of their former presence are numerous. Potsherds, ollas, and other artifacts can be seen by the diligent searcher. The crumbling walls of rock houses near Cottonwood Spring (dry), however, date from a later era when Nicholas Swartz and other prospectors combed the region for mineral wealth. From these remains Rockhouse Canyon received its name.

This wintertime trip ascends the narrow confines of Rockhouse Canyon to the lonely plain at the foot of the Santa Rosas. Chances are you will have this forgotten corner of the Santa Rosas to yourself. The only sure water is in Nicholas Canyon, just above the northwest corner of the sloping plain.

■ DESCRIPTION

This route is unsuitable for low-clearance vehicles. From Borrego Springs, follow the Borrego-Salton Seaway (S22) east to the signed Rockhouse Trail, 0.3 mile east of mile marker 26.0. (You can also reach this junction from Highway 86 by turning west at Salton City on S22 and following the latter 21 miles.) Rockhouse Trail becomes dirt in 0.3 mile. In 1.2 miles, stay left at a fork. Continue 7.9 miles along the west edge of Clark Valley, sometimes crossing deep sand, to a signed fork for Butler and Rockhouse Canyons. Most vehicles should park at the two-wheel-drive trailhead

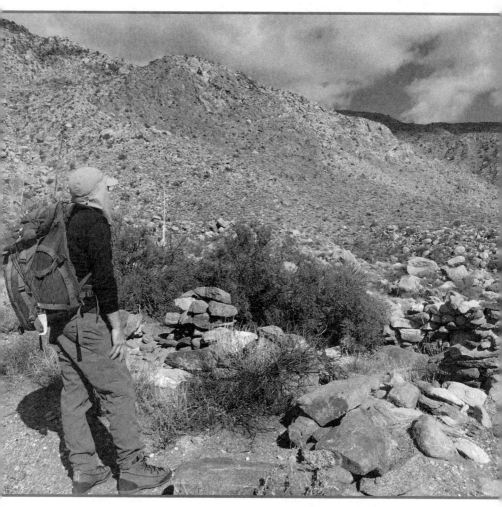

Old Santa Rosa site

here (**GPS N33° 23.236' W116° 21.954'**). High-clearance four-wheel-drive vehicles can take the right fork and attempt to drive as much as 3 miles farther up the rocky wash/road into Rockhouse Canyon to the signed wilderness boundary.

From the two-wheel-drive trailhead, hike up the jeep road toward Rockhouse Canyon. The wash is dotted with ocotillo, smoke trees, and cheesebush. The canyon soon narrows and you pass the wilderness boundary at 3 miles. Hidden Spring is usually dry. In 1.3 miles, a 20-foot dry waterfall blocks the canyon and can be bypassed most easily on the left. In 1.2 miles, the canyon widens and the wash makes an easily overlooked fork. Stay left and continue through the final 1.4 miles of narrows before emerging onto a huge alluvial fan at the foot of the Santa Rosa Mountains.

The wash splits, rejoins, and comes to a three-way split in 0.4 mile. Stay left. In 0.5 mile, watch for some prominent boulders on the low ridge to the right of the wash. The low walls of three rock houses are on the ridge just north of the boulders (**GPS N33° 27.411' W116° 22.345'**). This is a good spot to camp.

From here, you can pick out your route ahead. Toro Peak is the highest antenna-clad summit. Just to the right is a rocky mass locally known as Alta Seca Peak (7,597 feet). Look for dark green vegetation marking some seeps at the base of the peak where three washes converge. The Old Santa Rosa site is among the boulders by the easternmost seep labeled on the topographic map.

Return to your wash, which soon forks. Take the smaller right fork. Travel becomes more difficult because this wash has not been scoured clear of brush and rocks. In 0.6 mile, pass the spot labeled on the topographic map as Cottonwood Spring. This spring is now completely dry and the cottonwoods are long gone, but a thicket of honey mesquite is nourished by the groundwater. Birds nest in the thorny branches. Continue up the wash 1.7 miles until it becomes poorly defined at the valley's north edge. Here you can search for evidence of Old Santa Rosa. Look for a large, flat area below the boulders (**GPS N33° 28.923' W116° 23.042'**). You may find a granite slab with a metate where Cahuilla women ground their food. Slightly higher up, remains of two rock houses can be found. The village site and its artifacts are protected by the Antiquities Act of 1906. You'll find diverse desert vegetation, including nolina, Mojave yucca, desert agave, cat's claw acacia, and barrel, hedgehog, and gander cactus. There are a few seeps at the foot of the mountain wall, but your only sure water is in Nicholas Canyon, 1 mile west.

■ Contacts ■

SAN BERNARDINO NATIONAL FOREST
www.fs.usda.gov/sbnf
See the website above for contact information for specific ranger stations.

SAN GORGONIO WILDERNESS
Mill Creek Visitor Center
Highway 38 and Bryant Street in Mentone
34701 Mill Creek Road
Mentone, CA 92359; 909-382-2882
8 a.m.–4:30 p.m. Thursday–Sunday, 8 a.m.–3 p.m. Monday, closed most federal holidays
Wilderness permits: tinyurl.com/sgwpermits

SAN JACINTO WILDERNESS
Idyllwild Ranger Station
Corner of Highway 243 and Pine Crest Avenue in Idyllwild
54270 Pine Crest Ave.
PO Box 518
Idyllwild, CA 92549; 909-382-2921
8 a.m.–4 p.m. Friday–Tuesday, closed most federal holidays
Wilderness permits: tinyurl.com/sjwpermits

MOUNT SAN JACINTO STATE WILDERNESS
Mount San Jacinto State Park Headquarters
PO Box 308
25905 Highway 243
Idyllwild, CA 92549; 951-659-2607
Daily 8 a.m.–4 p.m.
Wilderness permits: tinyurl.com/msjpermits

SANTA ROSA AND SAN JACINTO MOUNTAINS NATIONAL MONUMENT
Visitor Center
Highway 74 (4 miles south of Palm Desert)
51500 Highway 74
Palm Desert, CA 92260; 760-862-9984
9 a.m.–4 p.m. Thursday–Monday

SAN BERNARDINO MOUNTAINS (OUTSIDE SAN GORGONIO WILDERNESS)
Big Bear Discovery Center
40971 North Shore Drive (Highway 38)
PO Box 290
Fawnskin, CA 92333
909-382-2790
8:30 a.m.–4:30 p.m. Thursday–Monday, closed most federal holidays

▪ Pacific Crest Trail ▪

THE PACIFIC CREST TRAIL (PCT), the most ambitious footpath in the United States, traverses the crest of the Pacific states for 2,650 miles from Mexico to Canada. The proposal to carve this wilderness path from border to border was conceived by a single individual in 1932—Clinton C. Clarke of Pasadena. He urged the US Forest Service and National Park System to knit together and extend the threads of high-country footpaths already existing, such as the Oregon Skyline Trail and California's John Muir Trail. Clarke achieved partial success before his death in 1957; he prevailed upon the Forest Service to call the footpaths in Oregon and Washington by the collective name "Pacific Crest Trail System." But not until 1968, when Congress, responding to pressure from outdoorsmen, created the PCT as a national scenic trail, did active work begin to join together a border-to-border system.

The PCT crosses the length of the San Bernardino National Forest. The route, from south to north, goes as follows: from Highway 74 up and along the crest of the Desert Divide, past Tahquitz Peak and down to Saddle Junction, past Strawberry Junction to the Fuller Ridge Trail, down the north slope to San Gorgonio Pass, west to Whitewater, north up the Whitewater River, across the ridge to Mission Creek, up the North Fork of the latter to Heart Bar Creek, up Coon Creek and across Onyx Summit, northwest down to Big Bear City, up Gold Mountain to Cougar Crest and down to Little Bear Camp, down Holcomb Creek to Deep Creek, west north of Lake Arrowhead to Grass Valley Creek, west down the East Fork of the Mojave River to Summit Valley, west to Cajon Pass, and up Lone Pine Canyon into the San Gabriels.

For more information on the PCT, see *Pacific Crest Trail: Southern California*, by Schaffer, Winnett, Schifrin, and Jenkins, published by Wilderness Press.

APPENDIX 3

▪ Bibliography ▪

GENERAL

Fletcher, Colin, and Chip Rawlins. *The Complete Walker IV*. New York: Alfred A. Knopf, 2002.

Jardine, Ray. *Trail Life: Ray Jardine's Lightweight Backpacking*. Adventurelore Press, 2009.

Olander, Ann, and Farley Olander. *Call of the Mountains: The Beauty and Legacy of Southern California's San Jacinto, San Bernardino and San Gabriel Mountains*. Las Vegas: Stephens Press, 2005.

Mountaineering: The Freedom of the Hills. 8th ed. Seattle: The Mountaineers, 2010.

NATURE

Booth, Ernest Sheldon. *Mammals of Southern California*. Berkeley: University of California Press, 1968.

Delisle, Harold F. *Common Plants of the Southern California Mountains*. Healdsburg: Naturegraph Company, 1961.

Furtz, Francis. *The Elfin Forest*. Los Angeles: Times-Mirror Press, 1923.

Grinnell, Joseph. *The Biota of the San Bernardino Mountains*. Berkeley: The University Press, 1908.

Grinnell, Joseph, and H. S. Swarth. *Birds and Mammals of the San Jacinto Area*. Berkeley: The University Press, 1913.

Hall, Harvey M. *A Botanical Survey of San Jacinto Mountain*. Berkeley: The University Press 1902.

Ingram, Stephen. *Cacti, Agaves, and Yuccas of California and Nevada*. Los Olivos, CA: Cachuma Press, 2008.

Lanner, Ronald M. *Conifers of California*. Los Olivos, CA: Cachuma Press, 1999.

Munz, Philip A. *Introduction to California Mountain Wildflowers*. Berkeley: University of California Press, 2003.

Pavlik, Bruce M., Pamela C. Muick, Sharon G. Johnson, and Marjorie Popper. *Oaks of California*. Los Olivos, CA: Cachuma Press, 1993.

Peterson, P. Victor. *Native Trees of Southern California*. Berkeley: University of California Press, 1966.

Raven, Peter H. *Native Shrubs of Southern California*. Berkeley: University of California Press, 1966.

Sudworth, George. *Forest Trees of the Pacific Slope*. New York: Dover Publications, 1967 (reprint of 1908 ed.).

Vaughn, Francis E. *Geology of San Bernardino Mountains North of San Gorgonio Pass*. Berkeley: University of California Press 1922.

HISTORY

Beattie, George William, and Helen Pruitt. *Heritage of the Valley: San Bernardino's First Century*. Pasadena: San Pasqual Press, 1939.

Belden, Burr, "History in the Making," *San Bernardino Sun-Telegram*, various issues, 1953–1964.

Big Bear Panorama. Big Bear, CA: Big Bear High School, 1934.

Brown, John, Jr., and James Boyd. *History of San Bernardino and Riverside Counties*. Chicago: Lewis, 1922.

Drake, Austin. *Big Bear Valley: Its History, Legends and Tales*. Big Bear: Big Bear Historical Society, 1970 (reprint of 1949 ed.).

Holmes, Elmer Wallace. *History of Riverside County, California*, Los Angeles: Historic Record Company, 1912.

Hughes, Tom. *History of Banning and San Gorgonio Pass*. Banning, CA: Banning Record Print, 1939.

Ingersoll, Luther A. *Ingersoll's Century Annals of San Bernardino County, 1769–1904*. Los Angeles: Ingersoll, 1904.

Jackson, Helen Hunt. *Ramona*. Boston: Little, Brown, 1884.

James, George Wharton. *Through Ramona's Country*. Boston: Little, Brown, 1909.

James, George Wharton. *The Wonders of the Colorado Desert*. Boston: Little, Brown, 1906.

James, Harry C. *The Cahuilla Indians*. Los Angeles: Westernlore Press, 1960 (reprinted 1969 by Malki Museum Press, Banning, CA).

Johnston, Francis J. *The Serrano Indians of Southern California*. Banning, CA: Malki Museum Press, 1965.

LaFuze, Pauliena B. *Saga of the San Bernardinos*. Bloomington, CA: San Bernardino County Museum Association, 1971.

Maxwell, Ernest, ed. *Town Crier* (newspaper); Idyllwild, CA, various issues, 1946–1971.

Patencio, Chief Francisco, as told to Margaret Boynton. *Stories and Legends of the Palm Springs Indians*. Palm Springs: Palm Springs Desert Museum, 1970 (reprint of 1943 ed.).

Robinson, John W. *The San Bernardinos*. Arcadia, CA: Big Santa Anita Historical Society, 1989.

Robinson, John. *San Gorgonio: A Wilderness Preserved*. San Bernardino: San Gorgonio Volunteer Association, 1991.

Robinson, John W., and Bruce D. Risher. *The San Jacintos*. Arcadia, CA: Big Santa Anita Historical Society, 1993.

Ruby, Jay W. *Aboriginal Uses of Mt. San Jacinto State Park*. Los Angeles: UCLA Department of Anthropology Annual Publications, 1961–62.

Saunders, Charles Francis. *The Southern Sierras of California*. Boston: Houghton Mifflin, 1923.

Shumway, Nina Paul. *Your Desert and Mine*. Los Angeles: Westernlore Press, 1960.

Williamson, Robert S. *Report of Explorations in California for Railroad Routes*. Washington: War Department, 1853.

Woodward, Lois Ann. *Mount San Jacinto*. Berkeley: WPA Project, 1937 (typescript in Bancroft Library).

▪ Index ▪

▪ About the Authors ▪

JOHN W. ROBINSON has been exploring, backpacking, and climbing throughout the Mountain West, from Alaska and Canada to Mexico, for more than 50 years. His first guide, *Camping and Climbing in Baja* (now out of print), set the standard for guides to the Baja California mountains. His *Trails of the Angeles,* now in its eighth edition, remains the definitive hiking guide to Southern California's San Gabriel Mountains.

He has authored or coauthored a number of the original Wilderness Press quadrangle guides, covering California's three major southern ranges: the San Gabriels, the San Bernardinos, and the San Jacintos. In addition, he has published numerous articles in *Westways, Desert Magazine, Southern California Quarterly, Overland Journal,* and *Summit.*

If the mines of Southern California's mountains revealed gold and other precious minerals, they cannot compare to the treasure trove of information contained in this one man. His love for these forests, peaks, and wilderness areas is apparent on every page of his many works.

DAVID MONEY HARRIS is a professor of engineering at Harvey Mudd College. He is the author or coauthor of six hiking guidebooks and five engineering textbooks. David grew up rambling around the Desolation Wilderness as a toddler in his father's pack and later roamed the High Sierra as a Boy Scout. As a Sierra Club trip leader, he orga-

nized mountaineering trips throughout the Sierra Nevada. Since 1999, he has been exploring the mountains and deserts of Southern California. He lives with his wife and three sons in Upland, California, and delights in sharing his love of the outdoors with their boys.